POLITICAL
▓▏▎▏▍▐▏▊▊ ANALYSIS

An Unorthodox Approach

POLITICAL ANALYSIS

An Unorthodox Approach

Charles A. McCoy
Lehigh University

Alan Wolfe
Richmond College

THOMAS Y. CROWELL COMPANY *New York Established* 1834

L. C. Card 70-187602
ISBN 0-690-64625-9

Designed by Jill Schwartz

MANUFACTURED IN THE UNITED STATES OF AMERICA

Preface

How can I, that girl standing there,
My attention fix
On Roman or on Russian
Or on Spanish politics?
Yet here's a travelled man that knows
What he talks about,
And there's a politician,
That has read and thought,
And maybe what they say is true
Of War and war's alarms.
But O that I were young again
And held her in my arms!

William Butler Yeats

IT IS RARE that one can preface a political science text with a poem, and rarer still with a poem by a great master of the language. Yet we can begin with a poem, for the lines quoted above constitute one of the best ways available to introduce students to the study of politics. Yeats expresses what we know many people feel—a

v

revulsion against things political. War, poverty, vituperation, hypocrisy—these are seen as the heart of politics. Far better to be a
romantic, to idealize something, to ignore the seamy. The authors
of this book strongly disagree, and one of the points we make, perhaps the main point, is that such a wish to be apolitical is both
impossible and dangerous. Given our commitment that politics is
an essential condition for human existence, we seek to enable the
student to find his or her political identity, to become politically
conscious.

It is impossible to be apolitical. Although Yeats may think that
it is better to dream of holding a woman than to be political, even
his simple poem reveals that he is a political person. What he does
in those few lines is to objectify a whole category of people, half
the human race, in fact. By reducing a woman to something he only
wishes to hold in his arms, he reveals a political attitude that today
is called male chauvinism. Such attitudes, particularly when held
by large numbers of people, are political, for they contribute to the
division of a society into unequal parts. So Yeats is not only being
political; he is also being politically conservative, perpetuating the
status quo.

This conclusion may seem like too much to read into what is
supposed to be a humorous poem, but it is important to search
behind the humor, for a general proposition is revealed thereby.
It has been our experience that those who claim to be apolitical
nearly always support the existing state of affairs. The state of the
world today—it has probably always been so—is such that those
who do not play an active role in trying to bring about a better
world are as political as those who do. The question, then, is not
whether it is possible to be apolitical, but whether one's inevitable
politics will be informed and intelligent or hidden and ignorant. In
that sense, trying to be apolitical is worse than impossible; it is
dangerous.

An important consequence of anyone's education, whether it be
in college or out, is to develop an appreciation for the importance
of politics. Presumably for that reason, all colleges in the United
States have courses in political science and most students take at
least one. Unfortunately, those courses rarely achieve this objective.
Instead, they often alienate students from politics in a variety of
ways and contribute to the idea that politics is a subject to be

avoided. This is reflected in the kinds of textbooks that most students are asked to read.

One type of textbook presents a detailed examination of American government. This frequently employed method has the disadvantage, in our judgment, of failing to lay the proper foundation for subsequent work in the discipline. It also reinforces an already existing parochialism (why learn about American government except for the fact that one lives in America?) and is viewed by many students as a mere rehash of secondary school work. Therefore, such an approach fails to take advantage of the incoming students' expectations that college will open new vistas and provide new and stimulating experiences.

A second alternative, introducing the student to basic principles of political analysis, offers a more promising manner of attaining the goal we have established. However, it is our opinion that the existing texts fail to live up to their promise. They frequently attempt too much, delving into the entire curriculum and subfields of political science, including, in most instances, chapters that purport to introduce students to political systems as diverse as those of the United States, the Soviet Union, France, Germany, the United Kingdom, and what is now called the Third World. Is it any wonder that students feel overwhelmed by such a mass of information? Alternatively, many such books treat politics in such an abstract and artificial manner that the study of politics becomes either the memorizing of jargon, the language of constitutions and formal governmental structures or the now more popular attempt to find the common functions underlying all political systems.

We feel that a textbook should do the following:

1. Make students intelligently political as well as students of politics.

2. Make students agents for political change and not mere spectators of politics. Not only do societies need to change in order to survive, but it is through the process of struggling to create a better world that political understanding often comes.

3. Make students aware that political decisions involve making moral choices and that individuals and institutions must be made to accept responsibility for the choices they make.

4. Help students sharpen their critical faculties and not be mere

celebrants of the existing political system. We are opposed to ideological thinking, which is most often defined as thought limited by a commitment to the existing political order. We want students to think for themselves.

5. Provide a foundation in theory and analysis for future study in the field of politics. Our aim is not to encourage people to become political scientists as such, for going to graduate school in political science is often one of the worst ways to learn about politics. Our aim, rather, is to aid any further study of politics, whether it be done in the streets or in the classroom.

6. Provide students with essential knowledge so that theory and practice may be united in a more reflective and conscious manner. There are not many facts in this book. We are more interested in providing guidelines for the student to follow in obtaining his own facts.

It is our hope that this volume will contribute more directly to the achievement of these goals than most existing texts have been able to do. We invite you to join us insofar as we have been able to go, fully aware that there may be a gap between what we wanted to accomplish in this book and what we may have actually accomplished. We encourage all students who are asked to read this book to communicate with us on whether they think we have done what we set out to do, for that is the only way we will ever know.

It is not only a tradition but a tradition we gladly honor to express our appreciation and indebtedness to others. Whatever one has to say is never the product of his or her own thinking alone, but is always produced in conjunction with others who think in a similar way. Our indebtedness to the great political thinkers from the past includes such distinguished personages as Plato and Marx. But we also recognize an obligation to our numerous contemporary colleagues and to our students, without whose constant interaction with us this book would never have been written.

In addition, from Thomas Y. Crowell we wish to mention in particular Mr. Stanley Duane who first encouraged the idea for the book and Mr. Herbert Addison whose persistence and dedication brought the book into print. Mrs. Joan Greene did great work preparing the manuscript, and a graduate student of Charles McCoy's, Mr. Morton J. Schoolman, provided bibliographical help. Charles McCoy wishes to express his appreciation to his wife, Elaine, for her forebearance and insightful comments as the manuscript progressed.

Alan Wolfe wishes to thank Allis Wolfe for critically reading the entire manuscript and suggesting important changes. He also feels that the book could not have been conceived or written without the intense political movement of the 1960s, to whose heroes, martyrs, and partisans he is thankful.

Again as is customary, we wish to acknowledge that we alone are responsible for the book's sins of omission and commission. But if people find virtue in the book, we like to believe that we may share some responsibility for that as well.

Contents

I THE MEANING OF POLITICS

ONE THEME OF this book is that politics is everywhere. This probably runs counter to the thinking of most people in the United States. They often talk about politics as if it were a distinct facet of one's existence, as if a person could decide to participate in politics at a certain time, like doing the dishes or driving a car. But this restricted view does not consider that much of our daily activity is ultimately political. Even doing dishes is a political act, since it is associated with a particular sex and a set of power distributions in the family. To appreciate the political dimension of human existence, we must first discuss what politics really means.

1 Problems of Political Analysis

THERE IS A deep-seated revulsion toward much of what passes as contemporary political science. Many people, with considerable justification, consider it both amoral and irrelevant. This leads college students, and to an increasing extent their teachers, to regard political science courses as a colossal bore. This might come as quite a surprise to the uninitiated for we are living in an age when politics is particularly relevant. Outside the classroom, students' interest in politics has never been higher. Young people today are also more aware of the moral character of political acts. We hope to demonstrate that studying politics can be as rewarding as participating in politics and that an understanding of politics can make students more effective agents of political change, agents that accept moral responsibility for their political actions.

David Easton's rather sterile description of politics "as the authoritative allocation of values for the community as a whole" [1] may obscure but cannot hide the fact that political decisions will determine for many—perhaps for all mankind—whether they will live normal lives or face premature and violent death; whether even

[1] *The Political System* (New York: Knopf, 1953).

3

in affluent America many will needlessly suffer from ignorance, ill health, and malnutrition.

How has this subject, filled with matters of vital concern for all of humanity, been separated from reality and become dull and uninteresting? Perhaps political science textbooks provide the key to this paradox. Many textbook authors seem to regard their writings as revealed truth. This "truth" takes various forms. The principal varieties include four types.

1. *Encyclopedic truth.* This kind of "truth" appears after "exhaustive" coverage of a given subject. Terms or concepts are meticulously developed and related to one another. The student who memorizes all the "facts," definitions, and details has acquired knowledge and is prepared for advanced work in the field. Medical textbooks provide the model for this approach, but it is used in fields like economics, history, psychology, and political science. There is something overwhelming and arrogant about such books. They convey the impression of an imposing edifice because of the monumental amount of work that went into them. Many students find this type of text formidable and consider the whole undertaking too staggering. Increasingly, the students simply refuse to buy or read the books. All those "facts" (which have probably changed since the last edition anyway) remain stored between covers, unread.

2. *Celebrated truth.* This type of text is most typical of political science and history. The "revealed truth" here is that our country is the greatest man has ever known. It may have had some problems in the past, but they were not major ones. Besides, the very history of the country is how the problems were satisfactorily resolved. Such books are commonly found in secondary schools, but they sometimes also appear at the college level. All popular high school and college textbooks in economics, history, and political science are based on a celebration-truth point of view to some extent. No matter how well they are researched and written, or how comprehensive their scope, all such books present a distorted view of reality. In the end, their "truth" turns out to be unrevealed falsehood.

3. *Disciplinary truth.* Many textbooks take as their subject matter the material taught in a university department. The university world is, however, a compartmentalized world. The tendency is to restrict one's knowledge of a subject to a constantly narrower and

narrower field, like the old adage about the scholar knowing more and more about less and less until he knows all there is to know about nothing at all. When knowledge is presented in this highly compartmentalized and restricted fashion, it is extremely difficult to grasp the whole. Elementary texts often attempt to include every subdivision of political science by devoting a chapter to it, or to cover comparative politics by describing the systems of various nations in separate chapters. This "disciplinary truth" tends to oversimplify the range and complexity of politics, giving students a distorted sense of political reality.

4. *Parochial truth.* Closely related to the other types are texts with built-in limitations to their subject matter. This defect can take the form of the ahistorical text, which concentrates on the present and ignores history. Economic texts, for instance, often fail to consider how the Great Depression shaped subsequent economic development. Frequently, the text reveals its parochialism by building on an unproven premise. For example, international relations texts often assume that war is inevitable and ignore anthropological studies of societies where peaceful relations usually prevail. Cultural parochialism is probably the most significant variety. Its two principal biases are a Western orientation, in which the non-Western experience is either ignored or judged inferior, and a middle-class orientation, in which the experiences and values of the middle class become the basis for judging other behavior.

It seems to us that the time has come for an antitextbook textbook, one that will consciously try to avoid "revealed truth" of whatever variety. This book will acknowledge that the allocation of human values involves great moral choices and that certitude and exactitude are deceptions for the teacher and student alike. Further, this book will acknowledge that the existing social and political order in the United States and the world is far from perfect—that it does not provide a physical, cultural, or political environment where people can realize their true potential. We, the authors of this book, desire to use our knowledge to change the world, to make it a "better" more "just" place where men and women can come closer to being "truly human." However, we are aware that to change society one must understand it and must also help others to understand it.

To begin with, we need an accurate description of political behavior and how that behavior is structured by the institutions within which it takes place. Therefore the first six chapters of our "anti-textbook" deal with political phenomena—with governmental and nongovernmental institutions, with the way political decisions are made, and how they are implemented. Although this section is descriptive, we have tried to avoid some of the weaknesses of traditional textbooks—such as limiting oneself to the study of governmental institutions. Frequently, the procedure has been to examine the formal rules of a particular governmental institution, and this has given political analysis a legalistic and formalistic cast. There is no doubt that studies of this type were thorough as far as they went. The essential purpose was descriptive, not explanatory. But the major weakness of this approach was that it ignored human behavior—perhaps the most significant determinants of institutions. Psychological or sociological dimensions were not taken into account. The descriptive section of this book, however, focuses upon these human dimensions.

There is another form of descriptive analysis, which developed in reaction to the one just discussed. The adherents of the second type believed that politics could be studied scientifically, like physical phenomena. They tried to eliminate all "value" considerations and to limit description to those phenomena that could be observed and measured with precision. With this approach, the collection of political data grew immensely. Voting returns were studied; budget information was gathered; interview schedules were constructed, and the answers to them scaled in ways that could be expressed numerically and compared with one another. As this approach gained strength in the profession, taking control in most graduate departments and shaping many doctoral theses, it expanded in scope. At the present time, it is complex and mathematically sophisticated. However, the approach has frequently sacrificed relevance for exactitude, often concealed a conservative ideology, and on occasion lost contact with reality.[2] In the descriptive section of this book, we shall emphasize those facets of reality that are most relevant to understanding the problems facing society.

There is yet another aspect of politics that needs careful and critical explanation—political philosophy. Introductory texts usu-

[2] See Charles A. McCoy and John Playford, eds., *Apolitical Politics* (New York: Thomas Y. Crowell, 1967), pp. 1–10. See also David Easton, "The New Revolution in Political Science," *The American Political Science Review* 63, no. 4 (December 1969):1052.

ally ignore it altogether or treat it summarily in one brief chapter. We have devoted the third and fourth parts of our book to this important aspect of politics. Part III traces the history of political philosophy from Plato and Aristotle to Marx and Lenin. Part IV deals with the more contemporary aspects of political philosophy and theory.

We believe that political philosophy should be an integral part of our text because it introduces the student to a tradition, one that is both humbling and liberating. It is humbling to realize that a writer like Rousseau was offering answers to questions that twentieth-century thinkers have not even had the insight to ask. But it is also liberating in that it removes the reader from the limited world of contemporary existence. Political philosophy also helps us develop criteria for making decisions. It provides a framework within which reasoned judgment can take place. And political philosophy helps us maintain a proper priority in our inquiries. It develops the ability to distinguish the trivial from the significant, the eternal from the transitory. Finally, political philosophy is instrumental in opening new avenues of thought. It helps us transcend the barriers of time, place, and culture, freeing the imagination and opening up the future as well as the past.

In conclusion, politics is somewhat like a child's kaleidoscope: each time it is shaken new patterns emerge. Since our world is also being shaken a great deal, we need all the insights we can get to understand these ever-changing patterns. Hobbes's vision of reality is different from that of Marx, but both are enlightening to the student of political science. This is not to say that all visions are of equal value. What we do know is that society cannot be changed or understood without a theoretical framework and that man's best creative efforts are needed to produce an adequate theory for our times. In Part IV of this work, we reaffirm the significance of politics as a permanent aspect of the human condition.

2 Identifying the Political

PEOPLE IN AMERICA have a bad feeling about politics. To be sure, there is a good deal of rhetoric about loving our flag and country, and taking an active part in its affairs. And no responsible states- man or politician would ever claim that political work is all bad. Yet many people have an aftertaste in their mouths when the word is mentioned. To some, politics is sin, to others it is a waste of time or sublimation, but most people consider it dishonest. There is often wisdom in popular conceptions, and such is the case here. Much of what is meant by the term "politics" is not ideal and people are justifiably suspicious of it. But to condemn all politics is not to understand what the phenomenon is really about.

If the present politics is not satisfying, only politics itself can change that state of affairs. It is not enough to assert, as Charles Reich did in *The Greening of America,* that the world will change as more and more people become conscious of its deficiencies. First what people perceive is a political process; consciousness is shaped by a person's social position. Besides, a retreat from politics is in any case illusory. You cannot go to the country until you have obtained resources from the city. In other words, divorcing oneself from the political world can be done only by ignoring problems like racism, sexism, imperialism, war, and exploitation. Trying to avoid politics means ignoring all those things, which means tacitly accepting them, which means stagnation instead of revolutionary change. But, the question of what constitutes politics persists. It is an old and a long-disputed subject, and learning about these disputes is a good introduction to politics.

PHILOSOPHY, SCIENCE, AND POLITICS

There are two basic approaches to politics: one emphasizes philosophy, the other science. The philosophical approach is essentially a normative exercise: it deals with questions of what should be, and only incidentally with what is. In general, this approach to politics begins by identifying a political value—for example, equality, freedom, or order—which is viewed as the ultimate goal of all political undertakings. Then, the writer usually suggests a procedure for obtaining the goal or value. These values are idiosyncratic; one man may feel that security is of the highest value, while his equally intelligent and perceptive colleague may just as sincerely feel that insecurity is something for which we all should strive. Each has to make his case, for when questions of value are at issue, it is not possible to prove scientifically that one is superior to another. The political philosopher may try to show what will happen if a society adopts a particular value. This can be done by creating artificial societies that highlight the effects of a surplus of one value or a decline in another. Or he may try to construct a logical system which will prove that, granting certain premises, a certain political value will logically follow. The important thing about the philosophical approach to politics is that it is concerned with ultimates involving the pursuit of the good life. But these ultimates cannot be proved; instead they are contrasted with one another to demonstrate through internal consistency, depth, and persistence the superiority of the chosen values. A few examples may help.

Plato felt that justice was the major political value, and could only be obtained through order. Any society faced with disorder was subject to turmoil and inconsistency. To prove the superiority of order, he started with an examination of the individual, showing that when an individual's mind was in proper balance, he was able to function best. The same is true of society. When each piece of society works in harmony with every other, when each segment has a job to do and does it without complaint and with respect for all the other segments, then order will be guaranteed. Only in such a society is justice possible, because a just society is one in which everyone has a role to play and plays it.

Marx, on the other hand, believed that the primary value of a political system is humanity. A system is not healthy when its subjects are inhuman—to one another or to themselves. He tried to demonstrate, with a mass of facts, that this inhumanity was caused by a peculiar configuration of the economic aspects of society. And he believed that by changing these economic aspects, the primary value of humanity could be preserved. But before this could happen, the most inhumanely treated segment of society would have to become aware of its treatment and overthrow the economic system that produced the inhumanity.

It should be clear that both Plato and Marx followed a similar intellectual process: a certain value was identified as important, and the way to make that value predominant was delineated. (For more on Plato and Marx, see Chapters 8, 11, and 12).

In nearly all the political philosophies examined in Part III, the value is obtained by utilizing a political institution. In the case of Plato, it was an entire society following his principles of justice. With Rousseau, it was a general will, probably operating through the state, that would guarantee equality. Montesquieu and later the American founding fathers, particularly Madison, felt that political institutions had to be multiple and antagonistic in order for both commonness and individuality to be realized. Finally, Lenin saw in the revolutionary political party the means of overthrowing an economic system. The fact that all of these political philosophies looked to political institutions to realize their ultimate value should make us aware of the key role institutions play in the political world.

While the philosophical approach to politics is essentially normative, the scientific approach is basically explanatory. It is not concerned with what ought to be, but with what is, or was, or will be. What values are to the philosophical approach, facts are to the scientific. Its method is to identify a certain fact about the way people behave politically and then relate that fact to a theory of how politics operates in different types of political systems. (See Chapter 14.) But the value of this procedure of logical reasoning based on facts is doubtful; if you start out with one fact, no matter how intricate your logic, you will always wind up with one fact. Similarly, the process of constructing ideal models to examine the

role of certain facts, while often used in scientific analysis for purposes of insight, is not the basis of the scientific approach to political analysis. The political scientist (in this chapter we are referring
to those who study politics scientifically, but, in general, we will
use the term to describe people who follow either approach to political science) is not concerned with ultimate questions; rather he
seeks to understand the way politics operates by collecting as many
facts as possible and by trying to fit those facts together into some
framework that makes sense. Once again, some examples should be
helpful.

Suppose one discovers that in the seven-year history of the local
Democratic club, there has never been a contest for the presidency.
By itself, this is of interest merely to the people who belong to the
club, and then not to all of them. What the political scientist would
do is to explain that isolated fact by pointing out that in nearly
all groups, leadership is shared by a few and most of the membership is content to have it that way. The fact has now been explained
in terms of a general pattern. The scientist might then go on to
conclude that the local club is part of a series of groups that make
demands on the political system. The turnover in leadership within
the group thus becomes a phenomenon related to the political system of the entire society. Political institutions are as essential to the
explanation of facts as they are to the fulfillment of values. Within
a political institution, an isolated fact becomes part of a general
pattern.

In short, both scientific and philosophical systems are designed to
make sense out of a basic unit—but in the scientific system the unit
is a fact, while in the philosophical system it is a value. Both approaches seek the meaning of the unit in political institutions, another indication of how important such institutions are to our general understanding.

The philosophical and scientific traditions probably have more in
common than either side will admit. Both, after all, are ultimately
concerned with understanding the political world. Since this is our
primary interest, we certainly want to use any tools that might help
us. The question is whether the two traditions can be combined
in some way, or whether the analyst must pick one or the other.
Perhaps these traditions could be reconciled by first selecting a
particular value, then using the scientific apparatus to analyze it.
Suppose, for example, that our main concern was maximizing free-

dom. Toward this end, we could compare various political systems, seeking out and trying to understand the conditions promoting freedom. After we knew more about those conditions, we could speak with greater authority about different means of achieving the political value of freedom.

Reconciling the philosophical and scientific approaches, then, is not only possible but inevitable. To begin with, science that does not try to take values into account is bad science. Values are part of the political milieu; besides, the scientist himself has values with which he must come to terms, otherwise his analysis will be totally sterile. A "value-free" social science is inconceivable, because nothing is value free. The great social scientists—Karl Marx, Max Weber, Karl Mannheim—were all aware of values, and they built social theories from, rather than around, their values. However, the fact that social science cannot be value free does not mean that social science itself is impossible. Marx, Weber, and Mannheim were brilliant social scientists whose understanding of the social world was greatly enhanced, not obscured, by their personal values.

Just as it is bad science to be unconcerned with values, it is bad philosophy to ignore facts. The most elaborate and logically constructed philosophical system is meaningless if it does not explain basic facts about the social world. If a value is really to be preserved, we must understand the culture in which it exists. The great political philosophers started with a concern for the facts they perceived in order to achieve the values they desired. Montesquieu stated his theory of the separation of powers from an interpretation of British political practice (an incorrect interpretation, as it turned out). Hobbes turned the world around him into a complete political theory. The inspiration for John Stuart Mill came from the conditions of his day. Each of these political philosophers were also political scientists, just as all the great political scientists are political philosophers.

There is another reason for reconciling the philosophical and scientific strains of political analysis—both, as we have seen, end up by studying political institutions. It is in the political institutions that descriptions, explanations, and prescriptions merge. We are concerned with political institutions because we want to understand and make some judgments about them. When we examine bureaucracy, for example (in Chapter 7), we will not simply define it and measure its impact on the world. Instead, we will try to understand the phenomenon of bureaucratization because we really want to find out if bureaucracy has led to a decline in popular control, and if the bureaucratic society is dangerous because of its impact on people's minds. In dealing with questions like these, we shall be both descriptive—because we want to understand the phenomenon—and normative—because we are human beings seeking a relatively decent world. To understand without wanting to perfect is an incomplete activity. The study of political institutions, then, is an area where some degree of completeness can be achieved. But before examining what a political institution is, we must define politics.

THE MEANING OF POLITICS

The word has meant many different things over the years. At one time, politics referred specifically to certain institutions that were formally called government. Anything dealing with an aspect of a society's government was political. But this type of definition was really too narrow. Some activities that occur outside the realm of formal government should be included in the term "political"—for example, the conflict between a trade union and its management over working conditions, the employment of private detectives by a corporation to investigate the possibility of a strike, a riot in an urban area, or the writing of *Das Kapital*. None of these activities involves a specific governmental institution, yet something is lost if we declare that they are not political. In other words, something called politics does take place in nongovernmental institutions (and we will discuss this further in Chapters 3 and 4).

Once we abandon strictly governmental criteria, we can treat politics as a process. We must then decide what aspects of social life to include in this process. Many students of politics resolve the matter by selecting areas that are of special concern to them— which produces a wide variety of definitions. Consider these three examples:

> The study of politics is the study of influence and the influential.[1]

[1] Harold Lasswell, *Politics: Who Gets What, When, How* (Cleveland: Meridian Books, 1958), p. 1.

Politics as power consists fundamentally of relationships of superordination and subordination, of dominance and submission, of the governors and the governed. The study of politics is the study of these relationships.[2]

If we were to sum up our commonsense conception of politics it might conceivably take the following form: Political life concerns all those varieties of activity that influence significantly the kind of authoritative policy adopted for a society and the way it is put into practice.[3]

The common element running through most of these definitions is *power* or *influence,* and we could conclude that power is the most important element in politics. This is in line with the definition by Max Weber: "Hence, 'politics' for us means striving to share power or striving to influence the distribution of power, either among states or among groups within a state." [4] Weber's definition has been so influential that we should examine it closely. To begin with, does Weber's definition fit into the scientific or the philosophical approach to political science? Is it trying to be descriptive or normative? At first glance, it seems that Weber is clearly scientific, giving us a definition of politics that applies to all societies. It is hard to distinguish Weber's values and preferences in this objective definition of the political. But a good case can be made for calling his definition normative instead.

In his essay defining power, Weber draws a distinction between two types of political conduct. One, which Weber characterizes as religious but we usually call "extremist," is characterized by a total faith in a set of ideas. Since these ideas are absolutely true, one does not bargain about them in a public forum. They are simply proclaimed. The other political style, which Weber much prefers, is based on a pessimistic view of man. It contends that since man will never be perfect, political action should proceed gradually through bargaining and compromise and with skepticism about

[2] V. O. Key, Jr., *Politics, Parties, and Pressure Groups,* 5th ed. (New York: Thomas Y. Crowell, 1964), pp. 2–3.

[3] David Easton, *The Political System* (New York: Knopf, 1953), p. 128.

[4] "Politics as a Vocation," in *From Max Weber: Essays in Sociology,* eds. Hans Gerth and C. Wright Mills (New York: Oxford University Press, 1958), p. 78.

revealed truth.[5] In short, Weber proclaims his values: he is moderate, nonrevolutionary, believes in gradual change, and distrusts any other course. So we would expect that if his definition of politics reflected any value bias, it would be toward these.

Most contemporary students of political behavior are biased toward stability and moderation, although they do not state this explicitly. They take Weber's definition at face value, concluding that politics is basically a matter of the struggle for power. Activities that do not involve a power struggle are nonpolitical, or, in the words of one contemporary writer, antipolitical.[6] The writing of *Das Kapital* was mentioned earlier as an example of an activity that was deemed nonpolitical by the narrow governmental definition of politics. Would it also be excluded by the Weberian definition? If Weber's definition is broadened slightly, then *Das Kapital* could be included, since Marx was seeking to influence the distribution of power in some future society. But according to the contemporary literal interpretation, it would not be political because it was not involved in the day-to-day struggle for power. This example reveals the bias of a definition of politics based upon the struggle for power. Two things tend to be left out: revolutionary activity, which seeks to change the nature rather than the distribution of power; and political ideas, especially those divorced from current struggles for power. Under the Weberian and post-Weberian definitions of politics, then, Karl Marx might not be classified as a political figure, but there would be no question about the eligibility of Richard J. Daley, Chicago's erstwhile mayor. Yet Marx is much more important politically than Daley. Something needs to be added to the strictly Weberian definition.

Since Weber's definition grew out of the scientific tradition (although it is more normative than Weber thought), the philosophical tradition might provide the rest of our definition of politics. One thing most political philosophers share is a desire to preserve their version of the good life. Nearly all of them dealt with ideas, rather than power with the notable exception of Machiavelli (see Chap-

[5] Weber calls these types of political ethics "the ethic of ultimate ends" and "the ethic of responsibility." Considering how his discussion foreshadows Hitler's rise to power, it is one of the most moving things he wrote. See ibid., pp. 117–28.

[6] John Bunzel, *Anti-Politics in America* (New York: Knopf, 1967).

ter 8). Underlying the thought of the great political philosophers was always the question: "power to do what?". The answer, of course, varied greatly—from the creation of a socialist society, to the provision of political stability, to the preservation of free enterprise. But we are more interested in the search for the good life than the individual answers. If we used this in our definition of politics, we could describe politics as conflict over the search for the good life. Under this definition, Karl Marx would definitely qualify as political, whereas Richard Daley would be a more dubious case. But of course it is silly to say that Richard Daley is not a political figure.

Eventually, we would be forced to conclude that all definitions of basic terms are normative. The scholar defines what he is going to study in going about his work. In other words, definitions are crucial because they determine the direction the social scientist will take. For this reason, people develop vested interests in defining certain things. It seems that all definitions are normatively chosen in the social sciences, but there is really nothing wrong with that. The question is not whether a definition is normative, but what norms are involved.

This is all well and good, but we still do not have a definition of politics. Instead, we have two—one stressing the struggle for power and the other emphasizing the search for the good life. But could they be combined? Could politics be the study of both power and ideas? Combination is possible, since all definitions of politics are normative anyhow, but not profitable. It is like taking two adversaries, sitting them down next to each other, and asking them to be friends, without ever finding out why they were not friends to begin with.

The two definitions are not compatible because their respective values are not compatible. In general, definitions of politics based on power have a normative point of view that stresses gradual change and a respect for the status quo. Since they exclude revolutionary activity and ideology from the realm of the political, they tend to glorify the pragmatic, the nonideological, the day-to-day struggle for power. In the broadest meaning of the term, then, these definitions are conservative because they seek to conserve some elements of contemporary society. Ideological definitions of politics, on the other hand, are not committed to either the status quo or revolution, since the good life could either be exactly what we have now or the complete opposite. But most political philosophies are committed to something other than the status quo. In that sense, the normative basis is radical, since society will have to be radically changed to achieve the good life. Radical is used here in its broadest sense, and it simply means radically different. Thus, the change could either be progressive, looking toward the future, or reactionary, looking backward. But whatever the direction, it is likely to be different from the present. These, of course, are special uses of the words "conservative" and "radical." Indeed, we use the terms in a different way in Part III of this book. Our purpose here is to examine the basis of each definition of politics and to show that reconciliation is no easy matter.

Still, since we remarked earlier that the philosophical and scientific traditions would inevitably be reconciled, there must be another way. If the purpose of a definition is to guide people rather than to become a substitute for understanding, then we can combine the two definitions merely as a guide. The struggle for power would tell us where to look for politics, while the search for the good life would help us discover what to do with politics when it is identified. In other words, only by understanding why it is difficult to reconcile the two definitions of politics can they be reconciled. The basic difficulty is that they are based on opposing values. What we have done is to structure the combination of the values so we could pick the ones most important to us. The search for the good life, which we consider the essence of political activity, comes at the end of the procedure. We much prefer definitions based on this tradition. As we said before, the study of politics seems pointless unless one is interested in perfecting society. And our point of view will, of course, influence our approach to politics, and our definition of it.

In short, politics is conflict over the search for the good life and the means of achieving it. Political science is the process of examining the structure and operation of political power to evaluate how the search is progressing. Both definitions of politics are involved, but the second tradition is more prominent. By this definition, the political scientist (now we use that term to mean anyone who studies political science, not simply those who study politics scientifically) will be interested in locating power in a political system, but not as an end in itself. He will always question the purpose of the power. He will study political institutions because they have power and because they must be perfected.

INSTITUTIONS

The concept of institution is less controversial than that of politics. It is usually defined as a series of regularized patterns of behavior. Thus, in the institution of marriage, people regularly go through a series of steps and then consider themselves married. Some institutions, like marriage, are unassociated with specific organizations, although the family unit can be viewed as an organization. Others—like a university, department store, or mental hospital—are specifically organizational; that is, the pattern of behavior becomes so regularized that some sort of bureaucracy develops to insure the continuity of the pattern.

Based upon these preliminary remarks, a political institution would be a regularized pattern of conduct that involves either the struggle for power or the search for the good life. The former will most likely be organized; the latter may or may not be organized. The Republican and Democratic parties are examples of organized political institutions that involve the struggle for power. Publishing one's ideas on social change to reach a wide audience is an unorganized political institution involving the search for the good life. But since the idea of a political institution is usually reserved for organized activities, we will refine our definition by saying it is an organization involved either in the struggle for power or the search for the good life. In this way, a political institution could still cover both governmental and nongovernmental areas. A governmental institution is a formal and official agency of power that is supposed to make decisions for the entire society. Nongovernmental political institutions, on the other hand, may be involved in a search for the good life, but they do not make decisions for the whole society. The Supreme Court of the United States is a governmental institution; the French Radical Socialist party is nongovernmental—but both are political institutions.

Political institutions, like politics in general, affect all of us because we are all the subject of political analysis. Nevertheless, the "nonpolitical" person—the individual who does not vote, read newspapers, hold opinions on important or unimportant issues, and who

expresses disdain for anything political—is an important part of any political system. Nonpolitical persons are counted on by the people who govern to continue to act as they have in the past. The governors know that apathy can be considered a form of support for their policies. Therefore, nonpolitical persons generally have a conservative effect on their political systems because of this indirect support. But sometimes the traditionally apathetic will, even though their knowledge has not increased, take a stand on some issue, particularly the fighting of a war. The "I am nonpolitical, but I support my country" theme was frequently heard during World War II. It is a contradictory statement.

We are all political because we are all affected by the actions taken by political decisions. Later, we shall define a political decision as one that affects everyone in a society. Paying taxes is the obvious example. Even if an individual has nothing to do with the decision-making process that created the tax, even if he has no opinion on the desirability of the tax—although this is unlikely— even if he is totally uninterested in trying to change the system, he cannot escape from the tax system. He pays, is exempted, or goes to jail. One simply cannot avoid being involved in such political decisions: in other words, one cannot avoid being political. The question, then, is not whether to be political or not, but whether to be intelligent about politics. And to be intelligent about politics, one must first learn something about the political process.

POLITICS AND VALUES

It is not easy to be intelligent about politics. Some political systems—rhetoric to the contrary—are based on an ignorant constituency, even the American. When Daniel Ellsberg released secret material on Vietnam, there was an uproar from a government that was shocked that its citizens might actually be permitted to learn the truth. The incident was enough to make one believe that political leaders in America want an ignorant population. In spite of periodic campaigns to "educate people in citizenship" or "train for democracy," too much knowledge about the nature of politics makes the governing group quake. Students in secondary schools are taught little about the American political system. Diagrams in textbooks describe how much power each institution has and how its power is utilized. There is generally no mention of the power wielded by people who are not in the formal institutions of government, people who hold positions in private associations like foundations, corporations, universities, labor unions, and churches. And, it is often concluded that the political system has few real problems. To be sure, there is racial trouble and occasional violence. But, in time, these will be taken care of by the system. The idea that the whole system could be in dire trouble is rarely considered. The authors and the teachers who use books of this sort do not want people to get the idea that anything might be wrong. Such a feeling would be unpatriotic. Whether it would be true or not is beyond consideration.

It is equally bad to conclude, without evidence, that everything is wrong with a country like the United States—that it is totally corrupt, evil, and ripe for revolution. That is a judgment for the student to make. It is, however, a proposition worthy of examination. If the system is as good as the high school texts say, then surely it can deal with a simple examination. If it is not so good, then perhaps it is time that people started to wonder why. Although our primary concern is to stimulate independent thinking about politics, that in itself can be partisan, because independent thinking often leads to political radicalism. The development of an individual's knowledge cannot be obstructed by blinders, like unthinking patriotism. Rigorous thought must be the goal of analysis, wherever it leads.

The study of politics should be a liberating experience. Wisdom is not wisdom because it is received. It must liberate in the sense of removing obstacles to a full understanding of the forces that affect an individual's life. In many ways, this liberation is primarily a humiliating experience. It should restrain the ethnocentrism that makes people feel that what they have is best. If we do not deal with feelings like these, then we have failed in our purpose. No one who is truly educated about politics blindly accepts the superiority of his own system. But there is nothing wrong with deciding it is the best, after completing a thorough comparative study.

A recent book, called *Teaching as a Subversive Activity*,[7] has caused a flurry among educators. Its thesis should be obvious from the title. Our conception of political science is that it, too, is a subversive activity—not of any specific country, but of prejudice, blind-

[7] Neil Postman and Charles Weingartner, *Teaching as a Subversive Activity* (New York: Delacorte, 1969).

ness, backwardness, and parochialism. For example, a remark that President Eisenhower once made about the cold war, "Freedom is pitted against slavery; lightness against the dark," [8] indicates how little he understood about political science. The statement had no bearing on the actual situation and could not qualify as political science. The idea that intellectual inquiry is subversive would be familiar to all the great scientists and would win sympathy from most philosophers. There is no reason to soften one's "subversion" because the subject matter is politics. On the contrary, it should be increased.

Just as a student should assume a critical attitude toward his own political system, he should be skeptical of received wisdom about other political systems. This is particularly true of Americans, who, as de Tocqueville noted in 1832, tend to be exceedingly ethnocentric. To achieve a better perspective about other countries, we will examine political systems outside of the United States in this book. Most of these fall into three political categories: industrialized countries of Western Europe and elsewhere, which very much resemble the United States; "underdeveloped" countries (a term so filled with values that we recoil at using it), which are found in Asia, Africa, and Latin America; and countries Americans call "totalitarian" but most people simply call socialist. The first type is familiar to most of us, through books and vacations. But a few words must be added about the other two categories.

Many prejudices have to be overcome in dealing with the so-called underdeveloped countries. The very term underdeveloped is more value-laden than it is scientific, and it reflects a common assumption on the part of most people, political scientists included, that the countries of Asia, Africa, and Latin America need only go through industrialization to achieve what everyone should want— a political system like that of the United States. This assumption is implicit in many discussions of these countries, where their alleged instability, lack of integration, and polarization are contrasted with the stability, integration, and homogeneity of the United States. Whether such assumptions are valid or not, they should not be accepted as true until more is known on the matter. Of course, ethnocentrism works both ways. It usually surprises Americans to discover that African political leaders shake their heads over the

[8] Quoted in David Horowitz, *The Free World Colossus* (New York: Hill and Wang, 1965), p. 143.

periodic outbursts of violence that seem to characterize American politics, that Cuban political leaders have a patronizing attitude toward the United States because it seems to have so much trouble dealing with its problems, and that the countries of the Middle East believe they were civilized thousands of years before anyone but the Indians (or native Americans) knew about North America. The point is simply that for every Westerner who thinks of the non-Western countries as underdeveloped, there is a non-Westerner who regards the West in a similar light. Neither attitude contributes much to political science.

There are further consequences of an open-minded approach to the rest of the world. It might seem that the whole process of comparing countries to show the superiority of one to another—even if this could be proved—is a meaningless activity. A skeptical analysis of politics might lead one to conclude that every political system should be evaluated on its own terms, not contrasted with an alien system. This does not mean that all political systems should be praised because they exist. Even when evaluating a country on its own terms, negative judgments are possible (in a country like Haiti, for instance). But one should be receptive to new and unique experiments taking place in the Third World (another value term; why not First World?), even though they run counter to Western values. For example, in March 1959, Fidel Castro announced that in the interests of freedom and democracy, and with no ambition on his part, elections in Cuba would be abolished indefinitely. Most Americans were shocked, for time and time again they had been told that elections are vital to a political system. Many were convinced that Castro was indeed a mad dictator. Yet, an understanding of the priorities facing Cuba would have shown that most Cubans were not very interested in elections at the time, and since elections would divide the country in the midst of the first sustained attacks on a disastrous economy, most people were willing to forgo them. In other words, judgments about political actions should be based on an understanding of the milieu where the actions took place, as well as on knowledge.

This is particularly necessary in dealing with the countries of Asia, Africa, and Latin America, because there are so many of them with so many distinct political systems. Sierra Leone's problems and successes are different from those of Gabon, even though most Americans see them both as African countries. One quickly learns that sweeping generalizations about the Third World are inappropriate. There are just too many different countries covered by the term. Nearly all of the political experimentation in the world today is taking place in Asia, Africa, and Latin America, because these countries have to experiment to deal with difficult conditions. If these experiments are sometimes called revolutions, that should not put off Americans, for we have a revolutionary heritage. Other names—like guided democracy—may seem contradictory. But what is contradictory in the United States may make sense in Indonesia —or it may not. The point is to find out. We can learn a great deal about politics from these many revolutions.

Ethnocentrism and value judgments become even more troublesome in dealing with the so-called totalitarian countries. The term "totalitarian" was originally used to describe Nazi Germany, where a one-party government had almost complete control over all aspects of political life. Since Germany was the enemy of America during the war, the negative connotations of the term caused no problem. Later, when the Soviet Union became the enemy, the term was transferred to it. Then, in the post-war period, when the victors were dividing up the spoils, the "expansionism" of the Soviet Union was compared to that of Nazi Germany. And the term has stuck. But it should be clear that "totalitarianism" is more an expression of a country's foreign policy than a term that belongs in scientific inquiry. The most extensive attempt to define totalitarianism centers around a group of characteristics:

> The basic features or traits that we suggest as generally recognized to be common to totalitarian dictatorships are six in number. The "syndrome," or pattern of interrelated traits, of the totalitarian dictatorships consists of an ideology, a single party typically led by one man, a terroristic police, a communications monopoly, a weapons monopoly, and a centrally directed economy.[9]

Many difficulties are presented by such an approach. If all but one or two of the characteristics are present, is it still totalitarian? Which of these characteristics appear in all political societies? For example, all societies use propaganda, supported by force. Are these phenomena all permanent? Definitions of totalitarianism often do

[9] Carl Friedrich and Zbigniew Brzezinski, *Totalitarian Dictatorship and Autocracy* (New York: Praeger, 1963), p. 9.

not take into account the change in societies. Thus, the apparent "liberalization" of the Soviet Union, after Khrushchev's speech attacking Stalin in February 1956, was pronounced another totalitarian ploy by one of the authors of the above definition. Change cannot be permitted, or else the whole model is false. In other words, the ideological investment in a term like totalitarianism is so great that it inhibits scientific understanding of politics.

But if we reject the term, what can we use instead? Labels like "so-called totalitarian" and socialist are sometimes applied to the countries of Eastern Europe, China, and Cuba. The important point is that the labels should be simply for purposes of identification, not for judgments—positive or negative. It is hard to avoid a value-oriented approach, but since the political organization of these countries is generally unfamiliar, we must learn as much about them as possible, so that we will understand as much as we can about politics.

As we move on to examine political institutions, it is important to remember that a particular definition of politics will determine our subject matter; that the authors have certain value biases, which should become clear; that the political phenomena discussed occur in all societies; that we are trying to make generalizations that apply to politics everywhere; that our examination will not be confined to specific political institutions. Rather, it will be concerned with questions and dilemmas facing political institutions in all parts of the world.

II THE INSTITUTIONS OF POLITICS

THIS SECTION OF the book deals with the aspect of the political process that affects our lives most—political institutions. When a social activity occurs in a regular and predictable way, it becomes an institution. Those concerned with the struggle for power or with improving the conditions of life are political institutions. Since we are all affected by an extraordinary number of these political institutions every day, we should know something about them—not factual things primarily (although facts are important in understanding the world), but some basic theory about political institutions that could make the political world more meaningful.

3 Political Parties

CERTAIN INSTITUTIONS ARE political, even though they are not part of the formal governmental apparatus. If an institution holds power and is involved in the struggle for a better life, it belongs to the study of politics, whether it is governmental or not. In general, such nongovernmental political institutions are divided into two types—political parties and interest groups—which will be discussed in this and the next chapter.

Although nongovernmental institutions are not part of a formal governmental structure, they often become very powerful. And when they are in a position to make decisions that affect the entire society, they tend to become indistinguishable from governmental institutions. Nongovernmental institutions frequently act in a dual capacity: proclaiming independence from formal government, yet operating as if they were part of it. This may sound confusing, but we hope to make it clear in the pages that follow.

Instead of giving an abstract definition of a political party, we are going to examine the functions parties perform within a political system. Then, a definition should make more sense, since it will grow out of the discussion. In most societies, political parties recruit people from positions of power in the formal governmental structure, define and focus conflict and consensus in the political system, and engage in the de facto governing of a society. After we have reviewed these functions, we should be able to evaluate the role political parties play in all political societies.

THE FUNCTIONS OF POLITICAL PARTIES

To begin with, political parties act as mediators of conflict and consensus, two processes that add a good deal of excitement to the political process. Conflict—disagreement among contending factions in a political system—is often denounced as a divisive influence in political society:

> The common and continual mischiefs of the spirit of party are sufficient to make it the interest and duty of a wise people to discourage and restrain it.
>
> It seems always to distract the Public Councils, and enfeeble the Public Administration. It agitates the community with ill-founded jealousies and false alarms; kindles the animosity of one part against another; ferments occasionally riot and insurrection. It opens the door to foreign influence and corruption, which find a facilitated access to the government itself through the channels of party passions. Thus the policy and the will of the country are subjected to the policy and will of another.[1]

So spoke George Washington in his Farewell Address in 1796. But Washington had good reason to be upset. The country he had served as first president was founded by gentlemen who were convinced that they could run the country well through consensus. Political parties were not foreseen, and conflict, especially partisan conflict, could do nothing but ruin consensus. Now, as he was retiring, factions were springing up and vying for power. Washington's dream was falling apart.

There are still frequent calls in the United States to eliminate the baleful effects of party. Many older people consider foreign policy to be outside the scope of partisan conflict, too important to be left to the political parties. We are being warned constantly that unity is imperative because we are threatened by an external

[1] George Washington, "Farewell Address," in *Documents of American History, Volume I: To 1898*, 7th ed., ed. Henry Steele Commager (New York: Appleton-Century-Crofts, 1963), p. 172.

enemy who will take advantage of our disunity and destroy us. How little things have changed since Washington's time! In both cases, internal conflict was considered conducive to weakness in the international sphere. In both cases, unity was considered a cardinal virtue. But in both cases, the appeal to unity seems to have failed because conflict cannot just be wished away. In spite of all the negative things attributed to it, people continue to come into conflict. Then, perhaps, there are also some positive aspects to conflict.

It could be argued that conflict is inherent in human nature and that is why it never disappears. But our contention is that conflict serves a positive function in political systems. For one thing, it is a way in which people express genuine grievances, especially those related to social and economic differences. Washington expressed indignation at conflict because it agitated, kindled, and fermented the community. But every political system has aspects that need to be protested. Some people are poorer than others; some are discriminated against; and some have lost their rights. If there is no means of expressing discontents, conflict will find other "illegitimate" outlets. Political parties are supposed to give legitimacy to that conflict. In their election contests and their appeals to popular support, they are expected to transform discontent into support through governmental redress of the grievances. All this seems simple enough, yet George Washington, our first president, was aghast at the idea.

Without conflict political systems would probably stagnate and become unworkable. It is apparent to any observer that political systems that have maintained themselves over long periods of time did so because they were able to undergo significant changes as they were needed. Other systems have collapsed because they could not cope with pressures for change, caused by conflict. Frequently, one party to the conflict presses his claim to the government when he cannot obtain redress elsewhere, forcing the political system to confront his demands. For example, in the continuing conflict between the races in the United States, the whites successfully appealed to the government in the nineteenth century to stop the advances being made by the newly freed slaves. So ended reconstruction. Then, in the twentieth century, the blacks appealed—less successfully—to the government to end what reconstruction had done to them. In both cases, conflicts within society forced the system to change. But this example should also illustrate that change in itself is not necessarily good. Conflict is associated with change; what form that change takes is another matter.

Consensus, the opposite of conflict, is a shared agreement on the fundamental issues facing a political system. It works in rather strange ways. In a famous study conducted in two American cities, people were asked which fundamental issues they agreed with. Nearly everyone agreed that "Public officials should be chosen by majority vote," but half of them no longer believed that "In a city referendum, only people who are well informed about the problem being voted on should be allowed to vote." Similarly, there was general agreement that freedom of speech was a vital thing for a political system to have, but the same respondents turned around and said that a Communist should not be allowed to teach in the local college.[2] It is only rarely that there is overwhelming agreement on a *specific* policy. For example, when asked: "Are you in favor of government old-age pensions for needy persons?" 94 percent of the American population in January 1939 answered "yes."[3] There is often agreement on a *general* question, but disagreement over *specific* points. In other words, consensus must be reserved for those aspects of a political culture that are so vague and indefinite that most people will support them. It is generally unwise to speak of consensus on a particular issue, like medicare, social security, or the war in Vietnam. When there is agreement on specific issues of this type, it has probably grown out of a more general consensual issue —like a domestic policy honoring the welfare state, or a foreign policy that is anti-Communist.

Consensus (or unity, solidarity) is as praised as conflict is damned, and, of course, it too is necessary to a political system. Without some form of consensus—and writers disagree where the line should be drawn—there is nothing to hold a system together. It ceases to be a system. For example, in Nigeria, a consensus existed for many years around the idea of independence from Britain. After the goal was achieved, regional and tribal differences came to the fore again, and civil war became inevitable. And we all know what happened when the American consensus broke down in 1860. Many other examples

[2] James Prothro and Charles M. Grigg, "Fundamental Principles of Democracy: Bases of Agreement and Disagreement," *Journal of Politics*, 22 (1960): 276–94.

[3] Cited in Lloyd A. Free and Hadley Cantril, *The Political Beliefs of Americans: A Study of Public Opinion* (New York: Simon and Schuster, 1968), p. 10.

make the same point: political systems need some "glue"—consensus—to hold them together.

The proper function of political parties in an ideal political system would be to provide for conflict while maintaining a basic consensus, to reconcile the two forces so that one never dominates the other. This can be done by restricting consensus to fundamental issues—the basic philosophy of the system, the constitution, national defense—while permitting conflict to take place on how to reach those goals. In the United States, it would seem that this ideal situation has been achieved. The Republican and Democratic parties are united on the basic questions, each trying to outdo the other in its loyalty to the basic ideals, but they disagree about means. One party generally relies on private initiative, the other on public action. According to the general model, everything should be working well. Yet this is not entirely true. Large segments of the population claim that they are not represented by those in power, and many people complain that the political parties are not "speaking" for them. What has happened to this model of democracy?

Perhaps the trouble arises because no allowance has been made for change in the consensus. If two parties agree all the time, then consensus becomes a static phenomenon, good for all time. It is more valuable, however, to regard consensus as open to change. But where will this change come from? How will conflict over the consensus be expressed? In most political systems, the consensus is challenged by "extremist" political movements, those whose ideas are so different from the prevailing ones that they are, by definition, outside the consensus. These movements develop when the prevailing consensus is in trouble, when it no longer commands universal loyalty. If it did, movements would not exist outside of it. When the consensus is threatened, political movements become more important: they can alter the consensus with their activities. And, usually, the political parties are still arguing about the means to a goal that is no longer shared. In fact, when faced with a threat to their hegemony, political parties usually move closer together. This seems to be the situation in the United States today. Although everything appears to be in order, both the right and the left are unhappy. So long as the consensus resists change, the political system will be unstable no matter how well the machinery is working.

It is a complex situation. All we can say is that political parties are supposed to find a balance between consensus and conflict that will keep the system stable. In most cases they succeed. But in periods of crisis, that is, when the basic values come under attack, the political parties will have trouble performing this function, and political movements, which are more relevant to the situation, will assume the initiative.

Another function of political parties is recruitment. This can be broken down into two categories—recruiting people into the system and recruiting leaders to run the system.

Political parties are expected to be able to involve the uninvolved. A political campaign in a local area generally incorporates many people in the political system who would ordinarily remain outside. Studies of this in the United States have focused on the work of the recruits. For example, the active campaign workers in Los Angeles County in the 1956 election campaign were making speeches, planning strategy, coordinating, fund-raising, and canvassing. Commitment varied with the party. Sixteen percent of Democrats worked full time, 32 percent half time, and 52 percent part time; for the Republicans the corresponding figures were 25 percent, 38 percent, and 37 percent. The workers within each party had varying motives for their work and different political ideologies.[4] A similar study in Detroit showed that local party leaders were more likely to be middle class than their constituents, but they had significant roots in the lower-class constituencies.[5] However, we still know very little about the type of person who is drawn into political activity by a campaign.

Whether these people stay involved in politics is difficult to answer. Party activity is cyclical: it reaches its peak at election time and is much quieter the rest of the year. Some people devote nearly all their time to political activity, others devote some time, others none. Political parties make it possible for those who want to spend a great deal of time in politics to do so, but they also provide an outlet for those who wish to be less active. Parties barely touch those who consider politics an alien activity. They are most helpful to full-time party members.

[4] Dwaine Marvick and Charles P. Nixon, "Recruitment Contrasts in Rival Campaign Groups," in *Political Decision Makers: Recruitment and Performance*, ed. Dwaine Marvick (New York: Free Press, 1961), pp. 193–217.

[5] Samuel Eldersveld, *Political Parties: A Behavioral Analysis* (Chicago: Rand McNally, 1964), pp. 153–60.

Two outstanding examples of individuals who rose to power through political parties are Lyndon Johnson and Leonid Brezhnev. Both came up through the party ranks, as the following summaries of their careers show:[6]

LEONID I. BREZHNEV	LYNDON B. JOHNSON
Born 1906.	Born 1908 in Johnson City, Texas, son of farmer, school teacher, local politician.
Joined CPSU in 1931.	
1927–1930, land surveyor in Kursk.	1924, graduated from high school.
1930–1935, in raion and then oblast land department in Urals.	1924–1927, worked as laborer.
1935, graduated from the Dneprodzerzhinsk Metallurgical Institute.	1927–1930, attended Southwest Texas State Teachers College.
1935–1937, engineer at Dzerzhinsky Metallurgical Plant.	1930–1931, taught in Houston public schools, helped Kleberg in campaign for Congress.
1938, Department Chief in Dnepropetrovsk Oblast Party Committee.	1931, went to Washington as secretary to Representative Kleberg, wealthy conservative Texas Democrat.
1939, became Propaganda Secretary in the same oblast.	1935, was appointed Texas director, National Youth Administration, youngest state director in country.
1941–1945, served as political commissar for the 18th Army, part of the 4th Ukrainian Front, rising to rank of major-general.	1937, elected to Congress on strong New Deal platform, became favorite of Roosevelt.
1946–1947, First Secretary of Zaporozhe Oblast Party Committee and member of Ukrainian CC.	1937–1949, Representative from Texas.
1948–1950, First Secretary of Dnepropetrovsk Oblast.	1941, lost close race for Senate to isolationist Pappy Lee O'Daniel.
1950–1952, First Secretary of the Moldavian Republic CC.	1941–1942, served in Navy in Pacific.
October 1952–March 1953, Secretary and Candidate member of CPSU CC.	1948, won Democratic nomination for Senate, 494, 191 to 494, 104.
1953–1954, head of the Political Administration of the Navy.	1949–1961, United States Senator from Texas.

[6] Reprinted from Zbigniew Brzezinski and Samuel P. Huntington, *Political Power: USA–USSR* (New York: Viking, 1965), pp. 164–67.

LEONID I. BREZHNEV	LYNDON B. JOHNSON
February 1954, appointed Second Secretary of the Kazakhstan Republic CC, under Ponomarenko.	1951, elected Senate Democratic whip.
August 1955–February 1956, became First Secretary of the Kazakhstan CC, replacing Ponomarenko.	1953, elected Senate Democratic leader, youngest man ever named floor leader by either major party.
February 1956, Secretary of the CPSU CC and candidate member of the Presidium.	1955–1961, majority leader, United States Senate, played constructive role in handling Eisenhower legislation.
1957, was elected full member in reward for supporting Khrushchev during June 1957 crisis.	1960, candidate for Democratic presidential nomination; selected by Kennedy as Vice Presidential nominee.
1957–1958, trouble-shooter in charge of industrial reorganization.	1961, Vice President of the United States.
1960, was elected Chairman of the USSR Presidium of the Supreme Soviet (nominal Head of State) and left the Secretariat of the CPSU CC.	1964–1968, President.
June 1963, returned to Secretariat of the CPSU CC—the man to watch.	
1964–present, First Secretary, CPSU.	

Both men used their political experience when they took on governmental responsibilities, but apparently both had some difficulty making the adjustment.

There are many points in the party system where people are recruited for national leadership. Most of these fall into three categories—initial activity, nominations, and elections. We have already talked about initial activity, participation in local campaigns, which can be the starting point for some people. At the local level, there are usually political party clubs (also called cells, branches, associations, depending on the kind of political party in question). These are permanent institutions; that is, although their activity varies according to the election cycle, they exist, with some staff, between as well as during elections. In many cities, especially in the United States, a person can rise to political prominence through his relationship with a political club—the urban political "boss" is one example. The boss's strength is based on the loyalty of these clubs to him, not on any position he holds. Some "bosses" have held no governmental position for years and yet been the most powerful political individuals in their area. Others may hold offices, like that of mayor, but their power really comes from informal ties to local associations; the office is incidental. Since power in the political system is highly decentralized, a person can become a national power through his ties to clubs in one city. This is clearly the case with Chicago's Mayor Richard Daley, and much the same kind of thing occurs in Italy and France.

When political parties nominate people for high office, they are recruiting them for leadership. The nominating process is generally most important in political systems where elections are not contested. When there is only one candidate, nominations become crucial. But when elections involve a real contest between candidates, the nominations themselves are less significant.

One-party systems take a variety of forms. In some cases (Nazi Germany, for example), second parties are illegal. In others, such as Ghana or Algeria, other parties are legal but so strongly discouraged in the interests of national unity that they have little significance. In a third type of one-party system, found in many states in the southern United States, second parties are legal but are discouraged by regional tradition, at least in local elections. Whatever the reasons for the lack of party competition, without it the nominating process assumes more importance. In the USSR, for example, most nominations for local positions occur at a meeting of the group the official is to lead. If the post is important, a representative of the CPSU usually picks the candidate; if not, the CPSU is likely to ratify the local choice. The important point is that ". . . the election itself is no more than a (virtually automatic) confirmation." [7] The same trend is evident in the American South, but national party elites exercise less power there. Candidates are usually nominated in a direct primary, that is, by the party members in a primary election. Since there will be no real contest in the

[7] Alfred G. Meyer, *The Soviet Political System* (New York: Random House, 1965), pp. 126–27.

general election, as many as ten or fifteen candidates may compete
for the nomination in the party. Competition does not occur between parties, only within one party.

In two-party systems, the nominating process is not as crucial,
but it still plays a major role (as the presidential nominating conventions in the United States show). Although a nominated candidate in a two-party system is not sure of election, without party
nomination he has almost no chance at all. Anyone seeking office
must be concerned about the nominating process. There are two
basic nominating procedures in a two-party system like the American
—convention and direct primary. The primary was devised to take
the selection of candidates out of the hands of professionals and
give it back to the party membership. It rarely works that way. In
fact, good relationships with the powers that be are essential, in
either procedure. This means that the recruiting process is usually
controlled by the leaders themselves; they determine who is to join
their ranks. It is possible for a candidate to be nominated without
their support, but it is difficult and unusual. Besides, when someone
is nominated on his own initiative, the battle is likely to be so ex-
hausting that he has few resources left for the general election
campaign.

Nominations are less important in multiparty systems. When political parties are numerous, it is not difficult to receive a nomination.
In the extreme example, a candidate could form his own party and
nominate himself. Although this tactic hardly guarantees election,
it is sometimes effective, even in two-party systems. For example, in
1968 George Wallace created a new party by putting himself on
the ballot in all fifty American states under various party labels.
Such a phenomenon is more characteristic of multiparty systems.
It happens so often in France and some Latin American countries
that it has become a regular feature of the political landscape.

The purpose of being nominated is to be elected—the final stage
in the parties' recruitment of new political leaders. In one-party
systems, elections are sometimes so *pro forma* they can scarcely be
recognized as elections. But, in other systems, where elections are
more important, money is spent, time is allocated, contacts are
made, speeches are delivered, and the results are eagerly anticipated.
If a potential leader goes through all the other stages brilliantly, but
fails in the election, then he is back where he started. In all countries where there are elections, they become the focal point of the

system. In systems where elections are unimportant, the recruiting occurs elsewhere.

In short, the recruitment of leaders is a vital function of political parties. Because this recruitment is necessary for all political systems, political parties or some functional equivalent will always exist. Different stages of the process become important, depending on the number of parties in the system and the role of elections. It should be emphasized that if a country proclaims the importance of elections, that by itself does not mean much. For instance, elections may occur for minor positions, while those in influential positions have either been appointed or have risen through the ranks. This can happen in heavily bureaucratic political systems, regardless of their rhetoric on elections. In other words, some elections are primarily important as symbols of popular control or indicators of mandates and trends, and only secondarily for electing people. But such theories have their limits. Recent events in the United States have shown that it really does matter who holds office, that different officials have different policies, and that some policies are better than others.

The third major function of political parties is the de facto governing of a political system. Once again, the way one-party, two-party, and multiparty systems differ is instructive.

Governing a political system is usually associated with one-party systems, where the major political party often becomes synonymous with the government. Important decisions are made in the party hierarchy, and then ratified and announced by the government. The leader of the party (first secretary) has more power in the country than the leader of the government (premier or president). For example, the names of the presidents of Cuba and the Soviet Union—Osvaldo Dorticos Torrado and Nikolai V. Podgorny—are not well known because the officials are obscure. The leader of the government in a one-party system is not particularly important; government positions are honorific and relatively easy to obtain, while party positions are important. In systems of this type, the political scientist interested in power will almost automatically turn to the party rather than the government.

De facto government by political parties also occurs in two-party systems. To head the government of the United States, for example, one must have the support of one of the major parties. It is virtually impossible, as we have seen, to be elected without a party nomination, and under the convention system, this invariably means support by the major figures in the party.

Once elected, a president of the United States serves simultaneously as leader of his party and leader of the country, a dual loyalty that is bound to create some confusion. Suppose an incumbent president travels to Seattle to tell an assembly of longshoremen how much their wages and way of life have improved in the last few years. Is he acting as the leader of his party or of the government? It could be argued that he is acting properly, because a president needs to build support for his policies. But a cynic would point out that "the last few years" refers to his administration, and that there is an implicit contrast with the "stagnation" of the previous years when the other party was in power. Besides, a reelection campaign is approaching, and he wants to be prepared. Now further suppose that the president spent $100,000 in government funds transporting himself and his staff to Seattle, and that while he was there, a crisis arose in the Middle East that made it necessary for him to return to Washington. The lines between government and party are becoming more blurred. Most Americans would not be too upset by this example. They give their political leaders much leeway in what they can do to further a partisan cause in office. Seeking reelection is considered part of the president's job, and as long as nothing dishonest is involved, partisan behavior is acceptable.

It is easier to see how de facto governing by political parties in a two-party system works in Britain than in the United States. There, when a party elects a majority of the members of Parliament, it automatically becomes the governing force at the invitation of the monarch, and the leader of the winning party becomes prime minister. So, a primary difference between party politics in the two countries is that the leader of the British government owes his position to his party status, rather than to a direct national election. After assuming office, the prime minister and his cabinet—all party leaders too—prepare a program to send to Parliament. Because party organization is tighter in Britain than in the United States, the government's program usually passes, supported by all the members of the majority party. The phenomenon of one faction of a president's party (Southern Democrats, for example) working to defeat his program is unknown in Britain. Laws passed by Parliament then become the supreme law of the land, comparable to the American constitution.

On paper, this process seems to be party government in its highest form, incorporating some of the best features of the one-party system. Yet it does not work out quite as well in practice. First, the British civil service, a theoretically nonpartisan body that supports programs of both parties, is often vital in formulating parliamentary programs. Second, because a party must win support for its policies from the general population, it goes to great lengths to appease followers of the other party. One strange result of this phenomenon is that Labour governments are becoming quite stodgy, while Conservative governments can be more innovative. (The present Conservative government of Edward Heath is an exception to this, being as stodgy as any Britain has ever had.) But despite these qualifications, party government is more genuine in Britain than in most other two-party systems.

The situation in multiparty systems is more confusing. Since no party generally obtains a majority of the seats in the legislature, coalitions must be established to form a government. These coalitions are highly unstable, so strong partisan policies that might upset the balance are avoided. A coalition government's programs tend to be compromises of the various party platforms. Cabinets are coalitions, too. In general, multiparty systems involve less party government than other types. Figures identified with national, rather than partisan, causes are likely to head the government. If they are connected with a party, it is a personal, not a partisan, association. The members of Charles de Gaulle's party had little in common besides loyalty to de Gaulle. In short, the function of de facto government by political parties is less important in multiparty systems than in other types.

PARTIES IN THE UNITED STATES

Having discussed the functions of political parties, we can now examine how parties work in specific political systems throughout the world—in an advanced industrial society like the United States, for instance, or in the dependent countries of the Third World.

Descriptions of the role of political parties in advanced industrial societies are virtually identical. They deal with a nonideological, two-party system, whose major characteristics have been set down by Clinton Rossiter:

(1) the persistence and ascendancy of the two-party scheme, (2) the hard times of minor parties devoted to narrow-gauge interests or broad-scale reform, (3) the loose, supple, interest-directed, principle-shunning, coalition-forming nature of the two major parties, (4) the decentralization of authority in the organization of these parties in the country at large, (5) the absence of effective discipline in the organization of these parties within the government, (6) the encirclement and penetration of the parties by a vigorous array of interest groups, and (7) the generally low-key, independent, skeptical approach of most Americans to the business of politics.[8]

The picture should be familiar enough to most people. Election contests characteristically have two major candidates for office, one of whom will win. Other candidates may add color and fun, but they are not really in the race. During the campaign, each candidate voices innocuous platitudes—or not such innocuous threats—but neither really discusses the major issues facing the country. If they did, the voters would be bored and not elect them. The party that wins is the one that gets the most people out to vote, and this is accomplished through local organization. Voters are canvassed, baby sitters and rides arranged, telephone calls made, announcements mailed. A few people volunteer to help in their candidate's campaign. The local candidate is virtually autonomous: the national party organization may make suggestions and provide some literature and funds, but that is all. And the candidate is under no obligation to support the party's national candidate or its national program. In many cases, he will ignore or oppose the national organization if this helps him out locally, and the national party has no recourse when the candidate's local power base is strong. Finally, the candidate is surrounded by small sources of financial aid, which assist in the campaign and expect favorable, but honest, treatment afterward. After the election, this activity subsides until the next campaign.

Not only is this a substantially accurate picture of politics in the United States, it also indicates the political trend in many European countries. Although European political parties are still centralized, they resemble American parties in their nonideological nature. In West Germany, for example, the Social Democrats, the historic

[8] *Parties and Politics in America* (New York: Signet, 1964), p. 45.

Marxist party, have formed a coalition with the Christian Democrats, a capitalist party. Similarly in Italy, what was called the "opening to the left" occurred when former Marxist Pietro Nenni led his Socialist party into an alliance with the Italian Christian Democrats. It appears that the trend in industrial societies is toward "interest-directed, principle-shunning, coalition-forming" political parties. Is this desirable?

Three points in Rossiter's list—the persistence of two parties, the lack of centralization, and the lack of ideology—merit closer examination, and we will discuss them in order.

The two-party system is usually considered desirable because it combines the advantages of the one-party and the multiparty systems without their disadvantages. As a rule, the number of parties is inversely proportional to efficiency and directly proportional to representativeness—in other words, the fewer the parties, the greater the efficiency. In a one-party system, duplication is avoided. And the government is not disrupted by constant conflict. Therefore, the one party can carry out policies that are best for the greatest number of people, and it need not worry about watering down its decisions to appease certain factions. On the other hand, a multiparty system is a more accurate reflection of the political situation. How can one party represent everyone when people differ so? Sixteen parties can represent sixteen points of view better than one or two parties. A multiparty system does not force the voter to compromise. If he believes in welfare but not civil liberties, there is a party for that. If he believes in civil liberties, but not welfare, another party supports that. He knows that the more parties there are, the closer he is to the leader of his party.

If two-party systems are only somewhat efficient and somewhat representative, at least they are not generally considered totally inefficient (like multiparty systems) or totally authoritarian (like one-party systems). Some choice is available, but not enough to cause paralysis. And enough duplication exists to guarantee that minorities will not be trampled in the interests of efficiency. The justification for two-party politics, then, is expressed in terms of less desirable alternatives.

For the two-party system to work properly, there should be two distinct parties, which differ significantly on programs. But, this ideal is rarely found. Further, in evaluating the two-party system, we must consider the role of minor parties. It is often said, even by advocates of two-party systems, that minor parties have provided the impetus to change society. In the United States, for example, the programs of the Populist and Progressive parties have in due course become the law of the land. This is a strange comment on the two-party system—that it has to deny itself to save itself. It seems there is nothing magical about two parties; in fact, two-party systems that work do so because they have more than two parties. There are both advantages and disadvantages to all party systems—whether they contain one, two, or many parties. Choosing one type rather than another is a function of one's values.

A second characteristic of the American party system is its lack of centralization—a uniquely American phenomenon. In a centralized party system, power is asserted at the top. It then filters down to the rank-and-file of the party. Decentralized systems work in reverse. Power exists on the local level, and the national leadership is really symbolic. The differences between the ideal and actual models can be seen in the diagrams below:[9]

The great advantage of decentralization is that it is democratic and highly sensitive to local and minority interests. In the United States, local power refers to the South and the cities in the Democratic party, and to rural areas and the suburbs in the Republican party. Because of decentralization, these areas have a say in party activity. They exercise a veto over policies, guaranteeing that no group will ever be completely ignored. In addition, decentralization makes it difficult for anyone to take over a party and use it for his own ends; this adds to the stability of the political system. The major disadvantage of decentralization is that it inhibits the creation of national policy. As the two diagrams show, the more decentralized the system, the greater the distance between voters and the elite. Furthermore, after a party has been elected the opposition within the ranks makes it doubtful that the policy will ever be implemented. Local veto power can be a permanent obstruction. Critics of decentralization claim that it has harmed American black people politically. Black representation from the cities had little effect as long as a veto power existed. In other words, defenders of decentralization generally emphasize negative government—preventing bad things from happening; advocates of centralization stress positive government—making it possible for good things to happen. Here again,

[9] Reprinted from John Fenton, *People and Parties in Politics: Unofficial Makers of Public Policy* (Glenview, Ill.: Scott, Foresman, 1966), p. 17.

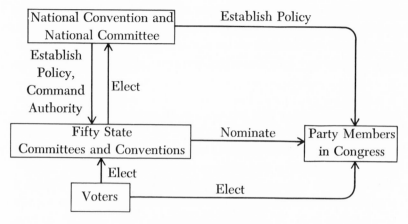

Strong National Party

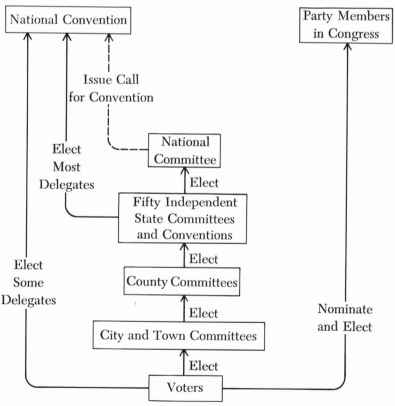

Actual Organization of American Parties

personal values determine one's preference—ours is for the positive approach of a centralized party.

The most important and controversial aspect of the American party system is its nonideological character. The defenders of nonideological parties consider them to be essential to the stability of a political system. If political parties based on extensive and conflicting world views divided the country, compromise would be impossible. Marxist would conflict with conservative, who in turn would conflict with liberal, who in turn would conflict with racist, and there would be constant shifting from one ideological faction to another. It would take demagogic or emotional appeals, calling for unity and national strength, to give some order to this disarray. In the end, the most ruthless and opportunist ideologies would win. Their extremist policies, whether Fascist or Communist, would lead the country toward disaster.

Nonideological parties, on the other hand, are supposed to promote stability. The argument in their favor runs as follows: people argue over the candidates, not the ultimate virtues of ideologies. The future of the system does not depend on an election campaign. In addition, a compromise-oriented party system produces excellent leadership and promotes responsible social change. To rise through the system, men must learn the difficult art of compromise. Thus, the man who makes his way to the top will be adept at reconciling hostile viewpoints. And compromise of this type engenders gradual, rather than revolutionary, change. Because the pragmatic leader wants to stay in power, he must follow public opinion. When the public demands change, he will change, and new policies will emerge. The result is democracy without mass action. The public will is heard, but it does not dominate.

Criticism of this point of view comes from two different directions. Fifteen years ago, some political scientists were saying that the United States needed "responsible party government." Based upon American impressions of the British system—impressions that were sometimes inaccurate—they argued for disciplined parties that would adopt definite and responsible points of view. Thus, the parties could unite around meaningful platforms that did not involve total ideologies. Avoiding ideology did not mean avoiding order and direction. If a party constituted a majority in Congress, it could put its platform into effect through disciplined voting. The party out of power would have an alternative program, and it would try to convince the voters of its superiority in the next election. The system would provide genuine choice, and once a decision had been made, the policy could be implemented.

Recently, a second wave of criticism of nonideological parties has appeared. This point of view, which comes from both the right and the left of American politics, is also critical of the lack of choice in American elections. "A choice, not an echo" is what the followers of Barry Goldwater called for in 1964. And Goldwater's famous declaration that "extremism in the defense of liberty is no vice" would hardly come from an advocate of nonideological parties. On the left, criticism is frequently addressed to the increasing irrelevance of party politics. Nonideology is seen as harmful, simply because it does lead to stability. So long as society faces basic problems like war, racism, poverty, and exploitation, any stability perpetuates injustice and is therefore reprehensible. A radical or revolutionary political movement is needed to replace the status quo, to transcend the irrelevance of party politics. Rather than a broker, a leader (or leaderless group) must arise, one that is aware of the problem and is committed to rectifying it. Politics must be concerned with the elimination of oppression, not interest. (For more on this, see Chapter 15.)

And the debate continues with no end in sight. Who is right depends on one's values. It is clear that, in general, defenders of nonideological politics are primarily interested in stability, while critics want change. Some social scientists, generalizing on the absence of ideological parties, talk about "The End of Ideology." According to Seymour Martin Lipset:

> This change in Western political life reflects the fact that the fundamental political problems of the industrial revolution have been solved: the workers have achieved industrial and political citizenship; the conservatives have accepted the welfare state; and the democratic left has recognized that an increase in overall state power carries with it more dangers to freedom than solutions for economic problems. This very triumph of the democratic social revolution in the West ends domestic politics for those intellectuals who must have ideologies or utopias to motivate them to political action.[10]

[10] *Political Man: The Social Bases of Politics* (Garden City, N.Y.: Doubleday Anchor, 1959), pp. 442–43.

We will have much more to say about the end of ideology later in
the book. For the present, it should be clear that those who believe
the fundamental problems have been solved value stability a great
deal. On the other hand, war protesters, rent strikers, urban rioters,
student activists, and many others certainly do not agree that society
is moving in the right direction. And in their proposed solutions,
many of these groups are developing ideologies, which seems to
indicate that we have not yet seen the end of ideology.

What has ended are traditional ideologies. When both de Gaulle
and the Communist party opposed the student strike in France in
May 1968, the leaders of the strike condemned them both as out-
moded and irrelevant. The old ideologies, like orthodox Marxism
and pragmatic liberalism, have been (or are being) replaced by
new ones. Thus the emphasis on the *New* Left, and on the one area
of the world where the old ideologies never really applied—the
Third World. Franz Fanon, Ché Guevara, and Mao Tse-tung have
become the intellectual guides for the activities of the new ideology.

POLITICAL PARTIES ELSEWHERE

So far little has been said about the Third World. We can begin
by stating that the "end of ideology" thesis is meaningless for the
countries of Asia, Africa, and Latin America. Revolutions are in
progress in those areas, and revolutions tend to create ideologies to
justify them. Negritude, Pan-Africanism, Pan-Arabianism, communism, socialism, and nationalism are a few examples. But instead of
examining these ideologies, we are going to work backward and
study the role of political parties in these societies.

Most countries in the Third World have institutions called political parties, and these were instrumental in the drive for independence. Very often the first stirrings of revolutionary activity occurred
in a coalition of legal, respectable moderates and secret, under-
ground revolutionaries. As independence came closer, their coalition
changed into a political association pressing for independence. Once
this was achieved, a political party was formed and began to govern
the country. Because unity was a necessity in the drive toward
independence, most Third World countries (except for Latin America, which achieved independence much earlier) have developed
one-party systems as the coalition turns, with less assurance, toward
economic development. Understandably, political parties in these

countries emphasize one function of political parties—the de facto governing of the political system. The other functions might be performed by other institutions, acting—though perhaps not looking—like a political party.

Political parties, in one form or another, serve as a basis for conflict and consensus. After independence has been achieved, the formation of consensus—in the face of linguistic, territorial, economic, and tribal conflicts—becomes a major goal of political activity. Rarely does the formal political party do this well. Mexico, a country with a wide variety of interests, including big corporations, small businessmen, large landowners, small farmers, peasants, urban workers, and professionals, has adopted an interesting system. To build a consensus, the one major party, Partito Revolucionario Institucional (PRI), is organized into sectors. One represents labor, another agriculture, and another "the popular sector," which covers most other groups. Although the attempt has met with mixed results, it is an interesting approach to the problem of building consensus in a Third World country.

More often, conflict and consensus take place outside the formal political parties. Conflict occurs because the new "nation" was never a nation in anyone's eyes but the European power that colonized the territory. Different languages are spoken within the "nation," and people are attached to their own language and do not want to learn another. Further, if the language of one group is also spoken in an adjoining country, the group may feel closer to people in the foreign country than to people in their own. Many Third World countries face conflicts of this kind. The conflict does not occur in the political party system, but in the nonpolitical divisions dating back hundreds of years. The same is often true for consensus, which will not be built by the political party, but by external forces. A drive for economic development, external war, and the international demonstration effect—what has happened successfully elsewhere in the world—have all served as nation-building forces.

Recruitment of people into the political system will take place both inside and outside the party system. It has already been suggested that in one-party systems the major party acts as a de facto government. Since most of these countries have one-party systems, people will be recruited to power through the party. And since most of these parties led in the struggle for independence, they will supply most of the country's leaders. In India, for example, the

Congress party was a leader of the independence movement and a source of political leaders, such as Ghandi, Nehru, Shastri, and Mrs. Ghandi. Political parties are very important in providing leadership, but recruitment also takes place outside the parties. Some leaders arise regionally or tribally; they become spokesmen for a local interest and eventually build a national constituency on it. Besides, the leaders in the independence movement were an elite group. To involve others in the affairs of the country, they must break out of their small circle and find leaders among the population. Institutions other than political parties serve that purpose.

To summarize, political parties are common to all systems, in function if not in form. (This does not mean, as Gabriel Almond suggests, see Chapter 14, that "interest articulation" is characteristic of all societies. It does mean that the functions discussed in this chapter take place everywhere, in one form or another.) We have defined a political party as a nongovernmental institution that performs certain functions, and we have examined those functions in various political systems. We classified any body that performed these functions as a political party or its functional equivalent. We have also seen that party activity is much quieter in developed than in underdeveloped countries. This lack of ideology within the party system, however, has been matched by ideology outside of it. One could conclude on the basis of this that parties are becoming increasingly irrelevant to advanced industrial societies, that conflict takes place outside the parties, that the parties do not mold a true but a false consensus, that recruitment takes place elsewhere, and that the parties no longer govern in any meaningful sense of the term. In fact, that conclusion is drawn in Chapter 15. But before we reach that point, we must look at another type of nongovernmental institution, interest groups, and then consider what it means to govern.

4 Interest Groups

ALTHOUGH THEY BOTH are nongovernmental institutions, and although they both intervene between citizens and government, political parties and interest groups are two different things. We defined a political party as a nongovernmental institution through which people attempt to gain control of the state. Interest groups differ in that they usually seek to influence those already in control of the state, instead of attempting to elect their own candidates. Occasionally a member of the American Medical Association (AMA) is elected to Congress, but most of the AMA's political activity is devoted to convincing nonphysicians in Congress of the justice of its cause. However, this distinction between political parties and interest groups is only a general one. Although minor parties in many systems run candidates for office, they are really interest groups because of their low standing in the race and because of their educational activities. Thus, Norman Thomas, former head of the American Socialist party, considered his party primarily a means of changing minds rather than changing incumbents. The Poujadist party in France, which was dedicated to the elimination of the French income tax, is another example of a political party that is really an interest group.

In other words, we should pay more attention to what a nongovernmental institution does than to what it is called. For that reason, we shall look first at the functions of interest groups in all political systems and then evaluate their role in advanced industrial societies and in the countries of the Third World.

INTEREST GROUPS AND WHAT THEY DO

Certain writers consider political groups the essence of political activity. One of them, Arthur F. Bentley, declared:

> The great task in the study of any form of social life is the analysis of these groups. It is much more than classification, as that term is ordinarily used. When the groups are adequately stated, everything is stated. When I say everything, I mean everything. The complete description will mean the complete science, in the study of social phenomenon, as in any other field. There will be no more room for animistic "causes" here than there.[1]

Why are political groups so important? Bentley regarded them as the basic datum of political analysis—like energy in physics, money in economics, or culture in anthropology. Further, everyone belongs to political groups, whether he is aware of it or not. No membership cards are needed, no meetings attended; people are group members because they are people. David Truman, a follower of Bentley, later called such groups "potential groups." Students, women, Polish Americans, people between eighteen and twenty-one, residents of the Southwest, salesmen, amateur jai alai players, tourists to the West Indies, and German-speaking Americans would qualify as potential groups. They were formed because of similar characteristics, rather than a specific desire to form a group. Such potential groups, according to Truman, operate in almost the same way as formally organized groups.

In the countries of the Third World, organized groups are less important than potential groups. Geographic groups play a crucial role in a country like Nigeria. There the eastern region of the country (which corresponds roughly to a tribal division) took its existence as a potential group seriously enough to secede and form a separate country. A similar merging of geographic and tribal divi-

[1] *The Process of Government* (Evanston, Ill.: Principia Press, 1935), pp. 208–9.

sions in the Belgian Congo led to the secession attempts of Katanga province. In India, hostile linguistic groups divide the country, intensifying political conflict. Another example of conflict based on potential groups is the division between landlord and peasant.[2] This can be seen clearly in South Vietnam, where land distribution is a major political issue (see Chapter 7). If you know how much land a Vietnamese possesses, you can predict with reasonable accuracy whether he will favor the government of South Vietnam or the insurgent forces.

Whether potential or organized, hierarchical or informal, national or local, interest groups exist in every political system. They perform many of the same functions as political parties—de facto government, recruitment, and shaping consensus and conflict—and are also active in support building within a political system. We shall examine all of these functions, but will concentrate primarily on support building, since that was not discussed in connection with political parties.

De facto government by nongovernmental institutions is not restricted to political parties. One interesting case of de facto government by an interest group occurs in the area of American agricultural policy. Each local farming area has a county farm bureau with a county agent. These bureaus are associated with individual state farm bureau federations and with the American Farm Bureau Federation—perhaps the single most powerful private interest group in the United States. Local bureaus, although ostensibly private, make public decisions on price supports and acreage allotments. And because they are combined with governmental institutions like the Federal Extension Service and the Agriculture Committee of the House of Representatives, local bureaus controlled by large farmers in effect make public decisions involving all farmers. Theodore Lowi has summarized the situation:

> Agriculture is the field where the distinction between public and private has been almost completely eliminated, not by public expropriation of private domain, but by private expropriation of public domain. For more than a generation, Americans have succeeded in expanding the public sphere without giving thought to the essential democratic question of how

[2] Barrington Moore, Jr., *The Social Origins of Dictatorship and Democracy* (Boston: Beacon Press, 1966).

each expansion is to be effected. The creation of private governments has profoundly limited the capacity of the public government to govern responsibly and flexibly.[3]

The field of agriculture is a typical case. The confusion of public and private, or who is governing whom, is common in American politics. In foreign policy formation, for example, there are many activities, particularly those involving propaganda or espionage, where it is advantageous to employ private groups. Then if a mistake occurs, the government can disclaim any knowledge of the affair, passing it off as the price of independence in a democracy. Yet at the same time, the government is actually responsible, since it finances and operates the private agency under cover. The Central Intelligence Agency (CIA) has subsidized "private" groups as diverse as the Asia Foundation and the National Student Association. Although there is no proof of government backing, propaganda groups like Radio Liberty (broadcasts to Soviet Union) and Radio Free Europe (broadcasts to Eastern Europe) are really quasi-public interest groups. Neither publishes any financial records, and the supporters of Radio Liberty are not listed, while the supporters of Radio Free Europe include prominent governmental figures. Both model their policies after those of the United States. These groups are examples of a rapidly increasing tendency to merge public and private, particularly in the realm of international affairs.

De facto governing by interest groups is also common in many socialist countries. Labor unions, for example, are frequently intended to make policy and transmit it down to the members, instead of representing the interests of the members to the government. Groups like the Soviet Writer's Union and the various congresses of Soviet writers exercise a similar function, determining what is acceptable to the government and can be published. Although these groups, like those discussed in the United States, are ostensibly private, they make authoritative decisions and are therefore acting as government.

Interest groups are also involved with recruiting people into the system. Like political parties, they recruit both part-time and full-time workers. When an interest group decides to support or oppose

---

[3] "How the Farmers Get What They Want," *The Reporter*, May 21, 1964, pp. 34–37. Reprinted in Lowi, ed., *Legislative Politics USA* (Boston: Little, Brown, 1965), p. 139.

a given policy, it often encourages its members to write those in government about their point of view. This involves many people who have never before communicated with their representatives. But this type of activity is not very important because the letter writers are not really participating; they are being used. Frequently, they are told what to say or given a prepared letter to sign. Most American congressmen are unimpressed by mass letter-writing campaigns. In any event, this type of recruitment is cyclical at best, arousing people only for a short period of time.

Many political leaders have been recruited from interest groups. The head of a major labor union is frequently asked to serve on various government commissions to investigate this or that and to recommend people for different offices. In other words, he becomes a decision maker, a "new man of power" in the words of C. Wright Mills.[4] But it is more common for governmental officials to be recruited from private corporations, which are very definitely political interest groups, than from labor unions. Most cabinet members in recent years have been businessmen of one type or another, in both Republican and Democratic administrations. David Packard, for example, started his own electronics firm and made millions working on contracts for the Department of Defense, before accepting the position of assistant secretary of defense in the Nixon administration. Another example is George Romney, who went from private industry to state government and then, after an attempt at the presidency, to the cabinet as secretary of housing and urban development. Finally, other governmental officials come directly from the interest group with which they will be concerned. The assistant secretary of health, education and welfare for medical affairs is expected to be cleared with the AMA; agricultural personnel often come from the American Farm Bureau Federation; the American Bar Association is called upon, by law in many states, to nominate judges. In these ways, interest groups become involved in the job of recruiting political leaders.

The third function interest groups share with political parties is that of providing a forum for conflict and consensus. Interest groups engage in conflict more often than in consensus. In fact, they exist principally to get what they can out of the political system—which of course leads to conflict with others of a similar mind. This func-

[4] *The New Men of Power: America's Labor Leaders* (New York: Kelley, 1969).

tion is so important that an entire political theory, usually called pluralism, has developed around it; most of this chapter will be devoted to the pluralist theory. We will come back to the function of conflict later; as for consensus, it simply is not expected from political interest groups. If consensus does exist, it usually has a bad name—like collusion, conspiracy, or monopoly. Interest groups are not expected to pursue the public interest, only their private interests.

The one additional function of interest groups is support building. Governments need support for their policies, and one of the primary tasks of political interest groups is to build that support. Consider the following item, which appeared in the *New York Times*:

> Arthur J. Goldberg, United States representative at the United Nations, lent his good offices last night in an attempt to reestablish harmony between the White House and some segments of the Jewish community.
>
> About 40 representatives of secular Jewish groups met with Ambassador Goldberg for two hours at his Waldorf Towers suite.
>
> The discussion concerned the controversy aroused by reports that President Johnson has singled out Jewish opposition to the war in Vietnam and linked it with American aid to Israel.
>
> [One of the participants] said he thought that each of the representatives would go back to their groups and report on the discussions and that the groups would then reassess their positions. He added that he expected a "spate of agreements" to be issued soon. The meeting was called, according to Mr. Goldberg, at the suggestion of Dr. Joachim Prinz, head of the President's Conference, an association of 19 Jewish organizations, and former head of the American Jewish Congress. . . .
>
> The 19 organizations affiliated with the President's conference . . . cut across all of the major rabbinical, congregational, fraternal, and service groups in American Jewish life.[5]

This is support building. The government (President Johnson) was using an informal leader (Ambassador Goldberg) of a potential

[5] *New York Times,* 14 September, 1966, p. 1.

group (American Jews) to win support for his policies (the war in Vietnam).

There are several interesting points about this example of support building. First, it involves only leaders. But if it is to succeed, it will have to work its way down to the ordinary people. This is suggested by the participant who remarked that each person in the room would go back and talk to the group he heads, then, the people in those groups would presumably go back to other groups, and so on down the line. Second, there was constant interaction between potential groups and organized groups. American Jewry, the potential group, was also well organized through the president's conference, bringing together a variety of Jewish activities. Third, the meeting was called by a private citizen, although its primary purpose seems to have been communication from the government to private groups. This suggests that the support building process may work two ways, from the government down and from the group up.

A successful political system must have upward, as well as downward, communication. And interest groups play a major role here. Classical lobbying by interest groups involves upward communication. When the National Rifle Association devotes its energies to defeating gun-control legislation in Congress, it is communicating the views of its members directly to the decision makers. The process is not so clear with potential groups. But a riot could be considered the expression of one dissatisfied potential group.

PLURALISM

In this three-part diagram, the middle figure represents the process of two-way communication.

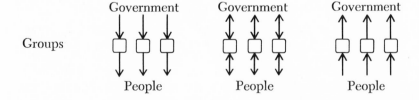

The figure at the left symbolizes, in oversimplified terms, a totalitarian or authoritarian state, in which all communication is directed downward to the population with no feedback. This same type of situation occurs when a private group becomes governmental. Then, the purpose of the group is to transmit decisions to the members of the group. Obedience is expected. This relationship does have the advantage of efficiency. As in one-party systems, groups and popular idiosyncrasies do not interfere with policy making. But there are also some serious disadvantages. Aside from the fact that such one-way communication is highly undemocratic and unrepresentative, contact between government and the population is broken. They become increasingly remote from each other, and this creates an atmosphere of unreality that will eventually cause instability in the system. The figure on the left, then, is elitist, unrepresentative, and inherently impermanent.

The figure on the right represents a system where all communication flows the other way, from the population to the government. This could be called pure democracy, although the terms direct democracy and populistic democracy have also been used. The closest approximation to this model is government by referendum —legislation approved or rejected directly by the electorate rather than by their representatives in the legislature—which occurs in France and the United States. The supporters of the referendum believe that it is extremely democratic and should be used extensively. People can control policy that affects them, without the intervention of selfish private interests and unconcerned representatives.

The opponents point out that the referendum has produced mixed results. In the United States, for example, open-housing legislation has inevitably been defeated when presented in a referendum. Some people think that pure democracy is inherently unstable because it stresses the irrational fears and anxieties of the general population. Some governments have found that by stirring up racial antagonisms they will win in a referendum—a point that was demonstrated in New York City during the police review board referendum of 1966. In short, its opponents believe that the referendum rarely results in purely democratic policies, and that, in any case, pure democracy would be as undesirable and unstable as authoritarianism.

Two-way communication, combining the advantages of both extremes without the disadvantages, has been called pluralistic democracy by William Kornhauser.[6] At its best, it is considered the most practical method of carrying out large-scale decision making without sacrificing popular choice. Advocates of pluralistic democracy argue that it is more stable than direct democracy. Popular will is expressed, but in a less direct form, so it is less likely to be manipulated by demagogues and end up irrational and emotional. It is filtered through interest groups, and the leaders of the groups pass the sentiment on to the governors, after "refining" it. A labor leader, for example, takes emotional statements about the company from his men and translates them into demands for higher minimum wages. These intermediate groups, the argument continues, help check authoritarian tendencies from the government. To gain acceptance of its policy, the government works through the leaders of interest groups, who will translate the message and relay it to the people. The people would never comply with a government decision to cut back spending to avoid inflation, unless interest-group leaders explained why cooperation was important to them. The virtues of pluralistic democracy are seen in contrast with the vices of the alternatives.

However, the case can be overdrawn. Most people would condemn authoritarian government, but they might hesitate before pronouncing pure democracy just as bad. It is only in recent years that referenda have resulted in repressive legislation. Forms of pure democracy have worked well in other periods of American history, leading to significant reforms in state and local government. And, on occasion, corrupt officials have been recalled from office by the voters. Legislatures controlled by private interests have been boycotted by the electorate in an attempt to pass legislation directly. Perhaps the voters are not responsible for recent bad experiences with direct legislation. It was not the ordinary citizen but the leaders of interest groups, particularly the Patrolmen's Benevolent Association, who turned the police review board into a racial issue. The problem was not the irrationalism of the masses but the irrationalism of the elites. Finally, pluralistic democracy does not really filter mass sentiment; it significantly changes it. People will have a voice in politics only when meaningful participation exists at every level of the system.

[6] *The Politics of Mass Society* (New York: Free Press, 1959), pp. 40–41.

All these arguments about pluralistic democracy boil down to
two basic questions: Does pluralism work? Should pluralism work?
The first question is descriptive, the second philosophical. Our discussion so far has been concerned with values, that is, with the
philosophical aspect. But pluralism is also considered a description
of political reality. In fact, there is as much unanimity on the subject of America as a pluralist society as there is on America as a
two-party system. This is not surprising because most advocates of
the two-party system also favor pluralism—the two have a lot in
common.

Pluralism is not simply a two-way communication between the
citizen and his government. Communication (or conflict) between
the groups themselves also takes place, which leads us to revise our
earlier diagram.

Government

Groups

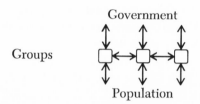

Population

This intergroup conflict is considered one of the great advantages
of pluralism. No single group can obtain everything it wants because another group stands in its way. Therefore, no group in society
can dominate all the others. Not only must business contend with
labor, but some businesses must contend with other businesses. The
truckers make sure that the railroads do not get everything, and
vice versa. From this clash of interests, policy emerges. Each participating group receives a share in rough proportion to its political
assets. No group is without political assets. Unorganized groups
have a potential voting strength that is readily translatable into
political capital. The result is regarded as the fairest way of making
policy, with no one group excluded.

Pluralism seems to impede the emergence of a power elite that
could dominate decision making by monopolizing the means of
political power. This does not mean that political power does not
exist, but rather that many political elites exercise power in many
areas. The people who make key decisions involving military policy
are not necessarily the same ones who dictate educational policy.

Both groups of people have boundaries. They have to work within confines set up by the interest group. We have, then, neither rule by the majority—which is pure democracy, nor rule by a small minority. Robert A. Dahl has coined a new phrase—"minorities rule"—to describe the situation in which a number of elites compete for the support of the general population.[7]

DOES PLURALISM WORK?

This description of pluralism in an advanced, industrial society has come under attack by another group of writers. Their argument is not with the values of a pluralistic society but with its failure to live up to the model. They say that the system excludes certain groups and that it misrepresents American political reality. The principal charges against pluralism are summarized below:

1. *Give-and-take occurs between some groups while others are totally ignored.* Certain groups have been excluded from American pluralism. The American Indian is perhaps the most obvious example. Others include people under twenty-five, who are not eligible to serve in Congress, but are directly affected by selective service policy, and advocates of marijuana, who have been excluded from legislative bodies. In fact, any group that has been labeled "deviant" by the majority for one reason or another cannot really change policy. Pariah groups, like homosexuals, find that the laws affecting them are often made and implemented by people who specifically want to harass or eliminate them.

The most prominent example of exclusion, however, does not involve an "outcast" group but one that constitutes 11 percent of the American population. Blacks in America have traditionally been denied access to the pluralist process, sometimes through disenfranchisement, sometimes through gerrymandering, sometimes through prejudice and ignorance. Pluralism means compromise, and most pluralists assume that the benefits of compromise will be random, that is, one group will benefit this time, another the next. But nothing in the pluralist system prevents the process from always favoring one group and always hurting another. This is essentially what has happened to American blacks. Whenever southern bigotry

[7] *A Preface to Democratic Theory* (Chicago: University of Chicago Press, 1956), p. 132.

or northern intolerance demanded appeasement, the interests of the American blacks suffered. This was obvious in 1880; it is still apparent today. No wonder black writers attack academic pluralism.[8] The pluralist system is simply not inclusive enough to reflect American political currents accurately.

2. *Democracy must exist within the interest groups before a pluralistic society can be democratic, yet internal democracy is decidedly the exception rather than the rule.* Interest groups play the role of intermediary in the political process; they are expected to transmit messages from the government to the people, and vice versa. Most of the transmitting is done through interest-group leaders: they translate the demands of their members into terms the governing elite can understand, and they meet with the governing elite and then instruct their members to obey certain decisions. Since interest-group leaders play such a key role, it is important to examine how they are selected. Unless they are chosen democratically, there is no reason to believe that they would represent the members any more fairly than someone outside the group. The pluralist model would then no longer make sense. On the other hand, if they are democratically chosen, and a democratic transmission system is set up, then pluralism might work. It would seem that the amount of internal democracy within political interest groups has far-reaching consequences.

The basic problem was outlined in 1908 when Robert Michels published his seminal work, *Political Parties.* Michels set out to show that the German Social Democratic party, by ideology a highly democratic organization, was under the control of a small oligarchy. According to what Michels called the "Iron Law of Oligarchy," leadership in any institution generally falls into the hands of a few (see Chapter 12). Although most interest groups in the United States preserve a democratic structure with annually chosen officers and regular balloting, they are actually far from democratic. The domination of the American Medical Association, for example, by a group of small-town, general practitioners is a matter of national concern and a source of continual consternation to hospital-affiliated doctors in urban centers.

The AMA is similar internally to many other private interest groups. For example, the authors of this book belong to the Ameri-

[8] See Stokely Carmichael and Charles Hamilton, *Black Power: The Politics of Liberation in America* (New York: Random House, 1968), pp. 6–16.

can Political Science Association (APSA). Since nearly all the political scientists in the country, men and women familiar with problems of power and governance belong to this group, one would expect that here if anywhere democracy would exist. However, 149 election contests for APSA officers were held between 1958 and 1967, and not a single one was ever contested. In every election, a nominating committee of six people—statistically unrepresentative of the general membership and appointed by the president—presented a slate of candidates that was not opposed. No wonder the members of the APSA agreed three-to-one that: "There has developed an inner group in the American Political Science Association which, in large part, controls the key panel assignments at the annual Association meetings." [9] Perhaps the problem for pluralistic democracy is one of a missing link. A decrease in democracy in one of the major elements of the system, private interest groups, decreases democracy throughout the system, and pluralism no longer becomes the best way to make complex decisions with some form of popular control—because the popular control is gone.

3. *A power elite does in fact exist.* Although different elites exercise influence in different areas, critics charge that all the elites together constitute a miniscule part of the population. In other words, the combined elite may total more than a few hundred men, but it is still an elite and it still exercises power. It attracts its own type of person with his own ideology. It is composed of the heads of the large, corporate institutions of the United States—business, labor, the universities, the military, the foundations, government. These men constitute an interlocking directorate, passing, like McGeorge Bundy, Robert McNamara, Dean Rusk, from foundation to university to government to business back to foundation. Clearly there is an unequal distribution of power in American society. Exactly how much inequality creates an elite is a controversial question, so we will devote Chapter 6 to this matter, as well as to an evaluation of the power elite theories of the pluralists and their critics.

4. *Policy often springs from one interest group that has made deals with the others rather than from a clash of diverse interests.* Pluralism regards conflict between private groups as vital to its proper operation. If this conflict is absent, if, in other words, the

[9] Albert Somit and Joseph Tanenhaus, *American Political Science: Profile of a Discipline* (New York: Atherton, 1964), p. 157.

private group with the greatest interest in a certain policy is permitted to dominate the formation of that policy, then another key assumption of pluralism would need revision. For that reason, we will examine some basic policy areas to see whether conflict over policy actually exists.

In our examination, we must think of private corporations as interest groups. Most large corporations have intimate connections with government. Some (or, in the case of Republic Aviation, all) of their business may be under government contract. Government research and science are basic to the activities of many corporations. Others rely on government not to enforce certain laws, like antitrust legislation. In contrast to the old ideology of laissez faire, all major American corporations accept the idea of working with the government because they have found it so profitable. We can regard corporations as interest groups in all areas of policy making that affect industry. The question is whether and to what extent other groups conflict with the demands of industry.

The oil industry is a good example, and one that has been heavily studied.[10] It is vitally concerned about its relationships in Washington. The government's policies on oil-depletion allowances, joint pipelines, off-shore drilling, and especially drilling in the Middle East and Latin America affect the industry directly. Therefore, the American Petroleum Industry, the trade association, maintains a lobby in Washington to look out for its interests and to conduct extensive advertising and public relations campaigns. In addition, oil men contribute heavily to both political parties; oil men frequently take positions in the government (in the Eisenhower administration, the secretary of state and undersecretary of state, the ambassadors to London, Saudi Arabia, and Lebanon, the secretaries of the navy, defense, and the treasury, the federal power commissioner and the federal trade commissioner, the consultant to the National Security Council, and the chairman of the Atomic Energy Commission were all associated with oil); in fact, oil interests have created an international government that makes the United Nations look impotent. The presence of oil is everywhere. When he needed an envoy to study conditions in Latin America, an area of vital im-

[10] See Robert Engler, *The Politics of Oil: A Study of Private Power and Democratic Directions* (Chicago: Phoenix Books, 1967). This book has been used as the basis of the following discussion.

portance because of its oil, President Nixon chose a man whose name is almost synonymous with oil—Nelson Rockefeller.

When an issue comes up that affects oil, all these resources mobilize to bring about a policy favorable to the industry. But does anyone advocate a counterpolicy to introduce the competition that is central to the pluralist conception? It seems that nobody does, at least nobody with effective political resources. Labor does not challenge oil's hegemony because few unions are directly involved. Most working-class people employed by the oil industry work for local service stations, whose owners make little more than their employees. Even if there were a union, it would probably be more interested in sharing the profits of the oil industry than attacking its power. And there are no consumer groups with significant political influence. Occasionally a senator comes along who defends the consumer's interests, but he must contend with the fact that the last two majority leaders of the Senate, the Senate whip, one of the last two Speakers of the House, and the present House majority leader all represent states that are heavily involved with oil production. The consumer-oriented senator is powerless next to the senators from Texas, Oklahoma, Louisiana, and Kansas. There are few checks on oil because its influence extends to all branches of government. In short, oil policy in the United States is determined by the oil industry, without any significant competition from other groups.

Few Americans see anything wrong with this. When President Eisenhower appointed a Standard Oil executive to fill a key position in the Department of Defense dealing with international petroleum, he responded to critics by saying: "It would be idle to employ as a consultant anyone who didn't know something about the petroleum business. He is bound to come from the petroleum industry." [11] In other words, only the experts can be expected to play a role in policy formulation. Since the only effective and profitable way to become an expert on a subject is to work for the industry involved, those who decide the policy affecting the industry are bound to be in the industry's pay.

This idea did not originate with Eisenhower, and the policy toward most industries is similar. An even better example is the so-

[11] Quoted in ibid, p. 334.

called independent regulatory commissions—the Federal Trade Commission, the Federal Power Commission, the Federal Communications Commission, and the Interstate Commerce Commission. These bodies were established to regulate certain industries that had abused the public. However, it turned out that the men appointed to these commissions—experts in the field—came from the industries that were to be regulated. In effect, the regulatory commissions became lobbyists for the industries they were supposed to restrain.[12] The same lack of competition that characterizes the oil industry also characterizes, to a greater or lesser degree, the mass media, transportation, agriculture, automobile, and many other industries.

Essentially what has happened is that the parties to the conflict have learned that cooperation is more profitable. So they cooperated. All major American airline companies belong to an international cartel that has standardized prices at a highly profitable rate. To be sure, airlines conflict somewhat with one another. Whenever the government distributes important new routes, the competition is fierce. It is not, however, conflict over policy, but over who will benefit from the policy. In all other areas of airline conflict, there is very little to dispute. Interestingly enough, charter flight companies, who were not members of the cartel, did force price competition to occur by showing how high the artificially created prices were. This suggests that conflict over policy rarely occurs, and when it does, the outcome barely affects those who are not directly involved.

5. *Although theoretically a call for social change, pluralism more frequently defends the status quo.* This criticism, perhaps the most inclusive, draws an analogy between a "laissez-faire" system, with its competing economic units, and pluralism, with its competing political units. Just as laissez-faire ideology became a defense of the economic order in the 1890s, so pluralism defends the political order in the 1960s and 1970s. Economic laissez faire was unworkable, producing huge monopolistic concentrations of economic power;

---

[12] See Marver Bernstein, *Regulating Business by Independent Commission* (Princeton: Princeton University Press, 1955). Gabriel Kolko has effectively argued that the Independent Regulatory Commissions were never expected to regulate. Instead they were supported from the beginning by businessmen to rationalize the economy and stabilize profits. See Kolko, *The Triumph of Conservatism: A Reinterpretation of American History, 1900–1916* (Chicago: Quadrangle, 1967).

in the same way, critics contend, pluralism leads to monopolies of political power that will eventually need regulation. The conservative nature of pluralism is revealed by its distrust of any political activity that does not take place through established institutions. Pluralists are apt to dismiss mass movements, demonstrations, sit-ins, and riots because they occur outside the rules of the game. But the rules of the game consign a protesting group to political impotence. Consequently, the pluralist call for participation through channels is essentially a call to leave things the way they are. As Robert Paul Wolff puts it:

> . . . pluralist theory functions ideologically by its tendency to deny new groups or interests access to the political plateau. It does this by ignoring their existence in practice, not by denying their claim in theory. The result is that pluralism has a breaking effect on social change; it slows down transformation in the system of group adjustments but does not set up an absolute barrier to change. For this reason, as well as because of its origins as a fusion of two conflicting social philosophies, it deserves the title "conservative liberalism." [13]

Pluralism, then, appears to be inadequate as a description of the operation of interest groups in advanced, industrial societies. It seems that some interest groups, particularly corporations, have enormous powers to influence decisions, while other groups, like blacks, have been consistently excluded from power. Even if all groups had about the same amount of power—an almost impossible situation—pluralism would still need to establish internal democracy for better upward and downward communication—another objective that is far from realization. Our criticisms of pluralism, therefore, are not matters of degree but of kind. We need an alternative model of power structures in America, and Chapter 6 will address itself to that problem.

INTEREST GROUPS ELSEWHERE

We have examined the role of interest groups in advanced, industrial societies, but have barely mentioned their role in the Third World. In fact, we find pluralism somewhat out of place there (just

[13] "Beyond Pluralism," in *A Critique of Pure Tolerance*, Wolff et al. (Boston: Beacon Press, 1969).

as we found the "end of ideology" theory irrelevant). There is no question that certain types of interest groups can completely dominate the political system of an economically underdeveloped country. The irony is that the groups are the same ones that dominate advanced countries. For example, to take the case of oil again, the Rockefeller family controls nine of the most powerful interests in Peru—the International Petroleum Company, Cerro Corporation, Banco Continental of Peru, the Compania de Petroleo Chevron, S.A., the Refineria Concham-Chevron, S.A., three wholly owned subsidiaries of Mobil Oil, and the International Basic Economy Corporation (sugar, insurance, food stores, poultry-breeding).[14]

The problem in Third World countries is that political independence was granted, but not economic independence. Since many firms act as interest groups in the political system of any country in which they are involved, economic dependence can become translated into political dependence on matters concerning international corporations. The difference in the Third World is that no one tries to explain things pluralistically.

Yet interest groups do operate in the Third World. As we mentioned earlier, it is the functions performed by political parties, not the name of the institution performing the function, that is important. The same is true of interest groups; there is no exact equivalent to the American Legion in Bolivia. Actually, the so-called underdeveloped countries have developed some unique institutions for performing the functions of interest groups. Although Western experiences may have provided a starting point, it is best to deal with these institutions on their own terms.

We suggested earlier that a primary function of interest groups is to build support between government and the population. We should, therefore, look for "things" that build support in the Third World. A number of unconventional institutions perform this task— the Chinese Cultural Revolution (CCR), or Red Guards, for example. They have been cited as examples of random, violent terror on the part of a sadistic, totalitarian dictatorship. The CCR was in reality not that at all but in some ways a nongovernmental, support-building institution. It represented an attempt by the Chinese leadership, particularly Mao Tse-tung, to win support for his policies from certain elements of the population. In fact, it is surprisingly

[14] David Horowitz, "Rocky Takes a Trip," *Ramparts,* August 1969, p. 60.

analogous in terms of function to the attempts by the Johnson administration to gain support for its Vietnam policies in the Jewish community. The methods may be different, but the basic function is the same.

There is also much to be learned about support building from the civil war in South Vietnam. This, it has been suggested to the point of cliché, is a war for the hearts and minds of the people, or a war for their support. Both the government of South Vietnam and the National Liberation Front (NLF or Viet Cong) have built institutions to win popular support. The South Vietnamese government has created Revolutionary Development Cadres in an effort to secure parts of the countryside, while the NLF uses a variety of techniques from land distribution to political reprisals. Our point here is simply to note the unique forms that interest groups can take in a support-building situation as unconventional as this one. Support building will always occur. The institutions involved are interest groups or something like them.

Both political parties and interest groups, the two main examples of nongovernmental institutions, are found in all political systems. This is an indication that all political systems need ways of relating those who govern to those who do not. How this need is met varies greatly in different political systems. But whatever course they follow, they use nongovernmental institutions—political parties or interest groups—to do the job. How well they do it is a question we should constantly ask about each institution.

5 Political Decisions

WE ALL KNOW how difficult it is to make a decision. Choosing between two or more alternatives, when each seems equally desirable (or undesirable), is enough to paralyze a person. Similar tensions exist within the body politic. One of the primary duties of a government is to decide things. Should the problem of air pollution be tackled? Will the new highway go through the suburbs or the slums? Should taxes be raised? And, if so, by sales tax or by income tax? Questions of this sort present decision makers with a series of alternatives, one (or none) of which must be chosen. The process by which the choice is made, political decision making, is one of the most complex political processes.*

There is one important difference between decision making on the individual level and political decision making at the societal level: the former mainly concerns only the individual involved, whereas political decisions, by definition, involve everyone in the society. Moreover, certain political decisions can affect the future of the planet. The decision of the United States government to confront Soviet missiles in Cuba with a blockade was one such

* The distinction between adequacy and acceptability used in this chapter developed out of discussions with Professor Neil McDonald of Douglass College of Rutgers University.

case. Arthur Schlesinger, Jr., has given us a vivid description of what John F. Kennedy, the chief decision maker, went through at the time:

> He never had a more sober sense of responsibility. It was continuous; there was no day and no night. In the intervals between meetings he sought out his wife and children as if the imminence of catastrophe had turned his mind more than ever to his family and, through them, to children everywhere in the world. This was the cruel question—the young people who, if things went wrong, would never have the chance to learn, to love, to fulfill themselves and serve their countries. One noon, swimming in the pool, he said to David Powers, "If it weren't for these people that haven't lived yet, it would be easy to make decisions of this sort." [1]

"If things went wrong"—with all this riding on the outcome of a political decision, it is easy to understand why the decision-making process occupies a key place in introductory political science.

THE DECISION-MAKING PROCESS

Despite the importance of many political decisions, most people remain ignorant of the decision-making process. Every young American male between the ages of eighteen and twenty-six has faced the selective service system. It has dominated the lives of some, forcing them into jobs, marriages, or schools they did not want. It has led to the deaths of others in countries around the globe. The selective service system has radically affected marital patterns, parental patterns, and the separation of church and state. Yet in spite of its importance as a political decision, most people assume that it was just made, springing intact from Congress or the president. Of course, the truth is that the selective service law was passed by Congress and signed by President Truman in 1948, amid partisan and sectional debate. Most of its provisions were implemented by the bureaucracy created by the law. No aspect of the system was inevitable. Every part of it was determined by the pulls and pressures of contending political forces within the country. To study these pressures is to realize that political decisions are

[1] *A Thousand Days: John F. Kennedy in the White House* (Boston: Houghton Mifflin, 1965), pp. 818–19.

the creations of men, not gods, and that it is possible for the student of political science to understand and affect the decision-making process.

There are countless aspects to a political decision: When was it made? What procedures were used? Were they fair? Were they effective? Who opposed it? Were there any amendments? Why was it amended? Was the change an improvement? and so on, and so on. In other words, it is possible to study almost anything about a political decision. And people have. Many full-length books have been devoted to a single political decision—the Cuban missile crisis, the Full Employment Act of 1946, the decision to adopt independent television in Britain, the politics of codetermination in West Germany, Khrushchev's assumption of power in the Soviet Union, the decision to drop the atomic bomb, the Hawley-Smoot Tariff of 1930, and the Japanese peace settlement.[2]

Faced with this complexity and multiplicity of factors, we will concentrate here on two crucial aspects of the decision-making process—acceptability (Will the people in the system comply with the decision?) and adequacy (Will the decision effectively deal with the problem for which it was designed?). Under these two criteria, much of the fascination and difficulty of the decision-making process can be incorporated.

Acceptability is often called "legitimacy," which occupies a distinguished place in the history of political philosophy. For some writers, such as Max Weber, legitimacy has played a central role (see Chapter 12). Weber believed that men obey decisions for three main reasons: tradition, accepting decisions because they were always accepted; charisma, accepting decisions because of the magnetism and extraordinary qualities of the decision maker; and legality, accepting decisions because a certain generally agreed

[2] For examples, see Elie Abel, *The Missile Crisis* (Philadelphia: Lippincott, 1966); Stephen K. Bailey, *Congress Makes a Law* (New York: Columbia University Press, 1950); H. H. Wilson, *Pressure Group: The Campaign for Commercial Television Broadcasting in England* (New Brunswick, N.J.: Rutgers University Press, 1961); Herbert Spiro, *The Politics of Co-Determination in Germany* (Cambridge: Harvard University Press, 1958); Lazar Pistrak, *Grand Tactician: Khrushchev's Rise to Power* (New York: Vintage, 1965); E. S. Schattschneider, *Politics, Pressures, and the Tariff: A Study of Free Private Enterprise in Pressure Politics* (New York: Archon, 1963); and George R. Packard, *Protest in Tokyo: The Security Treaty Crisis of 1960* (Princeton, N.J.: Princeton University Press, 1966).

upon body of rules calls for their acceptance.[3] Weber's typology is particularly useful because he is describing *any* form of political system. He does not fall into the trap of making statements like: "In a democracy people accept decisions because they are legitimate, whereas in a dictatorship decisions are forced upon people against their will"—an imaginary statement but one that could have come from a high school civics text. The truth, alas, is much more complicated. Decisions must be partially acceptable in any society—democratic or authoritarian, developed or developing, old or young—or else the political system cannot exist. What makes a "totalitarian" government different from a democratic one is not that its decisions are illegitimate, but that legitimacy is achieved in different ways.

This important point about acceptability can be illustrated by two examples. Sometimes, decisions made in a democracy are unacceptable, even though democratic procedures were followed. A good case, of course, is prohibition. Few things are more "democratic" than a constitutional amendment in the United States. It must pass by two-thirds vote of two popularly elected (since 1923) branches of Congress. In addition, three-fourths of the state legislatures, also popularly elected, must pass it by majority vote. In spite of all this support from democratically chosen legislatures, prohibition was just not acceptable, and the reaction to the measure is well known. A second example involves "totalitarian" decisions that are considered legitimate. Adolf Hitler's policy to exterminate Jews led to few popular uprisings. Although they had no part in the decision, most non-Jews approved (if often in silence) of what was happening. Moreover, recent events in the Soviet Union and other socialist countries seem to indicate that so-called "totalitarian" regimes will almost inevitably turn toward legitimacy. This digression is relevant because the phenomenon of acceptability transcends our common typologies of political systems and applies to all governments, whatever they are called.

In other words, we must pay close attention to the factors that lead to acceptability. As a rule, the greater the degree of popular participation in decision making, the more likely it is to be ac-

---

[3] See Chapter 7 and Chapter 12. A good summary is in Hans Gerth and C. Wright Mills, eds., *From Max Weber: Essays in Sociology* (New York: Oxford University Press, 1958), pp. 78–81.

cepted—which may seem to contradict the preceding paragraph. However, though acceptability must be achieved in any political system, its chances of success are greater in a democracy than in any other type of political system. (Remember, though, both the Soviet Union and the United States call themselves democracies.) Therefore, the first consideration in acceptability is who makes the decision, or rather, who do the citizens in a political system think makes the decision. If the citizens feel they have participated in the process or (more commonly) that they were represented by someone who participated, they will be more likely to comply with the decision. This single proposition is the basis of representative government and majority rule (as well as the various forms of socialism.) To use the example of selective service cited earlier, if a young man facing the draft believes that Congress is a democratically elected body representing him, he will probably choose to go along. But another young man may decide that the older men who run Congress have nothing in common with him and resist the draft. Both acknowledge that the decision was made by Congress, but they disagree about how representative and democratic that body is.

A second factor in acceptability is the way decisions are made. Democratic methods appear to be more conducive to acceptability. In general, a decision made by procedures that are regarded as fair and just will be more legitimate than one made by arbitrary methods. The effort to establish nonarbitrary procedures is often related to Weber's third form of legitimacy—legality. In England, this concept is summarized by the phrase "rule of law"; in the United States, by "due process of law." In both systems the concepts refer to a series of procedures, usually specified in a written or unwritten constitution, by which decisions must be made. If President Truman had tried—to continue the selective service example—to establish a conscription system by executive fiat, he would have been charged (rightly) with bypassing constitutional procedures. If he had persisted, draft resistance would no doubt have intensified because people would refuse to accept a decision that was not made according to procedure.

A third factor that affects the acceptability of a political decision is the reason it is being made. All political systems stress legitimacy by relating the decision to some high or noble purpose. Conscription is necessary for national defense and security. Nationalizing the steel industry will produce economic stability. Continuing to fight guerrilla wars will show the tenacity of communism and the cowardice of "paper tigers." Arguments of this sort represent attempts to legitimize decisions. They are usually reserved for decisions that call for some sacrifice by the people and they are often a last step in the process of legitimization. Most decision makers try to win acceptance under the first two factors, reserving the third until all others have failed. And unlike the other two, this rationale is not specifically related to democracy. Neither democracy nor totalitarianism has a monopoly on patriotism, loyalty, and noble purpose.

The second important aspect of political decision making is adequacy—the effectiveness of the decision in accomplishing its objective. The many unsolved problems in the world today testify to the permanent nature of the adequacy problem. For example, consider the economic difficulties of postwar Britain. While the countries of continental Europe rebounded from World War II with expanding economies and rapid improvements in living standards, England's economic growth was sluggish. A variety of decisions were made to strengthen the economy. The Labour government that came to power after the war nationalized certain key industries, like steel and coal, in an effort to stabilize the economy. When the Conservatives took over, they denationalized steel, in the hopes that the incentives of private enterprise would hasten economic growth. In addition, the National Economic Development Council was created to combine public and private resources in economic planning. Both parties eventually supported Britain's entrance into the Common Market (although the Labour party had serious second thoughts), another device designed to stimulate consumer purchasing. Then, the second postwar Labour government took the drastic step of devaluing the British pound. All of these measures were acceptable to the British people, although there has been some disenchantment with devaluation. Yet none of them, it seems, were technically adequate. For Britain's economy is still sluggish. In short, a decision can look beautiful on paper, but unless it deals with the problem that prompted it, it has little value. We must look, then, at the factors that tend to produce adequacy.

We can begin with the same factors that determined acceptability. The first, who makes the decision, also affects its adequacy.

The decision makers must be able to command the necessary technical resources for a policy to be effective, and in an advanced industrial society, these can be enormous. A decision involving agriculture, for example, might require specialists in rural sociology, economics, meteorology, environmental science, ecology, microbiology, botany, biology, chemistry, biochemistry, physics, political science, transportation, and many subdivisions and combinations of these. Governments have to find these people, sometimes train or retrain them, attract them to government service, provide them with laboratories, resources, and funds, give them the decision to be made, and then hope the experts will agree. All this is vital to the adequacy of the decision, and many political systems, including the American, devote large portions of their national budget to the recruitment and utilization of scientific and technical manpower.

In the difficult process of recruitment, the industrialized countries have a definite advantage—at least the manpower is available. Few, if any, of the underdeveloped societies have the technical knowledge or personnel to solve their problems. In much of Africa and Asia, technical expertise often came from the colonial power. But after independence, these British and French scientists and civil servants were asked to leave or stay on new terms because they were a symbol of a hated oppressor. While this often satisfied the anticolonialism of the newly independent nation, it left the country without technical help. Thus, as if the problems of linguistic and religious diversity were not enough, many of these countries also faced a crisis in trained personnel. Various United Nations activities, the Peace Corps, and the Soviet Union's lease of scientists are designed to promote the accumulation of technical skills in societies where they are missing. Of course, they serve the interests of the assisting agency as well.

The "how" of the decision-making process is also relevant to considerations of adequacy. The electoral procedures designed to produce acceptability are often unsuitable for incorporating scientific information in the governmental process. The American Congress, for example, contains many lawyers, but very few physicists, sociologists, or, since the defeat of Paul Douglas, economists. For that reason, the administrative branch of government, sometimes called the bureaucracy or the civil service, is often called upon for assistance. This development, unforeseen by the framers of the American constitution, has had many political consequences, some of which will be explored in Chapter 7. For the time being, it is enough to indicate the dimensions of the problem.

Because universities and research institutions contain most of the scientific manpower in the United States, the pursuit of adequacy has led to close cooperation between government, industry, and the university. To the dismay of students at Princeton and Columbia, the Institute for Defense Analysis, a consortium of twelve universities, sponsors research for the Department of Defense. Scientists and scholars at the Rand (for "research and development") Corporation in southern California conduct research for clients as diverse as the Air Force and the City of New York. Many industries like General Electric and Bell Telephone compete with universities in the hiring of scientists and cooperate with them through fellowship money, television quiz programs, research sponsorship, and other devices. The federal government, not to be outdone, aids the research process through the National Defense Education Act and through its own employment bureaus. These examples show the scope of the adequacy problem in the United States; resources from a variety of areas must be mobilized so that the decisions reached by the formally constituted governmental bodies will be effective in meeting the crises of twentieth-century life.

It should be apparent by now that there are four types of decision-making systems, based upon the two criteria we have been using. These four possibilities can be illustrated this way:

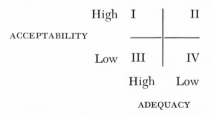

Obviously, Category I, in which decisions are both effective and legitimate, would be the most ideal decision-making system. However, Category I is extremely difficult to achieve. The explanation for this involves the dynamics of politics in many societies, and it merits a full discussion.

DILEMMAS OF DECISION MAKING

If the people in a political system could be persuaded to accept what is adequate, there would be no problem. But in many societies, particularly those with advanced and highly industrialized economies, the persuasion process becomes difficult. When people are relatively prosperous and comfortable, they tend to ignore those who argue that unless a certain course is taken in a specific area, a crisis of some sort will ensue. Consider the following example. In a recent national survey in the United States, 56 percent of those interviewed agreed that ". . . racial integration of Negroes in this country is going ahead too fast." [4] In spite of this general complacency, or perhaps because of it, there are dire warnings from many quarters that this attitude of nonacceptance of racial progress will lead to disaster.

> Black and colored peoples are saying in a clear voice that they intend to determine for themselves the kinds of social and economic systems they will live under. Of necessity, this means that the existing systems of the dominant, oppressive group— the entire spectrum of values, beliefs, traditions and institutions—will have to be challenged and changed. It is not to be expected that this fundamental scrutiny will be led by those who benefit or even have expectations of benefit from the status quo.[5]

> None of us can escape the consequences of the continuing economic and social decay of the central city and the closely related problem of rural poverty. The convergence of these conditions in the racial ghetto and the resulting discontent and disruption threaten democratic values fundamental to our progress as a free society. Only a greatly enlarged commitment to national action—compassionate, massive and sustained, backed by the richest nation on this earth—can shape a future that is compatible with the historic ideals of American society.[6]

[4] Lloyd A. Free and Hadley Cantril, *The Political Beliefs of Americans: A Study of Public Opinion* (New York: Simon and Schuster, 1968), p. 123.

[5] Stokely Carmichael and Charles Hamilton, *Black Power: The Politics of Liberation in America* (New York: Random House, 1968), p. 179.

[6] The National Advisory Commission on Civil Disorders, *Report* (Washington, D.C.: Government Printing Office, 1967), p. 229.

It is no coincidence that the racial crisis has been used to illustrate the difficulty of reconciling adequacy and acceptability. It is an area in which the problem is very apparent. The government has been active in the area: *Brown* v. *Board of Education,* the Civil Rights Acts of 1964 and 1968, a series of executive orders eliminating discrimination in various federal activities. And group activity is plentiful: ranging from the National Association for the Advancement of Colored People (NAACP) to the Black Panthers, to the Urban Coalition, to poor people's marches. Knowledge is also available: the *Report* of the President's Commission on Civil Disorders, quoted above, is a compendium of the causes of the present violence. Yet in spite of this commitment and activity, the living conditions of urban ghetto residents have not improved visibly. The reason for this may have something to do with the nature of political decision making in the United States.

Using the two criteria for evaluating decisions that have been elaborated in this chapter, we can arrive at the following conclusion: *the American people are prepared to accept decisions that cannot (by themselves) solve our racial problems, but they are not prepared to accept decisions that can.* Although this may sound harsh, it merely illustrates something fundamental about decision making in industrial societies. In societies where most people are economically comfortable, adequate decisions of fundamental importance will often result in severe displacement. And this displacement makes them unacceptable. To solve the racial crisis, Americans would probably have to spend huge sums of money, decrease foreign involvements, change their basic value schemes, admit mistakes, exist without scapegoats, and maybe lose some profits. That is a good deal to ask of any people, and so far there has been little indication that Americans are willing to make the effort. As long as no pressing crisis directly affects them—the urban riots have so far been confined to nonwhite neighborhoods—people will refuse to accept the severe displacement required for adequate decision making.

One consequence of this irreconcilability is that adequate decisions are often postponed for long periods. This is especially true in urban areas where the primary task of the mayor is often to make what a recent article called "non-decisions . . . the practice of limiting the scope of actual decision-making to 'safe' issues by manipulating the dominant community values, myths, and political institutions and procedures." [7] In the face of conflicting pressures, limited budgets, and voter apathy, the safe course for many urban decision makers is postponement. This may account for the periodic cycles of passive and active mayors in cities like New York. Long spells of postponement-oriented mayors are punctuated by youthful reformers who try to accomplish many things, alienate significant groups, and retire back to the sidelines, as the cycle returns to less colorful figures.

As we stated earlier, much of the difficulty is due to the prosperity and ease in the system. In the countries of Asia, Africa, and Latin America, severe displacement is a matter of course. In fact, in these countries the process is often reversed. Decisions that would solve their problems might be considered acceptable no matter how severe the displacement, but they lack the technical resources to make the decisions effective. Many Indian Moslems were willing to have their entire lives disrupted to create Pakistan, but the Pakistani leadership has not been able to take advantage of this sacrificing attitude because of the country's general poverty. Yet, Pakistan is more fortunate than most underdeveloped countries, where, because of divisive cleavages, a propensity toward sacrifice does not even exist and therefore neither adequacy nor acceptability is present.

We now have enough information to classify political systems on the basis of their decision-making abilities. Our classification will follow the diagram on page 75. The United States would fall into Category II, that is, high acceptability and low adequacy. A totalitarian country like Nazi Germany, on the other hand, would probably be closer to Category III, high adequacy and low acceptability. The underdeveloped countries might come closer to Category IV, low adequacy and low acceptability. Very few countries would qualify for Category I, which we have called the most ideal form of decision making. Although Great Britain has often been placed there, its status may have to be reviewed.

Whatever its decision-making ability, certain problems are inherent in any political system. A country patterned on democratic principles, for example, must confront the dilemma arising from the nature of Category II: How can a democracy force a justifiable decision on the people against their will? Or, to give a

[7] Peter Bachrach and Morton Baratz, "Decisions and Nondecisions: An Analytic Framework," American Political Science Review, 57 (September 1963): 632.

specific illustration: Should the recommendations of the President's Commission on Civil Disorders be implemented even though a majority of Americans are probably opposed to that implementation? If so, how? If acceptability is the primary consideration, then the answer to the first question is, no. Acceptability of decisions *is* a fundamental definition of democracy. If justice for all Americans and adequacy are the criteria, then the answer is, yes. But while following the end values of the system, imposing an unpopular decision violates one of its means. Methods would have to be found to carry out the decision over the majority's wishes. In the United States, that would probably mean bypassing Congress and implementing the policy through judicial or administrative fiat— a recourse that would generate even more resistance to the policy, since who makes the decision greatly affects its acceptability. Thus, reconciling adequacy and acceptability poses major problems for democratic countries.

A quite different problem exists in those societies called totalitarian. In the classic model of totalitarianism, a decision is reached because the decision makers consider it the most efficient way of achieving a given objective. Then the decision will be implemented without respect to the displacements it involves or the disenchantment it produces. The best example of this is probably Stalin's decision to industrialize the Soviet Union as rapidly as possible, whatever the cost. Stalin nearly tore the country apart in his drive: innumerable people were killed; labor camps flourished; people were moved around at will; families were broken up; terror was intensified. Yet the country was industrialized in a relatively short time. Whether the benefits of industrialization were worth the price is for each individual to decide. The point we are making is that adequacy is the supreme consideration in a classic totalitarian state, and acceptability is relatively meaningless.

Nonetheless, dilemmas arise here too because totalitarianism does not always exist in this "classic" form. The question is whether nonacceptability is a permanent phenomenon in a totalitarian system. If decisions can be implemented without acceptability over a long period of time, then we can assume it is a permanent condition. If, on the other hand, the search for total adequacy produces a crisis in legitimacy, then the system will have to change to accommodate the feeling that decisions should be acceptable. Political scientists are currently divided over the per-

manence of totalitarianism. Writing in 1956, two well-known scholars indicated their doubts about increasing acceptability in totalitarian states:

> What then is going to be the course of totalitarian develop-
> ment? If one extrapolates from the past course of evolution,
> it seems most likely that the totalitarian dictatorships will
> continue to become more total, even though the rate of inten-
> sification may slow down.[8]

In the sixteen years since that statement was made, developments
in both the Soviet Union and the so-called satellite countries have
led some to doubt that these societies would become more "total."
The attack on Stalin's crimes, the nonviolent displacement of leaders in the Soviet Union, student unrest in Poland, relative afflu-
ence in East Germany—these may indicate a relaxation of the
drive toward adequacy and greater responsiveness to factors involving acceptability.

CONCLUDING GENERALIZATIONS

In this chapter, we have introduced a scheme for evaluating
and understanding the decision-making ability of a political system. We should now be able to use some of these observations
on decision making to generalize about comparative political systems.

To begin with, political decisions are often made in places
where they are not supposed to be made. Many political systems
have constitutions, with a large section devoted to enumerating
the powers of the various parts of government, or in our terms,
enumerating the locus of decision-making power. But the constitution is only a first step in the search for power. The American
constitution provides for three coequal branches of government.
The Soviet constitution states that "All power in the USSR belongs to the working people of town and country as represented
by the Soviets of Working People's Deputies" (Chapter I, Article 3). Neither of these is an adequate description of the country's
decision-making process. It is obviously necessary to go beyond the

---

[8] Carl Friedrich and Zbigniew Brzezinski, *Totalitarian Dictatorship and Autocracy* (New York: Praeger, 1963), p. 300.

constitution and scrutinize the whole political apparatus. In the process, we will discover that political decisions are often made unconstitutionally, extraconstitutionally, and aconstitutionally.

The search for the locus of power may end in the same place, regardless of the political system being examined. The trend today, particularly in the advanced industrial societies, is for decision-making power to become centralized in the administrative branch of government, the bureaucracy. The British civil service, the Soviet *apparatchiki,* and the American cabinet departments have grown immensely in recent years. The reason is simply the pressing need for adequacy in political decision making. Since adequacy is dependent on scientific and technical expertise, and since this expertise is provided by the bureaucracy rather than the elected or representative institutions, there has been a natural shift of power to the bureaucracy. This trend is so important that Chapter 7 will be devoted to it.

The trend toward administrative decision making could deemphasize the acceptability aspect of political decisions. Are we, in fact, witnessing the growing irrelevance of democracy in this movement toward centralized bureaucracy and away from representative government? Does it matter whether a legislature has been chosen democratically, if it has no power? What choice do we have in selecting that tax adjuster who wields (so much) power over us? Questions like these are bound to arise when technical adequacy supercedes popular acceptability as a primary criterion. They are not easy to answer, if indeed they can be answered at all. An attempt to exercise popular control over the administrative branch would probably decrease its efficiency, while adding technical expertise to the representative institutions would probably decrease their acceptability. If the democratic model is to have any relevance in a bureaucratic world, then some way must be found of reconciling adequacy and acceptability.

This task is perhaps the most difficult one a political system has to face. No country has ever been completely successful. But since Great Britain is often considered the most successful, let us examine how the British have dealt with the problem of adequacy and acceptability.

In one of the most perceptive essays ever written about politics, an Englishman named Walter Bagehot, writing in 1867, pointed to the heart of the British experiment. He drew a distinction between the "dignified" parts of the government and the "efficient" parts, which he defined as follows:

> . . . there are two parts . . . first, those which excite and preserve the reverence of the population—the *dignified* parts, if I may so call them; and next, the *efficient* parts—those by which it, in fact, works and rules.[9]

With a disdain for the common man typical of a Victorian gentleman, Bagehot showed how acceptability could be gained through the common man's preoccupation with the symbolic, or dignified, forms of government. While the masses watched and listened to the queen, the real work of government, that is, the adequacy criterion and the efficient parts, could be carried on unobserved by those who really had the power—the members of Parliament linked to the prime minister through the cabinet.

The forms of British government have changed somewhat since Bagehot's time, but his central distinction still applies. Today the members of Parliament (M.P.) can be considered "dignified" as power has flowed to the more "efficient" civil service. It is now the M.P. who adds acceptability by being democratically elected. With attention focused upon him, the real work can be carried out by the civil servants. This process is facilitated by two special arrangements. In England, a cabinet member, who is also an elected politician, is considered personally responsible for the decisions made by the nonelected bureaucrats in his department. This provides an outlet for blame when a decision is considered unacceptable. Second, the British civil service is a gentlemanly fraternity composed basically of upper-class people. With no need for personal ambition, these men can perform their work in a spirit of national, rather than parochial, interest. (Of course, they define the national interest as the interest of their class.) This British experiment in reconciling acceptability and adequacy is both unique and fascinating.[10]

But does the British system work as well as it is supposed to? Bagehot's theory is based on the respect of the "common people"

[9] *The English Constitution* (Garden City, N.Y.: Doubleday, Dolphin Books, n.d.), p. 63.

[10] See Sir Charles Percy Snow, *Corridors of Power* (New York: Charles Scribner's Sons, 1964), for a revealing picture of the British system.

for their rulers. Undeniably, an establishment exists in Britain—in the clubs, Oxbridge (Oxford and Cambridge universities), and the civil service—an establishment that is by definition non-democratic. It would appear though that deference toward this establishment is not universal. As we mentioned earlier, many Britons did not support Harold Wilson's austerity program and do not support Edward Heath's European plans. This is one reason why the British have not been able to resolve their economic crisis. It is hard to say whether this is a temporary exception to Bagehot's Law—which may stop at the pocketbook—or whether it indicates a permanent decrease in political deference in Britain as bureaucracy increases. In any event, it is clear that the British have not been completely successful in reconciling adequacy and acceptability, although they have come closer than any one else.

Less developed countries also have to concern themselves with the reconciliation process. Basically, there are two different routes these countries could follow, although the actual course will probably lie somewhere between the two. A so-called under-developed country could develop new forms of political decision making and new institutions to provide acceptability and adequacy. Or it could simply copy the major industrial powers and become more and more like them. While some may consider the first route more desirable, the second may be more realistic.

There have been attempts to search for new forms in some of these countries. A charismatic leader, a man of the people, can inspire acceptability. Picture Fidel Castro in work clothes, cutting sugar in the fields outside Havana with local peasants. An action of this sort, inconceivable in Russia, America, or England, is an attempt to gain acceptability through the appearance of a general equality—"All men and women work." Or, take the concept of "guided democracy" associated with Mohammad Ayub Khan in Pakistan: it provided a vehicle for combining the forms of democracy with modified one-party rule, in other words, an attempt to reconcile acceptability and adequacy in a Third World country.

At this point we cannot predict where these attempts will lead. There is some evidence, though, that as countries become more economically developed, they begin to take on the political coloration of the advanced industrial societies. Perhaps then the decision-making patterns in the Third World will result in large bureaucratic structures like those in more advanced nations. This is an area where the student of political science can expect to see many developments in his lifetime.

In our discussions, we have not learned how to make a political decision, for this is not a "how-to-do-it" book. Instead we have explored some of the factors that affect political decision making. We have tried to indicate the complexities of the process and to point out its more important aspects.

6 Decision Makers and Nondecision Makers

BECAUSE POLITICAL DECISIONS are so important, we naturally want to know who makes them. Many before us have pursued the question. It has been a central concern of such diverse political philosophers as Edmund Burke and Karl Marx. Burke was very aware that not everyone could participate in the decision-making process. He felt that a member of Parliament (that is, a decision maker) was justified in considering himself an independent who could vote as he pleased, even if his view conflicted with that of his constituents (see Chapter 10). An examination of the relationship between decision makers and nondecision makers raises questions about representation.

This relationship also introduces questions about power. Marx also wanted to know who makes the important decisions. In a capitalist society, he found the decision makers among the captains of industry and other economically powerful groups of people, not in the political institutions. Thus, attempts to create representative government are irrelevant: they express a relationship between people and their political leaders, but the leaders actually take their orders from other places. Further, workers are quite distinct from their employers; their styles of life, their relationships to private property are too different. The only way to achieve parity is for the workers to take the power away from the real decision makers through revolution (see Chapter 11).

THE POWER ELITE

There are two general schools of thought today on the relationship between decision makers and nondecision makers: one follows Burke's interest in representation and one follows Marx's interest in power. Surprisingly, the most widely read account of this situation in the United States, *The Power Elite* by C. Wright Mills, is in the Marxist tradition. According to Mills, the powerful are those who ". . . are in positions to make decisions having major consequences." These decision makers tend to congregate in three areas of American life—the corporations, the military, and certain key positions within the formal political institutions. Each of these areas is important because political power is highly institutional, that is, it grows from specific positions within institutions in society: "For such institutions are the necessary bases of power, of wealth, and of prestige, and at the same time, the chief means of exercising power, of acquiring and retaining wealth, and of cashing in the higher claims for prestige." After examining how people attained these key positions, and what they do in them, Mills concludes that American society is out of balance. While decision makers at the top determine policy, nondecision makers form a mass society with no sense of community, only vastness and powerlessness. The result is a triumph of a "conservative mood"; alternatives are not discussed, and the various segments drift along, doing what they do, in what Mills calls ". . . the American system of unorganized irresponsibility." [1]

The Power Elite is ideal for introducing the relationship between decision makers and nondecision makers. Mills seems to suggest that this relationship (or, rather, this lack of relationship) is responsible for many of the problems of advanced, industrial societies. All questions become political ones, that is, they deal with who has power and why.

In answering these charges, critics of Mills have had to develop their own theory of power in American society, which sent them back to the works of Burke and John Stuart Mill. The critics con-

[1] C. Wright Mills, *The Power Elite* (New York: Oxford University Press, 1959), pp. 4, 9, 325, 342.

tend that Mills attributed too much sagacity and skill to his power elite. There are very real limits on its power. For one thing, the power elite is hardly as homogenous as Mills suggests. Eternal feuding tends to be the rule among the three branches of the Millsian elite. And the "political directorate" is not the slave of the military chiefs. The House and Senate recently defeated an appropriation for a supersonic transport (SST) plane, which both the military and large industry wanted very badly. We also read of a rise in prices on the New York Stock Exchange whenever the prospects for peace in Vietnam seem better—hardly the reaction one would expect from an alliance between corporate leaders and generals. Furthermore, disagreements often take place within each power branch. In the first days of the Nixon administration, a sharp disagreement occurred within the political directorate—within the executive branch and between two very good friends—over the appointment of Dr. John Knowles as an assistant secretary of health, education and welfare. In this case, the most powerful group was a private one, the American Medical Association, a group that does not even fit into Mills's tripartite schema. The AMA, in fact, is representative of what Mills calls the "middle levels of power," and its elevation here to the top of the power situation is an example of the looseness of Mills's categories.

Mills's tendency to bipolarize the distribution of power in American society also leads him to ignore the role of a third category— middle level men, like the members of the AMA. Mills's critics say that he underestimates the role of politics and politicians in American society. Ultimate power in the United States, even if it is a negative power, does lie with political institutions (like the House of Representatives), which are not composed of Mills's powerful elite. Members of the House represent the middle levels of power in American society. They are middle class in origin and middle-of-the-road in outlook. As politicians, they link the nondecision makers to the decision makers. They sound out their constituents on issues of special concern and incorporate those views into legislation. The result is neither mass democracy—decision making by everyone, nor restricted democracy—decision making by a very few. These two extremes are combined into a middle course that preserves some of the better features of each type, but eliminates their most odious characteristics. In this way, Mills's critics reemphasize the importance of representation in political systems. Since all cannot have equal power in policy making, a modern political system should listen to but not be directed by mass opinion.

Finally, critics of Mills note that the "powerless" in a mass society are not really that way. For one thing, through social mobility a member of the powerless group can rise to a position of prominence in the power elite, especially in the corporations. The presidents of the three major television networks in the United States are descended from Russian Jewish immigrants, who had no money, contacts, or facility with English. But more important, even those who stay at the bottom levels of power in America are not totally excluded from participation in the decisions that affect their lives. They have their politicians, many of whom become powerful on the basis of the many votes they collect from the powerless. The powerless also are represented through groups they belong to, labor unions at work, political clubs in the neighborhood, even social and athletic groups. These private groups (as we discussed in Chapter 4) tend to channel the views of their members upward toward the decision makers, and wise decision makers listen to these sources.

To summarize, Mills's critics agree that America is both more fluid and more complicated than Mills indicates. In examining specific political decisions, particularly those at the local level that Mills tended to ignore, we do not find that power is totally controlled by an elite or totally removed from the majority of the people. A subtle process of interaction takes place between the formal decision makers and the rest of the population. And though the process cannot always be seen, its effects are always felt. It is the process by which decisions become acceptable. And, as Chapter 5 pointed out, no political system can last if the people find its policies unacceptable most of the time.

Faced with compelling arguments on both sides, it is hard to decide which view is correct. We can, however, draw certain conclusions. First, it is clear that political power and political decision making are closely intertwined; indeed, political power can be defined in terms of an individual's control over the decision-making process. The more an individual helps shape an eventual political decision, the more powerful he or she is. In this sense, any discussion of political decision making will inevitably lead to a discussion of power. Second, both sides agree that political power as it has just been defined is never distributed equally throughout society:

some people will be powerful and some powerless. The question, then, is the relative size of each group. Are there any other groups? What forms of contact take place between the groups?

We have still not determined who was correct—Mills or his critics. Each student will have to decide that for himself, but since we have detailed the critics' arguments, we should also include the responses of Mills's followers, who believe that the critics have missed the central points of the book.

The Millsians concede that differences do exist within the power elite, but they make two other points. In the first place, these disagreements occur over relatively minor matters. Whenever crucial decisions have to be made, the power elite presents a unified face. What are some of these crucial decisions? The most obvious is anything involving the power elite's power. Thus, in its commitment to the present political system, the power elite stands united. On the importance of America's power in the world, there is no dissent either. The power elite agrees that communism is reprehensible compared to capitalistic democracy and should be stopped, if it poses a threat. To be sure, there are disagreements within the power elite over how to stop it. While some, like James Gavin and George Kennan, two of the authors of America's cold war foreign policy, feel that America should assert itself primarily through good works, others feel that a strong stand against communism is needed wherever a country is in danger of "falling." Both "doves" and "hawks" agree that communism is bad and that America's mission is to stop it. In the long run, the disagreements within the power elite are much less important than the broad areas of consensus.

The second point concerns competition within the power elite. When internal disputes occur, they tend to be resolved in such a way that all the factions in the elite obtain something, but those outside remain empty-handed. In the example of the disagreement within the executive branch over the appointment of Dr. John Knowles, a Millsian would point out that all factions won. The AMA won because it demonstrated the strength of its veto power. Former Secretary of Health, Education and Welfare Robert Finch won because the eventual appointee shared the same liberal views as Knowles. The president won because he saved face with the public while indicating to conservatives in Congress that he was responsive to their feelings. The only people who lost, a Millsian would conclude, were the powerless who suffer under an oppressive medical system because they do not participate in the decisions that shape it.

Mills's defenders point out that the hypothesis of the politician as broker between the powerless and the powerful does not work. Even though in theory power remains in the hands of Congress, in reality, as Marx predicted, corporate leaders are the ones who exercise the power. And people at the bottom of the system have no recourse to decisions made by businessmen at the top. Their private associations are ineffective. Although representatives of the working man bargain for concessions from employers, the bargains are never about power. Workers obtain higher wages, but this is their reward for not asking for or taking a share in decision making. Furthermore, the representatives of the powerless begin to deal so much with the powerful that they become more and more like them, "new men of power" in Mills's terms. They no longer have much in common with the people who gave them power. Thus, followers of Mills argue that the pursuit of representation ends up nowhere, and that the real question still is, as it always has been, one of power.

We are therefore back where we started from. The questions on the relationship between decision makers and nondecision makers have two sets of answers: one stresses representation, the other stresses power. Each set of answers is very convincing. Since little progress has been made in resolving the arguments involved, let us return instead to the areas of agreement. Both sides agree that complete equality of power does not exist. At any moment, therefore, some people will have more power than others over decisions. What kind of people have the power? What kind of people do not? Perhaps the answers will lead to some more concrete generalizations about decision makers.

WHERE THE POWER IS

"The very rich," F. Scott Fitzgerald once said to Ernest Hemingway, "are different from you and me." Are they very powerful? We all know, or think we know, who the rich are, what they are like, how they live. They are often the sons and daughters of an aristocratic elite. Their pictures appear on the society pages of the *New York Times*. They live in places like Oyster Bay, Mount Kisco,

Sneden's Landing, and Redding Ridge. They really do not have to work, and can spend their time fox hunting, collecting art, attending balls, sponsoring charities, and commiserating with one another about the decline in taste in America. All that is clear to anyone who follows the gossip about the very rich. But who are the very powerful? Are they the same people? Some of them obviously are, but not all the rich are powerful and not all the powerful are rich. Besides, the very powerful are not as visible. A recent article by Andrew Hacker demonstrated this graphically. The reader was asked to identify six men from their pictures. Three were obvious—Governors Rockefeller, Reagan, and Romney—but the others seemed totally obscure. They were, however, the presidents of the three largest corporations in America, in control of assets that make them as powerful as the chiefs of state of many countries. Yet so little is known about them that few people could think of their names.

Although not all the rich are powerful, we would expect more of them to be. In his book *Who Rules America?*, G. William Domhoff came to the conclusion that any analysis of power must start with the rich:

> A governing class is a social upper class which receives a disproportionate amount of a country's income, owns a disproportionate amount of a country's wealth, and contributes a disproportionate number of its members to the controlling institutions and key decision-making groups in that country.[2]

Members of the governing class, that is political decision makers, have a great deal in common, according to Domhoff. They tended to be upper class within their ethnic group. Thus, if aristocratic, they attended the usual prep school and Harvard or Yale. If Jewish, they were generally members, if not through birth then through marriage, of the Jewish society described in Stephen Birmingham's *Our Crowd*. All of them were taught that they had a mission to govern. Public service, by which was meant high office in government or corporation, was to be their lot, as they assumed the responsibility of governing America for the less fortunate. Fanning out from college and club, these members of the upper class were situated in key places in American society: insurance companies,

[2] *Who Rules America?* (Englewood Cliffs, N.J.: Prentice-Hall, 1967), p. 5.

banks, communications industries, law firms, university boards, corporate boards, foreign-policy establishments, the military, intelligence operations, hospital boards, the foundations, the executive
branch, the diplomatic corps, the regulatory agencies, high-level
government bureaucracies, voluntary associations, the State Department—in short, wherever decisions of consequence were made.

Domhoff shows that many of the very rich are also the very
powerful. What he has left out of his account are those who are
powerful without being very rich. Few would deny that Lyndon
Baines Johnson was a very powerful decision maker in this country
at one time. Yet his origins hardly fit Domhoff's description of the
upper class. He came from Texas, where he was not among the
very wealthy, and his breeding, in terms of the eastern upper class's
definition of that word, did not exist. We could find numerous other
examples to show that a simple equation of very rich with very
powerful is unrealistic.

But not completely unrealistic. Something happens to the powerful but not rich. For one thing, powerful people often use their
positions to obtain financial wealth, as Johnson did at many points
in his career. In fact, because of the relative insecurity of their backgrounds, they may be more impressed with the monetary advantages of their position than wealthy members of the upper class.
Then, too, the powerful who are not rich must have another resource
to substitute for money. It may be popular appeal, especially in the
case of political figures, or financial or military genius. But some
quality is needed to make the powerful powerful. This quality becomes the functional equivalent of wealth. It can be traded for
money, kept in reserve for use in crucial moments, or invested in
long-range projects. It is a resource that the clever owner can substitute for wealth as often as he chooses or as long as the quality is
still in demand.

In other words, it seems that the very powerful are also different
from the rest of us. They possess something—whether money, political skill, or technical ability—which makes them distinctive. Their
lives tend to be spent making decisions for others. If they leave
the government, they are likely to return to their private positions
in corporations, law offices, and universities. In these private positions—deciding how much oil to produce, who has the patent
rights to what, what the status of the disputed island of X is—they
often exercise as much power over decisions as they did in the

government. Born to power, schooled in the desirability of using that power, and employed in the means of power, the decision makers constitute a class—Marx called it the ruling class. They share social and economic characteristics that make them different from everyone else.

From the very powerful, we will investigate the very powerless. Once again, it is easier to see a situation in its extremes. Identifying the least powerful people in the United States is relatively easy. But as we move up the ladder, it becomes more and more difficult to use the term powerless. Nonetheless, we shall see how far we can go by following this procedure.

THE UNDER CLASS

In our examination of the very powerful, we looked first among the very rich. Similarly, we will begin our study of the powerless among the very poor. Some striking similarities exist between the two extremes. Just as the members of the ruling class have a tradition that guides their lives, so do the members of what we will call the under class. Like the powerful, the powerless live in exclusive residential areas, exclusive, that is, of people other than themselves. Children of the members of the under class attend similar schools, and their classmates share similar values. In these schools, the students learn attitudes that will guide them through their lives: cynicism, violence, distrust, suspicion, and hatred. But they also learn pride, independence, and integrity. Members of the under class also belong to exclusive social clubs, called gangs, but their importance has declined in recent years. Fanning out from school and club, members of the under class begin to occupy strategic positions within the society: collecting trash in law firms, cleaning university bathrooms, serving drinks on the train between New York and Washington, shining shoes in the State Department, or wherever decisions of consequence are made.

The ironies in the preceding paragraph are, of course, fully intended. Like the decision makers, the nondecision makers are a relatively distinct political subdivision within society. No one denies the existence of such a group; but its size is often disputed.

One segment of American society that clearly belongs to the powerless is the American black. A few statistics can substantiate what nearly everyone knows. A study in Cook County, Illinois (Chicago and its suburbs), discovered that only 58 out of 1,088, or 5 percent of the policy-making positions in the public sector of the county were occupied by nonwhites. Within private institutions, including insurance companies, banks, universities, voluntary associations, labor unions, law firms, and welfare and religious societies, 227 blacks were in policy-making positions, out of a total of 9,909, or 2 percent. Furthermore, this study indicated that ". . . the number of posts held by Negroes tended to be inversely related to the power invested in these positions—the more powerful the post, the fewer the black policy makers." [3] These figures show that powerlessness is closely related to poverty. What this means in political terms has been graphically described by Kenneth B. Clark:

> The effective exercise of power in the urban ghetto is crippled severely by the inexperience of the ghetto's own political leaders. Their inexperience and political unsophistication have a fundamental root—the psychology of the ghetto with its pervasive and total sense of helplessness. It is difficult, if not impossible, to behave as one with power when all one's experience has indicated that one has none. Because their house of political power is built on sand without a solid base of economic or social influence, ghetto politicians are likely to accept a limited jurisdiction and to seek immediate and concrete rewards. They often subject themselves to the control of others they believe to hold the primary power, and some are prepared to make petty deals and to toy with political corruption. Negro urban leaders, to illustrate, seldom have access to decisions on bids for multimillion-dollar construction projects. Those who are susceptible to temptation are restricted to marginal graft like the numbers racket. Negroes felt it an ironic confirmation of their low status that when the first Negro to be borough president of Manhattan lost his position, it involved not a million-dollar conspiracy but a less than $5,000 apartment renovation. In political patronage, too, Negro politicians are restricted to the lower levels of reward. The hard facts generally tend to limit the outreach and the effectiveness of the ghetto politicians. Unable to compete successfully for power or patronage, they tend to compete among themselves

[3] These figures are taken from Harold M. Baron, "Black Powerlessness in Chicago," *Trans-action*, November 1963, pp. 27–33.

for the available crumbs; and this struggle, in turn, makes them more vulnerable to manipulation by real political leadership —i.e., white leadership. When no one has much patronage or much power, rivalry for a minimal share keeps everyone divided and everyone impotent.[4]

At the same rung on the ladder are other groups whose powerlessness is connected to poverty. Many Spanish-speaking Americans —the Puerto Ricans in New York and the Chicanos in California— fall into this category. Poor whites—in Appalachia, but also in their own ghettos within the cities, particularly Chicago—qualify too. And the aged, those on public assistance, and the inhabitants of skid row are other examples. What all these groups have in common is powerlessness: because of their poverty, other people make decisions for them. Although they may not realize it, their powerlessness results in a paternalistic relationship with the decision makers, in which the nondecision makers must play an expressively passive role.

All this is relatively clear. But when we begin to examine groups that are not poor but that claim to be powerless, the analysis becomes more controversial. A prominent example is students, particularly college students. No one who can afford to go to college is completely poor, but college students have been arguing that they are powerless, that they do not participate in decisions that shape their lives, such as decisions about the selective service system. But even now that they are no longer legally disenfranchised because they are under twenty-one, students complain about how little their vote means. Some who are old enough cannot vote because they are away from home. Others who do vote say that because they belong to a small (and unpopular) voting block, their representatives can ignore them. It is ironic (though typical) that the congressman who was chiefly responsible for blocking all draft reform was over seventy, and that the rest of his committee was not much younger. And the various commissions designed to propose draft reforms did not even include people of draft age. Many students believe that a paternalism exists here, similar to that between the decision makers and the poor. So they think of themselves as sharing a common fate with the poor and powerless.

[4] Kenneth B. Clark, *Dark Ghetto: Dilemmas of Social Power* (New York: Harper and Row, 1967), p. 156.

"Student as Nigger" is the title of a radical pamphlet that was a best seller on most college campuses.

Most students are middle class, and will probably return to a middle-class life one day. But it has often been asked whether the middle classes, in spite of their economic security, are also powerless. Certainly, they feel powerless. Numerous surveys of middle-class neighborhoods have reported feelings of alienation, anomie, and overall powerlessness. Moreover, the two areas that Mills's critics regard as the strongholds of middle-level power—Congress and private associations—seem to be gradually losing their power. Congressmen complain that they no longer make decisions of consequence. They say that in congressional hearings, where the congressmen are supposed to cross-examine skilled bureaucrats, the bureaucrats now condescendingly "brief" the congressmen about decisions that are going to be made (see Chapter 7). Similarly, with the exception of some very powerful private groups like the American Farm Bureau Federation, the American Medical Association, and trade associations within the major industries, most private groups seem to be losing power. These interest groups were organized to lobby Congress for their goals. But as power has shifted away from Congress to the executive branch, many of them found it difficult to develop new strategies. Mobilizing the local vote, their greatest source of power, is no threat to an executive with a national constituency.

If the middle class exercises power anywhere, it should be at the local level—a point Mills tends to ignore. There is a tradition in American political thought, going back to Jefferson, John Taylor of Caroline, and even John Calhoun, which suggests that power is more easily exercised at local levels. There, with greater intimacy and fewer people, an alien elite is less likely to emerge. But many people question the relevance of this tradition in contemporary America. They point out that, increasingly, important local decisions are made nationally. Since the Interstate Highway Act, road construction must be planned around a national system. Because of the need for a mobile population, housing is being transferred from the hands of local builders to huge national construction firms. Even education, traditionally a local institution, is becoming a national consideration, with the pressure for more experts and a system tied to the national defense. And agriculture, which used to be considered a local issue, has also become nationalized. Quotas and parities are established by Congress. County agents, residents who make many important local decisions, tend to be more responsive to the interests of national institutions, like the American Farm Bureau Federation or Congress, than to local farmers. In many areas, then, local middle classes find that they are losing power to the national elites.

One other group that claims it is powerless—even though it includes a majority of the population and cannot be considered a financially poor group—is women. Throughout American history, women have complained that political decisions are paternalistically made for them by men who do not represent them. (One panel studying abortion, a problem of special interest to women, consisted of nine men and a nun.) It was only in this century that American women received the right to vote. But because of social customs, women's liberation groups argue, women are still disenfranchised. Only a few are able to gain political office, which is only one kind of politics. "Sexual politics" occurs in the home, at work, wherever the sexes meet. Women argue that a sure sign of their oppression is that many people consider their demands for liberation a joke, while they accept similar demands from other groups.

What we need now is some criteria for evaluating the various claims of powerlessness. If all these claims were valid, then Mills would be right. For the segment of society without power would be growing, while the segment with power would be getting smaller. To illustrate:

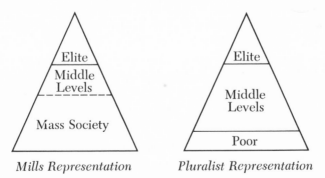

Mills Representation   *Pluralist Representation*

In the Millsian model on the left, the group without power is large and merges imperceptibly into the middle levels. But the pluralists believe that the powerless group is small, and a distinct middle level exists. Both agree that a separate group is at the top, though its size is often disputed.

Who is correct? Earlier we defined power as being closely related to decision making. The converse is helpful. Powerlessness is related to nondecision making. The less influence an individual has over decisions that affect his life, the more powerless he is. Paternalism, therefore, is a synonym for powerlessness, no matter how many rewards, financial or otherwise, the paternalized group receives for its passivity. In this sense, many of the claims made by the not-poor-but-powerless groups are valid. In comparison with the poor and powerless, these middle-class groups are obviously well off. But compared to the well-off and the rich decision makers, they are not.

We are now in a better position to evaluate the hypotheses of *The Power Elite.* One group in American society constitutes the political decision makers. They are either wealthy or have some functional equivalent of wealth. A second group is powerless. They are generally poor or bear some stigma that is the functional equivalent of poverty. This stigma could be race or sex, or a characteristic that society regards as "deviant"—political extremists, criminals, the insane, nonmajoritarian types in general. Finally, there is a middle group that has certain forms of power through middle-level institutions. Congress, and the people Congress really represents, still make some decisions in domestic spheres. Selective-service reform was decided by Congress, which had killed reform attempts by a presidential commission, which, ironically enough, was composed of members of the power elite. But this middle level of power is not as large as most people think because many people in it belong to the not-poor-but-powerless category. And the middle level feels powerless when it comes to major decisions, particularly those involving foreign policy. In the end, we believe Mills was closer to reality than his critics. But that is really beside the point. The important issue here is the relationship between decision makers and nondecision makers, and little attention has been paid to that so far.

POWER IN OTHER COUNTRIES

First, let us look at power and representation in other countries. Although up to this point, our discussion has been focused on the United States, it should be clear that the questions raised apply to any political system. We can divide our discussion into three types of political system: other advanced industrialized societies; "totalitarian" societies; and "underdeveloped" societies.

The patterns of power in other industrialized societies are similar to those of the United States. If anything, because of historically important social (and, to a lesser extent, economic) elites in countries like England and France, the distance between decision makers and nondecision makers is greater than in America. Indeed, many writers on British politics point proudly to this phenomenon. Britain, they maintain, has a stable political system because there is an elite, which is expected to act like one and does, and because there is a large group of followers, who are expected to accept those decisions and do. The stability results from the respect each one has for the other, so the distance between the groups is really irrelevant. In the remaining countries of Europe, there have been studies of national "power elites," and talk of an establishment is so common that the word has become part of every intelligent citizen's political lexicon. In fact, the elites of Europe and America have so much contact with each other—in banking, commerce, diplomacy—that they are beginning to resemble each other more than their fellow countrymen.

The picture of so-called "totalitarian" countries varies with the speaker. As we pointed out earlier, "totalitarianism" is more an ideological than a descriptive term. Taken at face value, it implies that an elite controls all the power, leaving none for other groups. This conception misses some of the subtleties that exist in those countries where the term is applied.

After the Bolshevik revolution in the Soviet Union, the Communist party definitely represented a power elite. Lenin's formulation of the party as the vanguard of the revolution was a direct call for the creation of an elite that could assume power when the time came. Even today, party membership continues to be a symbol of power-elite status. With membership in this elite comes the usual trappings of power—access to decision making, symbols of prestige, "more" equality. In nearly every respect these trappings are similar to power phenomena in other political systems. In fact, much about the power situation in the Soviet Union resembles the situation in Western countries. There is an elite; there is a group that is excluded from power. A middle group also exists, striving to obtain power while at the same time striving to keep away from the powerless.

However, a few important differences can be found. For one thing, the connection between wealth and power and between poverty and powerlessness is less pronounced in the Soviet Union. The wealthy aristocratic class was discredited during the revolution and has essentially left the country. The new class that replaced it, in the vacuum created by the removal of the wealth, had more of the functional equivalents, political skill, and technical ability, than similar groups in other countries. Its power was not based on its ability to make profits and own property. This situation has changed somewhat in recent years, because, for the first time in Soviet history, a power class has been able to pass its power on to its children. Also, the distance between decision makers and nondecision makers is not as great in the Soviet Union as in capitalist countries, although it is greater than egalitarian socialist ideology suggests. The predicted withering away of the state never occurred, and the USSR is far from a state of complete equality in decision making, yet real changes have occurred since 1917. (We will discuss this subject further in Chapter 15.)

The countries of Asia, Africa, and South America also have gaps between their decision makers and nondecision makers. Here, too, an historical vacuum was created, one involving not only wealth, but also administrative skills. When the colonial elites left these countries, those in power tended to draw their strength from political popularity, or more precisely, charismatic leadership. Those men (and women) who were active in the struggle for independence became the elite of the new country. But political ability was not enough in the face of enormous technical problems, and many charismatic leaders were eventually overthrown by less colorful but more efficient political leaders. The creation of an administrative elite takes a good deal of time, and in many countries, the process is just beginning. In general, the elite of the so-called underdeveloped countries is composed of a small group of people who established their reputations in the struggle for independence and who are developing technical skills. Since these skills require education and a cosmopolitan outlook, these elites are not representative of the country as a whole; they usually come from a small group that was trained by the colonial power. If anything, the distance between decision makers and nondecision makers in these countries is greater than in other types of political systems, not so much because the leaders want the separation, but because they were trained in the West.

COUNTRY	BASIS OF POWER		
	Wealth	Technical Skill	Political Skill
Advanced, industrialized	X	X	X
"Totalitarian" at revolution	O	X	X
"Underdeveloped" at independence	O	O	X
All systems eventually	X	X	X

X = most important   O = much less important

It can be seen, on the basis of this brief sketch and the diagram above, that the relationship between decision makers and followers is of primary importance to all political systems. There are always certain people who make decisions and others who have decisions made for them. What does vary from system to system, and what really determines the stability and character of a political system, is the relationship between these two groups. Are those for whom decisions are made willing to accept the authority of those who make the decisions? Because this question is so important, we should examine the conditions that promote acceptance or lack of acceptance. It should be clear that we are making broad generalizations here about all political systems, not just about the United States.

POWER RELATIONSHIPS

Let us begin with the relationship between the powerless and the powerful. Broadly speaking, the powerless could theoretically have three types of attitudes toward those who make decisions for them —positive ones, neutral ones, and negative ones.

Positive attitudes toward power elites are associated with

feelings of appreciation toward them. Sometimes the feeling is a direct one. The person will indicate that he is grateful to the decision makers for making complicated decisions that he could not possibly make himself. At other times, the gratitude will be more of an awe toward the position a power holder occupies. But most of the time, positive attitudes toward the decision makers are very indirect. They usually take the form of a strong identification with the country through some type of patriotic ritual without any reference to decision makers. But since the decision makers are, in a sense, the country, loyalty to them is loyalty to the country. The statement, "Our country right or wrong" actually means, "I support the decisions those in power in my country make, whether those decisions are good ones or not." Thus, when Americans are asked to support their country in time of war, they are really being asked to support the decision to go to war and the people who made that decision.

Feelings of appreciation toward the abstract entity "country" are often combined with negative attitudes toward the specific men who make decisions. A perfect example of this occurs at a baseball game, when spectators rise in solemn majesty to sing the national anthem and then proceed to boo the mayor as he throws out the first ball. This is an interesting paradox. Most people express their negative attitudes toward politicians, but have positive attitudes toward the things politicians do. A survey of American mothers showed that "politics" as a possible vocation for their sons ranked low in the order of their preferences, but their respect for presidents and other important office holders was high. How people become decision makers without being political is not considered. In short, positive attitudes toward decision makers are expressed indirectly either as respect for what they do or as respect for the country they do it in, not as respect for themselves as individuals.

Many nondecision makers have neutral or ambiguous attitudes toward the people who make decisions for them. Intensive interviewing of working-class men around "Eastport" made this clear.[5] Statements like the following are typical:

> President Eisenhower is not a big wheel. Tom Dewey is the big boss. It really surprised us. We figure he's [Eisenhower] a general and he knows what to do. . . . But he's taking orders like anybody else.

[5] "Eastport" is a made-up name for New Haven, Connecticut.

Congressmen know less and less about the people they are supposed to represent.

I belong to the group that might have too little power. But, I mean, we—as long as we exercise our political rights, our voting privileges, a group of little men become a big group.

I have nothing to do with the government; no, I've never had anything at all to do with them.

It [government] hasn't much effect on my life, you know. It could, I suppose, if they passed labor laws that could hurt me.[6]

Neutral and ambiguous political attitudes take behavioral forms. Nonvoting is a classic example of a neutral attitude toward the elite. Why do people refrain from voting? We know that a disproportionate percentage of nonvoters are located among the powerless group, particularly in poverty areas. However, two schools of thought exist, and neither views nonvoting strictly as a statement of neutral attitude. Both points of view suggest that nonvoting is an indication of the health of a political system. People are satisfied with the way things are going; if they were not, they would go out and express their dissatisfaction by voting. The contrary point of view holds that nonvoting is a sign that the political system is ill. If people in a democracy do not care enough to indicate their attitudes, then something must be wrong somewhere. What is interesting about these opposing views is that both refuse to accept a neutral category. They seem to imply that neutrality toward the decision makers is impossible, and that what appears as neutral must, eventually, be seen as either positive or negative.

Another form of neutrality (or alleged neutrality) is nonmembership in political groups, again most often associated with the powerless. Organizers among the poor can attest to the difficulty of bringing the powerless into groups that will be politically effective. Constant moving, pressure to get a job, the fear of getting in "trouble" and thus losing welfare checks, a general cynical attitude toward politics—all of these (quite legitimate) obstacles reinforce apathy. This form of neutrality leans toward the negative side of the neutral category. It would be difficult to regard nonmembership as a sign of positive attitudes toward the decision makers. Since

[6] Robert Lane, *Political Ideology* (New York: Free Press, 1962), p. 50.

political rewards often go to those who are organized to demand and receive them, group nonmembership creates a cycle in which the powerless tend to remain powerless.

Negative attitudes also take the form of resentment against the decision makers. Sometimes this is expressed directly—by civil disobedience, for example, or by noncooperation, resistance, rebellion, or violence. These take place in all political systems. We find urban rioting in the United States, food strikes in underdeveloped countries, and passive resistance under totalitarian regimes. Resentment expressed in this form presents a direct challenge to the political decision makers, and they have a variety of options to deal with it (which we will discuss shortly).

But resentment is more often expressed indirectly. Most subjects within a political system will obey decisions they personally resent because they believe the decisions were legitimately made and should be followed. In this case, their resentment is either internalized or assumes nonpolitical forms. Observers of the armed forces know that a draftee who resents being inducted may express his anger by becoming a supersoldier. Ashamed of his resentment, he will overcompensate, to the point of treating sadistically those who express their resentment more openly. Thus, resentment against political leaders is a highly subtle phenomenon. Even when it does not seem to be present, it may be potentially revolutionary. But it is very difficult to uncover. And when there is little overt discontent, many people conclude that nondecision makers are satisfied with the status quo. We are beginning to realize that if we persist in that attitude, we will still be sitting in our chairs scratching our heads when insurrection breaks out all around us.

To summarize, then, we have seen how the nondecision makers can be appreciative, resentful, or apathetic toward the decision makers. We will now turn to the decision makers' attitudes toward the people for whom they make decisions. And after examining this aspect, we should be able to see how the two fit together.

In general, elites have two basic approaches to nonelites (to introduce a convenient synonym for the powerless)—persuasion and coercion. People are asked to obey political decisions or they are forced to obey them. These two approaches have been used in all political systems in all eras; the first sophisticated, and still relevant, discussion of them appeared in Machiavelli's classic, *The Prince*:

. . . every prince must desire to be considered merciful and not cruel. He must, however, take care not to misuse this mercifulness. . . . A prince, therefore, must not mind incurring the charge of cruelty for the purpose of keeping his subjects faithful. . . . From this arises the question whether it is better to be loved more than feared, or feared more than loved. The reply is, that one ought to be feared and loved, but it is difficult for the two to go together, it is much safer to be feared than loved, if one of the two has to be wanting.[7]

Notice that in the following discussion we are not restricting the use of coercion to "totalitarian" regimes or persuasion to "democratic" ones. Coercion and persuasion occur in both types of government. And elites everywhere use both approaches. The proportions can, and do, vary. In England and Sweden, persuasion is more prevalent than coercion. Nazi Germany was a system that used coercion more than persuasion. But Germany had its propaganda ministries and England had (and has) its Northern Ireland. When persuasion failed, elites in both countries did not hesitate long before using force.

We are not saying that persuasion is better than coercion. Political systems have developed extraordinary methods of persuading their citizens. With constant bombardment through the mass media in the industrialized societies, with the manipulation of goods in less industrialized societies, and with self-criticism sessions in socialist societies, it has become difficult to say where persuasion ends and coercion begins. It has also become difficult to select one approach over the other. It is not inconceivable that a citizen of the not-too-distant future might plead, "Shoot me, shoot me, but don't let me see one more television commercial for savings bonds!"

Coercion of nonelites occurs when attempts at persuasion have failed. An excellent example of this process in the United States is provided by the Black Panthers. What made this group unique was that it refused to work for its demands within the context of the American political system, that is, the way other groups worked, by bargaining, compromising, and being "reasonable." In the words of Eldridge Cleaver, formerly one of its spokesmen:

[7] Niccolò Machiavelli, *The Prince and The Discourses,* trans. Luigi Ricci (New York: Modern Library, 1950), pp. 60–61.

Black people are no longer interested in adjudicating the situation, in negotiating the situation, in arbitrating the situation. Their only interest now is in being able to summon up whatever it will take to wreak the havoc upon Babylon that will force Babylon to let black people go. For all other avenues have been closed.[8]

And, as Cleaver concludes, "you are either part of the solution or part of the problem." Because this was not just rhetoric on the part of the Panthers, the pervasive power of the decision makers in the United States has been completely ineffective. As a result, most of the leaders of the group have been imprisoned, killed, or forced into exile.

Most elites are wary of using force and would much rather be persuasive. Therefore, we should examine some of the persuasive techniques that are available. In addition to relatively obvious tactics, such as the use of patriotic symbols and mass advertising campaigns, there are two other important tactics that are less obvious but frequently employed—civility and cooption.

Civility is a confusing word. We are using it to refer to a situation in which the elite presents a face of complete reasonableness. Lyndon Johnson was fond of quoting the prophet Isaiah: "Come, let us reason together." Civility suggests that the decision makers are not very different from the people for whom they are making decisions. If we all sit down together, we can work out our little disagreements. Impressed by power, for power is impressive, representatives of the nonelite group sit down with the elite (frequently on the elite's home ground) and work out a solution. Often the nonelite group accepts less than it had been demanding, because in this situation the elite group has most of the advantages.

Another form of civility appears in attempts by the elite to define the terms of political discourse. This is a very subtle process and needs some elaboration. Elites usually announce that they are willing to discuss any reasonable (or rational, or legitimate, or realistic) demands, but they will not discuss unreasonable (that is, irrational, illegitimate, unrealistic) ones. In this way, they attempt to define the terms of political discourse. Now what a member of the elite considers reasonable is a demand that does not challenge

[8] Eldridge Cleaver, *Post-Prison Writing and Speeches*, ed. Robert Sheer (New York: Random House, 1969).

his power. Therefore, what he is saying is: "I will negotiate on any demands that leave me where I am and leave you where you are (relatively speaking), but I will not negotiate on anything else." Nonelites can reject his definition and substitute their own, but this runs into two problems. One is that their adversary has power over the means of persuasion and can be successful at convincing everybody else that his position is reasonable and the other side is frenzied and irrational. And though the other side may have good reason for their frenzy, the label will probably stick. A second problem is that if they reject the elite's terms, they are in a position to have coercion used against them. So most nonelites eventually accept the decision-makers' terms for political discourse and, as a result, work from a disadvantaged position. This tactic is very successful and is used frequently.

Cooption has been more fully studied and discussed. The term refers to the process by which an elite group admits new members as a way of dealing with a nonelite group. It can also refer to what Harold Lasswell calls "restriction by partial incorporation." [9] In that sense, not only people can be coopted, but ideas and activities as well. Some examples will help illustrate the concept.

In the ideal cooptive situation, a recognized group makes concrete demands on the decision makers. The group has formally recognized leaders who speak for it. The elite offers something to the leader— a job, money, prestige, or the argument that more can be gained from working "within"—and expects him to maintain his ties with the dissident group. He then is placed in between the nonelite and the elite, carrying messages back and forth. The basic idea is to keep communication channels open so that bargains and compromises can be worked out. This was the pattern during the civil rights movement in the United States, particularly under the Kennedy administration. A former official of an organization like the Urban League or the NAACP would serve on the president's staff. He would communicate the groups' demands to the president, who would tell him what was realistic and what was not. The liaison man would then convey this information to the groups involved, and they would reformulate their strategies accordingly.

In other words, several conditions must be met for cooption to work properly. There must be a formally recognized group, and the

[9] Harold Lasswell, *Politics: Who Gets What, When, How* (Cleveland: Meridian Books, 1958), pp. 80–94.

group must have a spokesman or leader. When political activity is spontaneous, when it takes place before a formal group has been established, the elite should consider it as if it were a formal group. A representative from the dissidents can be considered their spokesman, so that there will be someone to coopt. But, then again, as reality becomes distorted, the whole strategy may break down. To continue with the example of civil rights, the organized movement was superseded by spontaneous and unorganized urban violence. The decision makers could no longer continue the same strategy. They tried. James Farmer was offered and accepted a position with the Nixon administration for a time. But anyone who joins the establishment loses his influence among the spontaneously political nonelites. He has no message to bring back and tends to be more a symbol than an active agent in the political process. This example illustrates the difficulties of cooption. The tactic is often attempted, but it does not always work.

Ideas are also coopted. When the ideology of an elite is threatened by an external ideology, an attempt may be made to head off the threat by incorporating some of the other ideology's basic tenets, enough to mollify the opposition without destroying the original ideology. Thus, Harold Lasswell has shown that by taking certain concepts from socialism, the New Deal prevented socialism from making inroads here. And Lenin was able to save his socialist revolution by partially incorporating some capitalistic ideas during the period of the New Economic Policy. Examples could be cited endlessly. The important point is that the cooption of ideas requires conditions similar to the cooption of men. The dissident ideas should be relatively well developed; they should be adaptable to cooption; and they should be broad enough so that the process appears legitimate.

At this point, we shall be able to make some generalizations about the effects of various relationships between decision makers and nondecision makers. We have seen that nonelites are either appreciative, resentful, or apathetic toward the elites, and that the elites are either persuasive or coercive toward the nonelites. When they are persuasive, they often use either the strategies of civility or cooption. This information should enable us to tell from the type of relationship whether a political system is working—that is, whether it is stable or unstable.

A high degree of coercion within a system usually means that something is amiss and the situation is potentially unstable. It is more difficult to judge the stability of a political system when persuasion is the basic tactic of the decision makers. If we combine the two types of persuasive strategies and the three types of nonelite attitudes, we arrive at six possible types of political situations:

		Appreciation	Apathy	Resentment
Elite Strategy	Civility	A Stable	C Potentially Stable	E Highly Unstable
	Cooption	B Stable (because cooption is unnecessary)	D Potentially Unstable	F Stable, if it works / Unstable if it does not work

ATTITUDES OF NONELITES

Situations A and B, the ones most desired by decision makers, are historically rare. Although Walter Bagehot would have us believe that pre-Victorian England fit the qualifications, reform agitation, wars, and developing colonialism hardly point in that direction. Situations C and D are much more common. Here, the equilibrium is potentially unstable, but nothing has happened yet. Nondecision makers are neither overjoyed nor tremendously upset about their status. They accept it for what it is. But because their attitude toward the status quo is not positive, decision makers cannot relax. They have to use their strategies preventively, heading off discontent before it develops. This was the situation in the United States during the 1950s, and in England throughout most of its history. In fact, most political systems fall into Categories C and D most of the time. The only problem is that apathy is usually either positive or negative. When it begins to move toward one of those poles, particularly the negative one, E and F situations result.

When nondecision makers are resentful, a political system is in trouble. If the elites decide to gamble on cooption, it may work, but it could also backfire. The coopted man becomes a traitor to the cause and is excluded; he is no longer helpful to the elites. At this stage, the elite may try civility. But if the dissident group is highly distrustful, they will reject the definition of the situation. If attempts to resolve the relationship peacefully fail, coercion is the next step. And when force becomes the order of the day, the instability of the system becomes apparent. A revolutionary situation has developed that will be resolved either by the complete repression or the victory of the dissident group—in which case a new elite comes into power. This is almost exactly what happened in Cuba. The Batista regime was unsuccessful in its attempts to deal with the dissidents through persuasion because of the generally poor conditions. When Batista resorted to wholesale repression, it strengthened the opposition. Castro could not be eliminated by force, and attempts to do so made him more popular among the powerless. Finally realizing his mistake, Batista tried to return to a policy of persuasion by coopting a more popular British figure. But it was too late. Castro's forces, with great popular support, routed his army and took control of the country. A new group of decision makers took over .

This chapter has taken a rather circuitous route. We have tried to show that decision makers are as important in politics as the decisions they make. The stability of a political system is often determined by who governs. We have seen that all political systems have decision makers and others for whom the decisions are made, that there are many possible relationships between these two groups, and that some of these relationships promote stability while others lead to revolution. We have indicated that we consider the pluralist model inaccurate and the relationship between decision makers and nondecision makers in pluralism so unhealthy that fundamental changes are needed, particularly in an advanced industrial society like the United States. But what makes the question of the relationship between decision makers and nondecision makers so fascinating is that we are all part of the relationship, and this chapter has discussed each of us.

7 Implementing Political Decisions

THE PROCESS OF carrying out decisions is easy to understand—on paper. After a decision has been made, it must be implemented. Making the decision is a political process; carrying it out is an administrative one. All political systems contain two groups—the politicians and the administrators. After each group has done its job, the process is completed.

So much for theory. It should be apparent, however, that there is not a sharp dividing line between making and implementing decisions. Consider the Civil Rights Act of 1964. After much tumult, including mass demonstrations, emotional speeches, and three assassinations, the American Congress passed a law designed to ". . . authorize the Attorney General to institute suits to protect constitutional rights in public facilities and public education." [1] To accomplish these ends, a procedure was developed that enabled the attorney general to sue in the federal courts to enforce desegregation policies in public schools. In the years since the law was passed, segregation has almost disappeared in public facilities, but it persists in the schools. In cities as diverse as Evanston, Illinois; Pasadena, California; Chicago; St. Louis; Albany; and New Haven, a

[1] HR 7152, the Civil Rights Act of 1964.

good percentage of the schools either have less than 1 percent or more than 50 percent black students. If anything, segregation in public education has increased since the passage of the Civil Rights Act of 1964, especially in the North.

No matter how perfect a law is technically, without implementation it is meaningless. For some political systems, implementation is a constant and recurring problem. Countries with a shortage of technical skills or a lack of desire to solve problems have a particularly hard time: decision makers may make decisions, but insiders know that many will never be implemented. One good example of this process is land reform in South Vietnam. Sophisticated observers concluded long ago that one reason for the popularity of the National Liberation Front is its program of land redistribution. The South Vietnamese have been urged to adopt a similar policy. Every year or so, the government announces a new land reform program with great flourish. Each time, the new decision, drafted with American help, reads perfectly. Yet nothing is ever done; the land distribution either remains the same or becomes more inequitable. The problem here is in implementation, not in decision making. Making decisions, in fact, is easy—one person or group of people proclaims a policy. But because the South Vietnamese elite do not really want to divide up their own land, the decisions are never implemented.

Nonimplementation also occurs when the desire is there, but technical ability is lacking. Egypt may genuinely want a new dam, and no social group may have enough power to obstruct the project. Unless there are people in the country who know how to operate a dam, that decision will suffer in implementation. In Chapter 5 we talked at length about the need for adequacy in decisions. Adequacy is even more important at the implementation stage than at the decision-making stage. Without it, the decision is useless.

Implementation seems to be a major problem for Third World countries. Decisions can be made fairly easily, but the implementation results in a major crisis. The opposite situation often occurs in the more advanced societies. In the United States, for example, it is usually not that difficult to carry out a decision once it is made, because the necessary technical skills are available. But the decision making itself can lead to a crisis. So many groups have to be pleased, and so many institutions—Congress, the Supreme Court, the executive branch—have to be consulted that the reason for the decision often disappears before the decision is made. In short, in the industrialized societies decision making is difficult while implementation (given popular support) is comparatively easy. In the less developed countries, making decisions is easy but implementation is a problem.

In all situations the distinction between what is political and what is administrative is helpful in understanding the entire process —but it should be emphasized strongly that there is politics in administration and administration in politics. In theory, decision making occurs in political institutions, that is, in institutions subject to popular feelings and manned by people whose abilities make them sensitive to the popular will. Implementation is carried out in administrative institutions, theoretically those where popular skills are secondary to technical ability and expertise. This chapter deals with the role played by this second group of institutions, often called the administrative branch, the civil service, or, more commonly, the bureaucracy. This does not mean that politics will be forgotten. Our contention is that politics is ubiquitous, that it pervades all aspects of organized social life, including areas where politics is not supposed to appear. Bureaucracy is one of those areas.

BUREAUCRACY

Everyone has had experience with bureaucracy. Anyone who pays taxes, works, rents or owns a home, or goes to school is familiar with the term. Since we have all had to adjust to bureaucratic situations, we have all become experts on bureaucracy. It is impossible to live in the United States today without being an expert in bureaucracy. Our schools are run bureaucratically (which is a description, not a criticism); our transportation, including walking, was provided bureaucratically; and this book was published by one bureaucracy and distributed by another. There is, in fact, very little social activity that is not connected with one bureaucracy or another.

When we talk about bureaucracy and its relationship to the implementation of political decisions, we are not referring to all these bureaucracies, only public ones. A public bureaucracy is one that implements decisions that affect everyone in the society. Decisions are often made and implemented for only a part of society. When, for example, a company decides to raise employee salaries, the payroll office is informed, the finance director and his staff are mobilized, and the treasurer and his staff are alerted to sign the new checks. These steps may be bureaucratic (if the company is a large one), but they are not publicly bureaucratic because the only people affected are those who work for this company. But when a legislature decides on higher taxes, a public bureaucracy will do the work involved because everyone is affected by the decision.

In nearly all cases, public bureaucracies are governmental, that is, they are part of the formal governmental structure and are charged with the implementation of political decisions. However, a public decision may sometimes be made by a private association. In that case, the decision may be implemented by either a governmental or a nongovernmental bureaucracy. But to simplify matters, we will confine our discussion here to governmental institutions. When we say bureaucracy, we usually mean the administrative branch of government or the civil service.

Bureaucracy is not a new form of social organization. The Mandarin Chinese developed a bureaucratic society in A.D. 600. There were written examinations for civil service positions, and the person with the highest score obtained the position. The civil service was organized by rank and skill, and promotion occurred along a continuum from the lesser positions to the higher ones. The entire process would win nods of approval from a modern public administrator.

As a matter of fact, the most brilliant treatment of bureaucracy as a social phenomenon dates back to the late nineteenth century to the writings of Max Weber. Weber, you will recall, discussed three kinds of legitimacy—traditional, charismatic, and legal. And as legal authority becomes routinized or rational, it develops into bureaucracy. Weber defined bureaucracy in terms of its essential features:

> (1) A continuous organization of official functions bound by rules. (2) A specified sphere of competence. . . . (3) The organization of offices under the control and supervision of a higher one. . . . (4) The rules which regulated the conduct of an office may be technical rules or norms. In both cases, if their application is to be fully rational, specialized training is necessary. . . . (5) In the rational type it is a matter of principle that the members of the administrative staff should be

completely separated from ownership of the means of production or administration. . . . (6) In the rational type case, there is also the complete absence of appropriation of his official position by the incumbent. . . . (7) Administrative acts, decisions, and rules are formulated and recorded in writing, even in cases where oral discussion is the rule or is even mandatory.[2]

Bureaucracy is, therefore, a highly formalized system of organization, in which individual discretion is minimized as much as possible in favor of systematic, collective procedure. Weber called this "the dominance of a spirit of formalistic impersonality . . . without hatred or passion, and hence without affection or enthusiasm. The dominant norms are concepts of straightforward duty without regard to personal considerations. Everyone is subject to formal equality of treatment; that is, everyone is in the same empirical situation. This is the spirit in which the ideal official conducts his office."[3]

DOES BUREAUCRACY WORK?

These two quotations from Weber highlight an argument that has been in progress since he put his thoughts down on paper. Was Weber's analysis purely descriptive or was he making value judgments in condemning or praising bureaucracy as a form of social organization? The first quotation, emphasizing the characteristics of bureaucracy, seems strictly scientific, but the second one contains traces of value judgment: bureaucracy promotes rationality and is therefore good.

Twentieth-century writers on bureaucracy fall into either the descriptive or the normative category. Those who have negative feelings about bureaucracy point out that it is basically antihumanistic, the substitution of impersonal criteria for personal responses. Every individual who confronts a bureaucracy is placed (must be placed) in a preexisting category. Any aspect of the individual's

[2] Max Weber, "The Essentials of Bureaucratic Organization," in *Reader in Bureaucracy*, ed. Robert K. Merton et al. (New York: Free Press, 1952), pp. 19–21.

[3] Ibid., p. 27.

problem that does not fit into the category is declared irrelevant, no matter how important it is to the individual. These categories have rules by which all cases must be judged, and the rules, originally designed to promote fairness and equity, become ends in themselves: RULES instead of rules. In one famous example of bureaucratic adherence to RULES, the man who served as Admiral Byrd's pilot in the first exploratory flight over the South Pole was not granted American citizenship because he did not meet the requirement of five years' continuous residence in the United States—even though he had done so much for the country with his flights. He did not meet the RULE, of course, because he had been flying over the South Pole, after discovering Little America, which, under the RULES of international law, was not American territory.[4] In such a fashion, bureaucratic procedure perpetuates itself.

This impersonality is usually more pronounced in public bureaucracies than in private ones. Perhaps private bureaucracies are more responsive to the individual as an individual because they are smaller. But size is not the only consideration. Robert Merton has described how public bureaucrats develop an inflated image of their own importance:

> The bureaucrat, in part irrespective of his position within the hierarchy, acts as a representative of the power and prestige of the entire structure. In his official role he is vested with definite authority. This often leads to an actually or apparently domineering attitude. . . . Protest and recourse to other officials on the part of the client are often ineffective or largely precluded by the previously mentioned esprit de corps which joins the officials into a more or less solidary in-group. This source of conflict *may* be minimized in private enterprise since the client can register an effective protest by transferring his trade to another organization within the competitive system. But with the monopolistic nature of public organization, no such alternative is possible. Moreover, in this case, tension is increased because of a discrepancy between ideology and fact: the governmental personnel are held to be "servants of the people," but in fact are usually superordinate, and release of

[4] Robert K. Merton, "Bureaucratic Structure and Personality," in *Reader in Bureaucracy*, ed. Merton et al., p. 366.

tension can seldom be afforded by turning to other agencies for the necessary services.[5]

Anyone who has been told by a postal clerk, supported by pictures of the president, the American flag, and other symbols of the majesty of the United States government, that his package cannot be mailed from one place to another—even though he has done it six times before—knows what Merton is talking about.

It is the thesis of Robert Presthus that bureaucracy is responsible for much of the poor mental health of modern society. In his book *The Organizational Society,* Presthus describes a particular kind of personality that has developed with the rise of bureaucracy. This personality avoids conflict and ambiguity because both are dysfunctional to the effective operation of the organization. Any conflict leads to an anxiety-conformity syndrome, in which superconformity is used to deal with the anxiety created by the ambiguous situation. A highly developed status system is an example of this; it eliminates doubt about who is higher than whom, thus permitting every individual to know his place. Those who adapt to the bureaucratic situation develop this type of personality; those who do not become ambivalent or indifferent. As the author concludes, "If meaningful work is essential to mental health, the human consequences of such orientations are disturbing." [6] Every big organization has its company psychiatrist.

These criticisms of bureaucracy as an antihumanistic institution are essentially apolitical. The criticisms are not related to any well-developed view of politics, in other words, to any ideology. But there are two ideological critiques of bureaucracy: one is basically conservative, the other radical.

Conservatives regard the development of bureaucracy as destructive of traditional values. Weber's discussion emphasized the rise of equality, which is associated with bureaucracy. Weber pointed out that bureaucracy led to "leveling"—the need for skilled personnel was so great that recruiting had to include the whole society, not just the traditional upper class. Conservative critics of bureaucracy carry this point further. They argue that bureaucratization created a "mass society" in which quality has suffered. It is not the

[5] Ibid.

[6] Robert Presthus, *The Organizational Society* (New York: Vintage, 1965).

best but the most efficient method that is adopted. The lowest common denominator, emphasizing both lowest and common, becomes the criterion. Aside from a decline in taste, this bureaucratization also has harmful political consequences. Traditional dividing lines between social groups break down in a bureaucratized society. People become grouped into large categories, with little in common but their relationship to the bureaucracy. They feel alienated, purposeless, impotent. If these feelings remain, the political system becomes unstable. If they are manipulated by demagogues, they assume purpose and potency through violence and symbolism. In either case, the result is a political disaster, the creation of bureaucratized society.[7]

Radicals, following Marx, also have developed a critique of bureaucratic society. Marx's early writings, particularly the *Economic and Philosophical Manuscripts of 1844,* were in the humanistic tradition. They emphasized the alienation of man from his work, which so often occurs in industrial societies. But many revolutionaries who followed Marx had a different conception of bureaucracy. Bureaucracy develops simultaneously in industry and in government, and the two types tend to become less distinguishable. The state bureaucracy implements the decisions made by the industrial bureaucracy. What is undesirable about bureaucracy is not bureaucracy itself, but the uses to which it is put. It becomes the means of making profits for the few, and exploiting and stultifying the rest of society. The significance of bureaucracy lies in its function as a power base in industrial societies. It is the power of bureaucracy, rather than its nature, that must be changed if society is to change.

Bureaucracy has been criticized and attacked from every political viewpoint. It has been blamed for neurosis, psychosis, fascism, communism, divorce, alcoholism, drug addiction, alienation, and for nearly everything else that is wrong in contemporary society. Yet there are some people who believe that there are positive aspects to bureaucracy.

These defenders of bureaucracy point out that no other form of social organization could give us the advantages of a modern society. Not only consumer goods, but also public benefits like social security and unemployment compensation emanate from bureauc-

[7] For example, see José Ortega y Gasset, *The Revolt of the Masses* (New York: Norton, 1932), and Gustave Le Bon, *The Crowd* (London: Ernst Bonn Ltd., 1947).

racy. People are likely to note when bureaucracy fails and to ignore the many times it works. We notice the foul-up in bus schedules, but do we appreciate modern society's ability to change our airplane reservations at the last moment, to keep track of our money in the bank, to provide an accurate record of the courses we have taken and the grades we received? All these things are possible because of bureaucratic organization. We could not live as we do without it.

In addition, it should be pointed out that bureaucracy is usually advanced through the efforts of exploited groups that want it. And they want it because it is fair. Nonbureaucratic authority was arbitrary and capricious. In manufacturing, for example, daily quotas could be raised or lowered at the owner's whim. To prevent this, workers fought for standardized daily quotas. It may have been bureaucratic, but it was also fair. Though the quota system may have hurt a few individuals, it helped many others. Similarly, the welfare bureaucracy we have now was created by groups who fought against the capriciousness of an unregulated business cycle. The welfare state has stabilized the economy and helped more people than it has harmed. Almost invariably, increases in bureaucratization come about when a deprived group seeks standardized rules of procedure to prevent its own exploitation.

Finally, although bureaucracy is associated with power, it is the most equitable power arrangement that can be found in the modern world. In an ideal bureaucracy an individual does not rise in the ranks because of his class, his last name, his race or religion, but because of his technical ability. Exceptions to this rule occur only in imperfect bureaucracies. The ideal bureaucracy is chiefly responsible for the great recent advances in human equality. The same "leveling" that conservatives deplore is chiefly responsible for social mobility. Bureaucracies cannot be inefficient. They must recruit from all society and procure the best talent if they are to work well. This recruitment will, in the long run, break down class, race, and religious prejudice, which are inefficient and antibureaucratic considerations. Without bureaucracy, society would not be less hierarchical but more. Bureaucracy does not deny the existence of hierarchy. It tries to make the hierarchy as fair as possible by fitting positions in it according to rational factors. Bureaucratic organization, as Weber always pointed out, is the most rational form of social organization we have, or could have.

Since there are many positive and many negative aspects to the

rise of bureaucracy, we should concentrate on the political significance of modern bureaucracy, the impact bureaucratization has on
politics in modern societies. It may then be possible to make a
more informed judgment about bureaucratization.

THE NATURE OF BUREAUCRATIC STRUCTURES

One of the first statements usually made about bureaucracy is
that its rise constituted an important social phenomenon, more important even than the industrial revolution. Thirty years ago it was
chic to argue that the bureaucratic revolution had replaced the
industrial revolution. Books with titles like *The Managerial Revolution, The Administrative State, The Organizational Revolution, The
Organization Man,* and *The Organizational Society* appeared.[8] The
line of reasoning in these books usually went something like this:
bureaucratization has brought with it the manager, a modern day
equivalent of the nineteenth-century capitalist. While the capitalist
obtained his fortune by building up his own investment through
enormous risks and shady finance, the manager invests other people's
money, usually in safer enterprises. In addition, the profit motive,
which formed the basis of the capitalist's activity, is gradually
being replaced by an efficiency motive. Large organizations are
more concerned about their growth and, especially, their continued
existence, than about making money. Society reflects this change in
the type of organizations it nurtures. Whereas nineteenth-century
society was dynamic, in constant economic, political, and social
fluctuation, bureaucratic society, symbolized by the triumph of the
manager over the capitalist, is staid and even. The primary goal
becomes conformity to the life style of organizational society. The
organization man emerges as a new social phenomenon. The organization's goals become his personal goals; the two are merged
together so completely that you would probably not even notice the
organization man, except for all the books written about him.

[8] James Burnham, *The Managerial Revolution* (Bloomington, Ind.: Indiana
University Press, 1960); Clifford D. Waldo, *The Administrative State: A
Study of the Political Theory of American Public Administration* (New York:
Ronald, 1948); Kenneth Boulding, *The Organizational Revolution: A Study in
the Ethics of Economic Organization* (Chicago: Quadrangle, 1968); William H.
Whyte, *The Organization Man* (New York: Simon and Schuster, 1956); and
Presthus, *The Organizational Society.*

Managerial society is run by generalists. A manager is a person who is adept at running organizations. He has no specific skills, or, at least, does not become a manager on the basis of them. What matters are his general skills. He collects information from technically trained subordinates and synthesizes it into a decision. Or he may be an expert at implementation, taking the decisions of others and guiding them to their final resting place. Just as the manager of a baseball team could have been a catcher, infielder, outfielder, or pitcher in his playing days, the manager can come from almost anywhere in the organization. It is because of his skills with people, public relations, industrial psychology, that he succeeds as a manager. He is something of a bureaucratic entrepreneur, adept at achieving his ends through bureaucratic organizations. He is Dean Rusk or Aleksei Kosygin, working his way up through organizations until he reaches the pinnacle of power.

There is much in the theory of a managerial revolution which is appealing. Clearly, political life and social life are different in the twentieth century than in the nineteenth. Even though bureaucracy is not a new phenomenon, there is something new about it—its enormous growth in recent years. All political systems that are relatively industrialized have experienced a great increase in the number of and size of bureaucratic institutions.

Big organizations—whether government, private enterprise, university, labor union, professional association, or anything else—have become characteristic of advanced societies. The following figures speak for themselves. In 1960, General Motors employed 500,000 people, United States Steel 270,000, Standard Oil 250,000, and General Electric 225,000. The State University of New York had about 220,000 students, as against 50,000 after World War II. There were some 11,000,000 civil servants in the United States. Union membership had increased from 791,000 in 1900, to 3,728,000 in 1935, to 16,000,000 in 1953, to 18,000,000 in 1960. Federal expenditures in 1860 were $63,000,000; in 1917, they reached $1 billion; in 1960 they exceeded $100 billion. These increases have produced a surge in bureaucratization that is staggering.

Moreover, there is a split between ownership and control in most organizations. That does not mean that control will become less important in a society dominated by managers, or that exploitation will disappear because it will be routinized. The split between manager and owner has not led to the situation described by German social scientist Ralf Dahrendorf, where ". . . the manager, unlike the 'full capitalist,' can ill afford to exercise his authority in direct and deliberate contravention to the wishes and interests of his subordinates." [9] On the contrary, control becomes impersonal and, if anything, more authoritative. The subordinate no longer is disobeying an individual, but a rule, which, though written by individuals, appears more frightening. In other words, we agree that there has been a split between manager and owner, but we do not agree that it is a positive development.

But the managerial revolution, in turn, is being superseded by yet another revolution—that of technocracy. Newer writers, particularly John Kenneth Galbraith in his book *The New Industrial State*, have been arguing that generalist managers have lost power to a specialist "technostructure." [10] The new men of power are experts on something—such as computer programming, program budgeting, systems analysis—and rise to power on the basis of that skill. They are not necessarily at the top of an organization (although like Robert McNamara, the prototype, they may be), but because the power at the top depends so heavily on these technocrats who have the expertise to make or implement decisions, they are the ones with the real power. These individuals have risen to power in every field. We can take C. Wright Mills's three classifications of power—the corporate, military, and political—and find examples of the transition from entrepreneur to manager to technocrat in each one.

The entrepreneurial style was flamboyant and highly individualistic; it had a certain flair to it. Whether it was General Sherman burning Atlanta without an apology (modern American generals burn villages with apology), John D. Rockefeller colorfully building up his fortune by forcing others out of business, or Theodore Roosevelt matching their antics from the White House, the essence of their style was personalism. Organizations, if there were any, took on the tone of their leader.

The manager gradually replaced the entrepreneur. Franklin Roosevelt presents an interesting contrast to his cousin. His skills were general ones; it is easy to picture FDR gathering a group of knowledgeable and dedicated men around him, his "brain trust," and

[9] Ralf Dahrendorf, *Class and Class Conflict in Industrial Society* (Stanford, Calif.: Stanford University Press, 1959), p. 45.

[10] John Kenneth Galbraith, *The New Industrial State* (Boston: Houghton Mifflin, 1968).

synthesizing or discarding their information. Theodore Roosevelt, on the other hand, tended not to trust those under him, and he often made decisions personally and impulsively. A similar contrast occurs in business and the military. The names listed as corporate leaders may be unfamiliar but they are, or were, the presidents of two of the largest private companies in the world—General Motors

	ENTREPRENEUR	MANAGER	TECHNOCRAT
Military	William Tecumseh Sherman	Dwight D. Eisenhower	James Gavin
Corporate	John D. Rockefeller	James M. Roche	Robert S. McNamara
	Andrew Carnegie	Frederick A. Kappel	Litton Industries
Political	Theodore Roosevelt	Franklin D. Roosevelt	Simulmatics Corp.
			Joseph Napolitan

and American Telephone and Telegraph. They, like General Eisenhower, managed big organizations through their general skills.

The emerging technocrats are even less likely to be known. Robert McNamara is an exception. He became president of Ford Motor Company through his expertise in budgeting and systems analysis. One of McNamara's protégés in the Department of Defense who had similar talents, Charles Hitch, is now president of the University of California, the largest university in the United States. Then too, certain industries have specialized in the new skills as corporations. Litton Industries, the leader in the field, has had a spectacular rise. One of its directors is General James Gavin, who argued for the new techniques and their applicability to the Armed Forces. He left the service, but his ideas were eventually accepted. Now most aspiring generals go to graduate school to become familiar with the new ideas in electrical engineering, mathematics, international relations, or psychology.

Finally, the new skills have been applied to politics. Simulmatics Corporation makes computer simulations of the American electorate and, on the basis of mathematical formulas, develops strategies for political candidates. Their division of the electorate into 480 categories was the inspiration for the title of Eugene Burdick's novel

The 480. On a less sophisticated scale mathematically, Joseph Napolitan represents the new type of campaign manager. His amazing success in electing his clients to office is based upon systems analysis techniques. If you have not heard of him, you probably will soon. He and the others mentioned above represent the transition from the managerial to the technocratic revolution.

THE INCREASING SIMILARITY OF ORGANIZATIONS

A second political consequence of the rise of bureaucratization is that the large organizations in a society tend to become more alike. Whereas, traditionally, the corporation served one purpose, the Defense Department another, and the university yet another, distinctive styles are being replaced by organizational style. This is most clearly seen in the university, the institution that has changed the most—and lost the most. It has often been noted that the modern university is so complex that the bureaucratic ethos of maintaining the organization becomes its primary concern and advancing and distributing knowledge becomes secondary. A huge staff is necessary. The staff members in the office of the president of the University of California outnumber the academic personnel in the political science department. Routinization and efficiency are demanded. Courses are dropped and programs cut back because they are inefficient. Faculties and student bodies are considered less essential to the university than administrators, and the difference in status is evident everywhere. In this sense, the university, traditionally the most distinctive of large organizations, comes to resemble the other big organizations in society more and more.

A parallel development is the diminishing distinction between public and private. As we mentioned earlier, public decisions are occasionally made by private groups. As the bureaucratization of public and private groups continues unabated, this tendency grows. The manager and the technocrat can apply their skills equally well in public or in private institutions. The president of the University of California learned his skills in the Department of Defense, but since fighting wars and teaching students are both bureaucratic activities undertaken by governments, the transition was a smooth one. It is just as easy to go from government to a private institution like a corporation. The similarities among all these institutions are much more striking than their differences. Consequently, the traditional distinction between public and private is no longer realistic.

As institutions within society become increasingly alike, more and more decisions are made and implemented at the national level. Originally, the United States had a federal system of government, in which the national government shared power with artificial governmental units called states. Now, although the federal structure remains, functional federalism is only historical. Governmental institutions must be national because the other bureaucracies have become national. We have already mentioned how decisions involving local matters like roads, education, and agriculture are now made at the national level. They are usually implemented there as well. The roads, for example, are built by huge construction firms, which may have a local base but are national in scope. After all, the program is called the *Interstate* Highway Program. Ninety percent of the funds come from the national government and 10 percent from the states, proportions that reflect the dominance of the national government. A similar pattern can be found in other areas of governmental activity.

This tendency toward national decision making is not the result of a conspiratorial plot by a few men to subvert the meaning of the American constitution. It is caused by historical forces, particularly bureaucratization, which have swept all the countries in the world. In this tendency toward nationalization, countries with federal structures face one of two situations: a great deal of activity at the national level, making federalism no more than a name; or local resistance. In that case, the local area generally splits off, developing its own political structure for making national decisions. The United States, the Soviet Union, and (to a lesser extent) Canada are examples of empty federalism, while the secession attempts in Nigeria and the Belgian Congo are extreme examples of local resistance. But in both cases, bureaucratization tends to remove decisions from local areas, the "grass roots," and substitute nationally made and implemented decisions.

The trend toward centralization has been deplored by people on all sides of the political spectrum. Conservatives in the United States lament the decline of federalism, whether out of a sympathy with "states' rights" or out of a distaste for the decisions reached at the national level. Their cries for a return to a less centralized government are echoed by some of the New Left. There are differences, to be sure. The right wants decentralization in order to give local elites, through state government, more control; the left wants to decentralize everything so that nonelites will have some control over their own lives. But the fact that both groups turn in the same direction for a solution is a sign that bureaucratic nationalization is a pervasive phenomenon.

A BUREAUCRATIC FUTURE?

If it is true that institutions within society are becoming more and more alike, and that more and more decisions are being made and implemented nationally, then it follows that countries themselves should begin to resemble each other. This is the basis of "convergence theories," the view that political systems are becoming so much alike, they will eventually converge into almost identical states.

Convergence theories are most fascinating in connection with the United States and the Soviet Union. These two countries started out at opposite ends, yet each has a vested interest in emphasizing the differences between them. Americans label their system "democratic" and the Soviet system "totalitarian," constantly comparing the two to prove the superiority of the American way of life. In fact, the state of Florida has a law that all secondary school students must be exposed to the difference between the two systems in order to demonstrate America's superiority. The Soviets, in a similar fashion, proclaim the superiority of their socialist regime. In their view, capitalism is a threat ideologically, even though a less effective system, and it is always trying to expand its influence throughout the world—which is almost exactly what Americans think about communism. If the two countries are indeed converging into a similar new form, that would be a powerful event, one that few citizens in either country could accept.

There is a good deal of evidence that a similar type of bureaucrat is emerging in both countries. Two political scientists, neither notably sympathetic toward the Soviet Union, have inadvertently demonstrated this by comparing the careers of two high-level bureaucrats, one Russian and one American.[11]

---

[11] Zbigniew Brzezinski and Samuel P. Huntington, *Political Power: USA–USSR* (New York: Viking, 1965), pp. 164–67.

Born 1902.

Joined CPSU in 1925.

1918–1931, various posts in the Red Army and oil and railway industries, Komsomol and Party posts.

1932, finished studies at the Moscow Institute of Transport Engineers.

1932–1935, in the political apparat of the Red Army.

1935–1937, engineer and group leader at All-Union Electrotechnical Institute.

1938, joined the CC apparat and became First Secretary of the Byelorussian Republic—until 1947.

1939, was elected to the CPSU Central Committee.

1948–1953, Secretary of the CC of the CPSU and from 1950–1952 Minister of Procurement.

October 1952–March 1953, member of the Presidium of the CPSU CC as well as Secretary.

1953–1954, Minister of Culture.

February 1954, appointed First Secretary of Kazakhstan Republic CC, an agriculturally critical area, which proved to be his undoing; also identified with Malenkov; after the latter's resignation as Premier in 1955, was appointed to increasingly less significant ambassadorial posts.

1961, dropped from membership in the CPSU Central Committee.

Born in 1896 in Richmond, Virginia, son of shoe-company executive.

1912, graduated from high school.

1912–1916, worked as traveling salesman for father's company.

1917, volunteered for staff of Herbert Hoover, served as assistant to Hoover in Food Administration Relief Work.

1919, joined Kuhn, Loeb, & Co., Wall Street banking house, at invitation of partner, Mortimer Schiff.

1929–1946, partner in Kuhn, Loeb.

1941, called to active service as Lieutenant Commander, USNR.

1941–1945, naval service in Ordnance Bureau, then assistant to James Forrestal, Under Secretary of Navy, and Secretary of Navy, promoted to rear admiral.

1946, was appointed by Truman as Republican member of Atomic Energy Commission.

1946–1950, as AEC member, pushed development of detection system and hydrogen bomb.

1950–1953, returned to private life, consultant and financial advisor to Rockefellers.

1953, was appointed Chairman of AEC by Eisenhower.

1953–1955, involved in controversies over Oppenheimer security case and Dixon-Yates electrical power contract.

1958, retired as AEC Chairman, was given recess appointment as Secretary of Commerce.

1959, Senate by a vote of 49 to 46 refused to confirm Commerce appointment.

The writers who compiled these sketches felt they proved that the two systems were still quite different: the American advanced by moving back and forth between governmental and private activity, while the Russian had to maintain his activity within the government or party. This is true, but it overlooks the striking similarities here. Both men learned early that to become powerful, one must go where the power is. In the Soviet Union this was the party; in the United States it was Wall Street. Then, both learned how to ride the "coattails" of powerful individuals: Malenkov for Ponomarenko; Schiff, Hoover, Forrestal, and Rockefeller for Strauss. Both became aware that the proper exercise of power in bureaucratic systems is through a combination of political contact and technical skill, so Ponomarenko studied electrical engineering and Strauss atomic energy. Finally, both were unable to meet the political demands of their job, either because of identification with the wrong person or an unpopular position on a crucial issue. Because of their errors, both men disappeared into political obscurity rapidly. In other words, the men themselves are less important than what they represent—the universalization of bureaucracy that occurs in all political systems, whether labeled democratic, totalitarian, capitalistic, or socialistic.

We will deal with the intriguing questions raised by convergence theories more fully in Chapter 15. We introduced the notion here to point out the universality of the trend toward increasing bureaucratization.

PROBLEMS OF IMPLEMENTATION

It may seem as if we have not yet reached the main subject of this chapter, the implementation of political decisions. Actually, it has been an important element in our whole discussion here. We have been dealing with a central question all along: has the bureaucratization of society made the implementation of political decisions more important than decision making itself? In other words, have those who carry out political decisions—the administrators, civil servants, and bureaucrats—become so important that they actually make, rather than implement, political decisions, or to be more precise, change the decisions so much in the process of implementation that new decisions emerge?

We have many theories, such as representative democracy, to

explain the relationship between decision makers and nondecision makers. But if decision makers are no longer crucial to a political system, then all these theories are irrelevant. For example, the system of checks and balances is designed to protect citizens against those holding political positions in places like Congress. However, if Congress no longer makes important decisions, the theory is meaningless. A new theory would be required to account for the relationship between bureaucrats and citizens. As yet, no such theory has appeared. If all this is true, citizens of a "representative democracy" may find themselves living in a system that is neither representative nor democratic.

We can see the changes in the role of Congress by following the thoughts of one shrewd commentator on American politics, Walter Lippmann. In some of his early writings Lippmann argued that legislatures were too large and even too representative to be trusted with important matters, particularly foreign policy. He felt that when it came to issues of war and peace, a force was needed that was more independent of the pressures of public opinion and could make decisions on the basis of what was good for the country. Lippmann believed that the executive branch could do this. About forty years later, in one of the great ironies of American history, Lippmann got just what he wanted. After an attack—actually an alleged attack—on American ships by North Vietnamese boats, the president asked Congress for a blank check to proceed with countermeasures, phrasing his message to Congress in good Lippmannese prose. Congress responded favorably by passing the Tonkin Gulf Resolution. Leading the chorus of private citizens who declared this action dictatorial was, of course, Walter Lippmann. He now argued that the passage of power to the executive branch meant too little public involvement and did not guarantee wiser or more sane foreign policy decisions.[12] The evolution of Lippmann's view on policy making is a good introduction to the problems we face in working out our solutions, for the passage of power to the executive and his bureaucracy has led to a decline in popular control. This may be regarded as either a positive or a negative development.

There has been a long history of mutual distrust between the administrator and the congressman; one achieves his position pri-

---

[12] See Walter Lippmann, *The Public Philosophy* (New York: New American Library, 1956), for his earlier view, and almost any of his newspaper columns on Vietnam between 1966 and 1968 for changes in that view.

marily on the basis of technical skill and the other on the basis of popularity. As Edward Shils observed:

> The civil servant, particularly the civil servant called before congressional committees, tends to be considerably more educated and probably of a higher social and economic status as regards his origin, than the legislator who is requesting a service of him or interrogating him. He is . . . not only more expert in the matter at hand, but he usually, either wittingly or unwittingly, is also more the master of the situation than the legislator. Resentment against those whose fortunate accidents of birth gave them educational opportunities which were not available to the legislator is heightened—it certainly was heightened during the Roosevelt administration—by an attitude of personal, social and intellectual superiority on the part of the administrator.[13]

Thus, the conflict can be traced to the administrator's technical expertise. In any society that values such expertise, the problem is how the power of the experts can be checked by the nonexperts. In the United States, there are two solutions—the purse strings and the "percolator."

A maxim of American politics is that whoever controls the money has the power. Since the constitution gave Congress ultimate authority over the budgetary process, it would seem to be the place that exercises control. Departments and agencies cannot function unless they have appropriations for their programs. The problem, however, is that even spending money has become a complicated and technical subject. To spend $100 billion a year, one needs fiscal experts, budget planners, mathematicians, economists, and so on. As a result, there is a subbureaucracy within the bureaucracy—the General Accounting Office and Bureau of the Budget—which develops the necessary plans and procedures for Congress to approve. Since these plans and procedures for spending money are as complicated as the plans for the use of the money, the congressmen are in a difficult position. They are being asked to formulate policy on a matter they do not understand. A classic response is the "across the board cut," chopping a certain percentage off every program. This makes Congress feel better, as it has exercised its jurisdiction.

[13] *The Torment of Secrecy* (New York: Free Press, 1956), pp. 113–14.

But the experts in the bureaucracy are not particularly upset because they had raised their figures to compensate for congressional
pruning. Everybody is satisfied, but popular control seems to have
been lacking.

The "percolator" theory holds that popular control travels from
one area of government to another until it reaches those who are
making and implementing the decisions. The president, as a nationally elected figure, must be responsive to popular will if he is
to be reelected or pass on the mantle of power within his party.
He, therefore, as agent of the people, checks the bureaucracy, which
is under him, by utilizing his own equally competent bureaucracy.
In the long run, this might be even more representative than the
congressional process, for the president has a national constituency,
whereas Congress is dominated by regionalism. As long as we elect
our president, we need not fear an uncontrolled bureaucracy.

There are a number of problems with the "percolator" theory.
In the first place, first-term presidents often do nothing, for fear of
antagonizing the public and not being reelected. And in the second
term, they are often neutral, or even hostile to the successor chosen
by their party. This proposed successor is likely to be the vice-
president, who was selected for that position because he represented
an opposite wing of the party. This, plus the usual irritations of a
president-vice-president relationship, make the president far from
enthusiastic about his successor. FDR would not have gone all the
way for Truman, and Truman had reservations about Stevenson.
Eisenhower expressed his doubts about Nixon, as did Johnson about
Humphrey. In short, there is really little to check a president in
his final term as he attempts to write his name into history. Second,
career civil service positions make some of the bureaucracy independent of the president. It is unclear who would win a confrontation between a president and the permanent bureaucracy because
no recent president has been willing to force the issue. Barry Goldwater threatened to make such a challenge by changing the nature
of the welfare state, but he did not get close enough to try. The
odds are good that in such a confrontation, the bureaucracy would
win.

It could even be argued that the bureaucracy would win because it represents the popular side, that is, it communicates directly with the people. This idea brings up the third and most
serious objection to the "percolator" theory: the popular control

associated with the rise of bureaucracy is essentially symbolic. In other words, if the people think they have control over a group of decision makers, they are satisfied. They never bother to find out whether their control has actually been implemented. The bureaucrats attempt to convince the public that control has been exercised. Once this is done, decisions can be made without regard to popular will because the populace believes its will is being actualized.

Murray Edelman has described this process in a book called *The Symbolic Uses of Politics*.[14] He takes the independent regulatory commissions as illustrations of his thesis. Around the turn of the century, the great public outcry over abuses by giant corporations, particularly railroads, led Congress to create commissions for regulating and policing various fields. Once the legislation was passed, however, the public lost interest in the whole matter. As vacancies occurred on the Interstate Commerce Commission (ICC), for instance, replacements were "suggested" by the railroads, in a spirit of "cooperation." And within a few years, instead of regulating the railroads, the ICC had become the chief lobbyist for them. This was partly because experts were needed to deal with the technical subject matter, and most experts in the field had been trained by the corporations, which could afford to pay for their services. The same public that had demanded the ICC, could not be convinced that no regulation was occurring; the ICC itself was regarded as an indication that regulation must exist. The railroads, therefore, continued to be as powerful, if not more so, as they were before the creation of the ICC. Thus, a bureaucratic situation can result in a lack of popular control.

If the things we have been discussing are all true, then those political systems called democracies are in deep trouble. So are all other kinds of political systems that have not made theoretical allowances for the class whose power is based on its technical ability to implement political decisions. As we have seen, the distinction between the making and the implementation of political decisions is no longer sharp. Those charged with implementation are making decisions, and theories dealing with the regulation of their activities are nonexistent or irrelevant.

A pessimistic conclusion appears inevitable. Those who empha-

[14] *The Symbolic Uses of Politics* (Urbana, Ill.: University of Illinois Press, 1964).

size the negative aspects of bureaucracy seem to have the stronger case. Aside from all the problems mentioned above—alienation, dehumanization, psychological adjustment—there is the power of bureaucracy, which exists essentially unchecked. This power, growing out of a mandate to implement decisions, is the single greatest source of governmental power in most advanced, industrial societies, surpassing legislative, judicial, and even executive power.

To avoid complete despair, we can mention one or two positive developments at this point. For one thing, a political theory could develop, which would describe the new patterns of power and attempt to do something about them. Urban blacks are aware of the situation. The recent controversy over school decentralization in New York City showed that the blacks knew that control would have to be transferred from the hands of distant, professional bureaucrats to the people it concerned before lasting progress could be made in the education of their children. A sophisticated political theory has not yet been developed, but at least in this case, an exploited group was arguing for less, rather than more, bureaucracy. A trend of this sort could have important ramifications in the United States.

The conflict over school decentralization highlights another source of hope for political systems—the ubiquity of politics. We defined politics earlier as conflict over the search for a better life. This idealism has not disappeared from political life; if anything it has increased in recent years. As long as some people are still practicing politics to build a better world, there is the possibility that political systems will change. Finally, it seems that in bureaucratic political systems of all kinds, politics has not been suppressed but is beginning to flourish.

III TRADITIONS OF POLITICAL ANALYSIS

THROUGHOUT HUMAN HISTORY, men and women have been concerned with the struggle for power and the desire for a better world. Those who have thought most about such matters are called political philosophers. Since their views have been extremely influential in shaping our perceptions, all students of politics should know something about them. This is not easy, for some of the political philosophies are rather complicated. But it is important to study them, all the same, to see how these thinkers handled some perennial political questions.

8 The Classical Tradition

THERE ARE MANY reasons for beginning our study of political theory with the Greeks, not the least of which is the chronological justification. Political questions do not spring out of thin air. We ask what is the best form of government because we have been shaped by a tradition, by numerous philosophers who lived before us. So our questions are both a reflection of their curiosity and a response to continuing problems. The question is not whether we wish to learn from the Greeks, because our world has already been so strongly affected by their concerns, but whether we will use the tradition in an intelligent or an ignorant way.

We turn to Plato and Aristotle, for they were concerned with many of the issues that trouble us today. Our primary interest is not in their answers but in their methods of inquiry, for this knowledge should help us formulate answers ourselves. We must keep this in mind as we proceed indirectly to the major consideration of what constitutes justice.

It is important to realize that ancient political theory reflected the social order of the time. Though the theory might be in conflict with the social order, the two were closely related nevertheless. But the classical philosophical tradition is of more than historical interest. In fact, probably no group of political philosophers transcended their environment as completely as the ancients. Alfred North Whitehead remarked that "all Western Philosophy is but a series of footnotes to Plato."

The central premises of classical political philosophy—particularly those of Plato and Aristotle—need some elucidation. The first of these principles concerns the nature of reality. Platonic realists believe that reality exists in the essence of things, not in their appearance, while nominalists believe that reality exists in concrete things that can be measured and verified by the senses. This the realists refer to disparagingly as the "world of appearances."

The best illustration of these distinctions occurs in mathematics. For example, no one has ever seen a real Circle, that is, a perfect Circle, for every circle that is drawn is imperfect. Its imperfections would appear if it were magnified 1,000 or 10,000 times. Yet, we all know what a circle is. Its essence is in its roundness. Its properties can be described in mathematical terms, such as, the circumference of a circle is equal to $2\pi r$. We can even speak about good and bad circles; for example, circle A might be considered a better circle than circle B because circle A comes much closer to the ideal Circle than circle B. Although this ideal Circle is an abstraction without concrete existence, it is hardly imaginary. It is an idea or form that is truly useful in mathematics.

According to classical political thought, all science, all true knowledge, is based on essences of this sort. The classicists would consider the ideal Circle real and material circles only appearances of reality. This concept of reality, almost the exact opposite of the contemporary view, is probably the most significant characteristic of the classical tradition. We must keep it in mind if we are to understand classical philosophy.

Closely related to the classical concept of reality is the concept of nature. The nature of a thing is understood by perceiving its essence. Its nature is not what it is, but what it would be if it realized its essence. Therefore, the nature of a circle exists in its roundness, and the nature of an acorn is its potential to be an oak tree, and not just any oak but a perfect Oak, the real Oak.

No one has ever seen the real Oak, for no oak ever experiences the optimum conditions of soil, water, wind, and so forth, in all its stages of development, so no oak will realize its essence as the perfect Oak. (Needless to say, the perfect Oak is not some abstract, statistically average oak, discovered by selecting 1,000 oak trees at random and taking their average height and girth to arrive at the dimensions of the perfect Oak.) Yet an expert in husbandry must know the true nature of oaks so that he can approximate the optimum conditions and come as close as possible to the real Oak. All art, therefore, rests upon knowledge of the real nature of things. And the real nature of all things, including man, is determined teleologically—that is, not by what they are but by what they would be if they were truly realized. Understanding a thing's nature, its real existence, is true knowledge, whereas belief rests on myths, dreams, poetic imagery, or merely the perception of how things appear.

It is also essential to understand the nature of man. The Greeks believed that it is man's nature (end) to be just (a concept that will be discussed more fully later in this chapter). A natural law, order, or purpose exists in nature that is independent of any man-made compact or convention. It is man's obligation to try and understand and live according to that natural law and by so doing come closer to realizing his true, just nature.

The Greeks believed that man's reason could lead him to justice, for just as our reason discovers the truth about circles, it also discovers that the true end or nature of man is justice (but through deductive not inductive reasoning). The road to truth starts with common assumptions, and then follows a dialectical process of careful, skeptical questioning of these assumptions to arrive at a more complete truth. Skeptical questioning does not lead to skepticism but to absolute Truth, which is unchanging and unshakable because it is based on knowledge rather than belief.[1]

Most of this may seem rather far removed from politics. However, the Greek philosophers believed that the end of the state was to make men live according to their nature, that is, to be just. This is not to say that all states were just—the Greeks were too wise to think that—but that justice was the virtue by which states should be measured. The perfect State, the real State, would be the perfectly just state. Like the perfect Oak or Circle, however, it was unlikely to be realized, for only the most unusual and fortunate of circumstances could provide all the optimum conditions.

---

[1] For example, while a man may believe, because he has often walked the distance, that the two sides of a triangle are greater than the third, it is only belief; to acquire knowledge he must examine the geometric proof of that proposition.

Nonetheless, the politician or statesman must *know* the true nature of the state. For the Greeks, political theory was more prescriptive than descriptive, that is, it attempted to evaluate rather than just describe political phenomena.

The two outstanding Greek philosophers, Plato (427?–347 B.C.) and Aristotle (384–322 B.C.), both had extraordinary lives. Plato was an aristocrat by birth and a student of Socrates; our knowledge of Socrates is almost entirely dependent upon Plato's writings. Aristotle, the son of a physician, tutor to Alexander the Great, was Plato's student for twenty years. Each man has left a valuable legacy in many fields of philosophy and science; but we shall limit our study to Plato's *Republic* and Aristotle's *Politics,* and further confine ourselves to certain central themes.

PLATO'S *REPUBLIC*

In the *Republic* Plato deals with the meaning of justice. He maintains that there is a parallel between justice in the individual and justice in the state, so he is equally concerned with defining the just state and the just individual.

Plato begins with a discussion of the soul, which he believed was composed of three parts. The lowest part, appetite, was related to the desire for food, water, sex, sleep, and so on. The middle part was spirit, and the highest part was reason. Reason and appetite are fairly easy to understand; spirit is more difficult. Plato meant something like will or willpower. A good example is presented by cigarette smoking. My appetite desires a cigarette. My reason tells me it is very harmful. But I smoke anyway because my spirit or will is weak.

Each part of the soul has a corresponding virtue. The virtue of a thing is the essential attribute that enables it to perform its function well. The virtue of a knife is its sharpness, the virtue of a craftsman is his skill. The corresponding virtues for the various parts of the soul are temperance or moderation for appetite, courage for spirit, and wisdom for reason. Plato believed there were class divisions in the state that paralleled the divisions of the soul. Some people are noted for their intelligence and intellectual curiosity. In any society, such a group would be the smallest class. A somewhat larger class, the warriors, excel in spirit. Finally, the largest class, the farmers and artisans, are mainly concerned about pleasure and comfort, and the desire for material things.

Justice is the proper and harmonious relationship among the parts of the soul, each exercising virtue. In other words, the appetite of the just Man would be ruled by his reason and reinforced by his spirit or will. He would be wise, courageous, and temperate. The just State would exhibit a similar order: those with true knowledge or wisdom, the philosophers, would rule and act as guardians of the just State. They would be aided in their administration by the auxiliaries, those noted for their courageous spirit; the bulk of the populace would pursue their separate vocations, whether carpentry or medicine or street cleaning, and be satisfied with the state's government and with their share of the fruits of their labor.

Such a state would be virtuous because it was just, if the rulers were true philosophers. But Plato was not unrealistic enough to believe this was likely to occur. Ideal circumstances would be needed to create the ideal State, where "Philosophers become Kings, or Kings become Philosophers." However, even if the republic were established, it would be a thing of this earth and like all earthly things could not endure forever. So Plato discusses the decline of the state, maintaining throughout the parallel between state and man. As the just State is inhabited by the just Man, so inferior states will be noted for the type of man each produces.

Plato traces the decline of the state through three stages: timocracy, rule by auxiliaries (Plato's military-industrial complex); oligarchy, rule by the rich; and democracy, rule by the common man. In a timocracy, the ideal citizen will no longer be noted for justice but for spirit. Honor and military glory—patriotism—will be his hallmark. In the next step in the decline, oligarchy, wealth will replace wisdom or honor as the criteria of worth. Finally, there is democracy and the democratic man. Plato's description of the democratic man is not very sympathetic:

> In his life thenceforward he spends as much time and pains and money on his superfluous pleasures as on the necessary ones. . . . he will set all his pleasures on a footing of equality, denying to none its equal rights and maintenance, and allowing each in turn, as it presents itself, to succeed, as if by the chance of the lot, to the government of his soul until it is satisfied.

So he spends his days indulging the pleasures of the moment, now intoxicated with wine and music, and then taking to a spare diet and drinking nothing but water; one day in hard training, the next doing nothing at all, the third apparently immersed in study. Every now and then he takes a part in politics, leaping to his feet to say or do whatever comes into his head. Or he will set out to rival someone he admires, a soldier it may be, or, if the fancy takes him, a man of business. His life is subject to no order or restraint, and he has no wish to change an existence which he calls pleasant, free, and happy.[2]

Is modern democratic man like Plato's democrat? Does he take up politics as a trivial and transitory pastime, of no greater significance than dietary fads or amusements? And, for Plato, this was not the worst of it; as the liberal spirit of democracy throws off all restraints, democracy can lead to tyranny.

A democratic state may fall under the influence of unprincipled leaders, ready to minister to its thirst for liberty with too deep draughts of this heady wine; and then, if its rulers are not complacent enough to give it unstinted freedom, they will be arraigned as accursed oligarchs and punished. Law-abiding citizens will be insulted as nonentities who hug their chains; and all praise and honour will be bestowed, both publicly and in private, on rulers who behave like subjects and subjects who behave like rulers. In such a state the spirit of liberty is bound to go to all lengths.[3]

In these passages, Plato raises questions about democracy that democratic theorists have been trying to answer ever since. On the one hand, the people appear to be irrational, as he suggests. In America, to digress for an example, racism, chauvinism, and militarism are found in many areas of society. These irrational (or in Plato's terminology, unwise or immoderate) sentiments have assisted many unprincipled leaders, demagogues (note the meaning of the word), concerned more with their fantasies and careers than with the public good. Consequently, some contemporary scholars, strongly influenced by Plato, have agreed that democracy is a poor form of

[2] F. M. Cornford, ed. and trans., *The Republic of Plato* (New York: Oxford University Press, 1945), p. 561.

[3] Ibid., pp. 562–63.

government, unless the irrationalities of common people can be controlled (see Chapter 6). But Plato's thoughts on democracy raise more questions than they answer. Do these attitudes develop naturally, or are they instilled in people? Are the rulers and military leaders in modern democratic societies any more rational than the people they rule? Do the common people support individuals like Joseph McCarthy or Governor George Wallace of Alabama, or do these men obtain their most important support elsewhere? We suggested earlier that contemporary elites are no more endowed with political wisdom than are the people.

Having dealt with the republic and its decline, we must return to Plato's concept of knowledge. After all, it is because the philosopher possesses truth—that is, he has more knowledge—that he is entitled to rule. Plato's discussion of the Four Stages of Cognition clarifies his distinction between the World of Appearances and the World of Reality. The following chart is particularly helpful in understanding Plato's epistemology (an inquiry into the nature or theory of knowledge):[4]

	OBJECTS	STATE OF MIND
Intelligible World	The Good	Intelligence (*noesis*) or
	Forms	Knowledge (*episteme*)
	Mathematical Objects	Thinking (*dianoia*)
World of Appearances	Visible Things	Belief (*pistis*)
	Images	Imagining (*eikasia*)

It should be noted that beliefs men form from their observation of the world of appearance (the empirical method) are not necessarily false. They may be true, but we have no proof of their truth or falseness. For example, Plato would maintain that there is such a thing as the form Beauty from which all beautiful things take

[4] Ibid., p. 222.

their character. This is why paintings by Michelangelo and Picasso can both be beautiful; they both partake of the form Beauty. There must be, however, a unity between the various forms, a principle that links Beauty and Justice. This, Plato calls the Good, but all he ever tells us about the Good is that it consists of the order and harmony of all things.

Because of its ineffable nature, one can best, or only, understand the Good through allegory. It is his allegory of the cave, from the seventh book of the *Republic,* that deals with this. Plato depicts man as living in a cave where what he takes for reality are actually shadows cast upon the walls of the cave by the firelight behind him. Only the philosopher who has left the cave and "seen the light" has true knowledge of the principles that should govern men's lives. But unfortunately, when the philosopher returns to the cave, he has great difficulty persuading men that the things they believe to be real and true are merely shadows. As Plato points out, men often resist the truth and prefer the comfort of their familiar myths and beliefs. Those who tell the truth, instead of what people want to hear, are often hated, even put to death, as Socrates was. Nevertheless, Plato affirms that there can be no Justice until men abandon their mistaken beliefs and politicians who play on their fears and ignorance, and turn instead to those who can lead them to Truth, Justice, Beauty, and the Good. In this way, Plato's concept of knowledge (epistemology) is related to his concept of politics. The following passage explains the connection between the two.

> . . . Here is a parable to illustrate the degrees in which our nature may be enlightened or unenlightened.
>
> Every feature in this parable . . . is meant to fit our earlier analysis. The prison dwelling corresponds to the region revealed to us through the sense of sight, and the fire-light within it to the power of the Sun. The ascent to see the things in the upper world you may take as standing for the upward journey of the soul into the region of the intelligible. . . .
>
> In the world of knowledge, the last thing to be perceived and only with great difficulty is the essential Form of Goodness. Once it is perceived, the conclusion must follow that, for all things, this is the cause of whatever is right and good. . . . Without having had a vision of this Form no one can act with wisdom, either in his own life or in matters of state.

It is no wonder if those who have reached this height are reluctant to manage the affairs of men. Their souls long to spend all their time in that upper world—naturally enough, if here once more our parable holds true. Nor, again, is it at all strange that one who comes from the contemplation of divine things to the miseries of human life should appear awkward and ridiculous when, with eyes still dazed and not yet accustomed to the darkness, he is compelled, in a lawcourt or elsewhere, to dispute about the shadows of justice or the images that cast those shadows, and to wrangle over the notions of what is right in the minds of men who have never beheld Justice itself.

. . . the truth is that you can have a well-governed society only if you can discover for your future rulers a better way of life than being in office; then only will power be in the hands of men who are rich, not in gold, but in the wealth that brings happiness, a good and wise life. All goes wrong when, starved, for lack of anything good in their own lives, men turn to public affairs hoping to snatch from thence the happiness they hunger for. They set about fighting for power, and this internecine conflict ruins them and their country. The life of true philosophy is the only one that looks down upon offices of state; and access to power must be confined to men who are not in love with it; otherwise rivals will start fighting. So whom else can you compel to undertake the guardianship of the commonwealth, if not those who, besides understanding best the principles of government, enjoy a nobler life than the politician's and look for rewards of a different kind?

There is indeed no other choice.[5]

ARISTOTLE

It has been said that we are all born either Platonists or Aristotelians. The remark, however, implies a greater area of disagreement between Plato and Aristotle than actually exists. After all, they were both Greeks, and they shared in large measure those principles enunciated at the beginning of this chapter. And, further-

[5] Ibid., pp. 514–21.

more, Aristotle studied with Plato for twenty years. It would be very surprising if their basic orientations differed radically.

The main difference between Plato and Aristotle is in method and focus of attention. Apparently, Aristotle believed that little could be added to Plato's efforts in the *Republic* (not that he accepted the *Republic* uncritically). He concentrated, instead, on how men actually live, on the nature of the polis, and how it might be improved. His more practical interests naturally led Aristotle to a more empirical mode of investigation. Because the writings of Aristotle are probably lecture notes compiled by Aristotle or his students, his literary style is not notably inspiring, especially in comparison with the liveliness of Plato's dialogues. However, many prefer Aristotle's straightforward and concrete presentation to Plato's circuitous style and his sometimes deceptive use of analogy.

Aristotle is often remembered for two phrases that may at first seem trite or nonsensical: "Man is a political animal," and "The state precedes man." But these two statements provide the key to an appreciation of Aristotle. He sees a hierarchical structure in society, starting with the individual, his family, his village, and culminating in the polity or the state. The family according to Aristotle is natural; within it, people's most basic needs—food, shelter, procreation—are naturally fulfilled. Although the family is natural and good, however, it is not peculiar to humans; animals also have these basic needs, and some animals, such as bears, even follow what might be called a family pattern.

But people are gregarious creatures as well. They can communicate with others and seek their companionship. It is, therefore, natural for men to live in a community, which also makes it possible for them to establish a division of labor and to participate in social and economic interchange. While this takes man to a higher plane of life requiring a more complex social organization, it still is not a unique and, therefore, distinguishing characteristic of man. Witness the complex social organization of an anthill or a beehive.

Finally, man lives in a political community or state, which is also natural since it is established for the good life. And, for man, the good life means the just life—justice to be determined by reason—which can only be realized within the state. Now, Aristotle did not mean that all states were just, but that questions of morality can only arise within the context of the polity. This is the area where man is unique: only humans can distinguish between good and bad, moral and immoral, right and wrong, just and unjust, legal and illegal. And it is only within the state that such distinctions can be developed to their fullest extent.

Therefore, when Aristotle asserts that the state precedes man, he means that man outside of the state is not man. He is either a beast or a god. This argument is based on logic rather than history; it affirms that in the area of politics the whole must precede the parts and that the whole is greater than the sum of the parts.

When Aristotle declares that man is a political animal, he means that humans, as distinguished from beasts, seek justice, which is inseparable from the political community, the state. Therefore if man wishes to be a man, to realize his essence as a man, he must be political. Even today it is at least partially recognized that a person must be political—not in the contemporary but in the Greek sense of being concerned about the public good—to realize his human potential. No matter how complex and efficient the state, unless it addresses itself to the problem of justice, it is no more than a large village, or worse, and its inhabitants cannot realize their potential. Perhaps St. Augustine summarized Aristotle's position best when he noted that a state is characterized by its moral purpose rather than by its formal authority or the monopoly on the use of force or sovereignty. "Justice being taken away, then what are kingdoms but great robberies?" [6] Many people today would readily apply St. Augustine's remark to the United States.

As we said, Aristotle was interested in the practical as well as the theoretical problems of politics. He believed that the main functions of political science were to (1) discover what sort of constitution is appropriate to which sort of civic body; (2) discover the best constitution for the best civic body; (3) discover the constitution that is generally appropriate to most civic bodies; and (4) discover the constitution that will suit a lower degree of human life. [7] Since all four rules refer to constitutions, it is important to understand what Aristotle meant by that term. He proposed the following criteria for a constitution (and they are still valid today): (a) An organization of offices in a state, by which their method of distribution is

[6] St. Augustine, "The City of God," in *Great Political Thinkers: Plato to the Present,* ed. William Ebenstein (New York: Holt, Rinehart and Winston, 1951), p. 173.

[7] *The Politics of Aristotle,* ed., trans. Ernest Barker (New York: Oxford University Press, 1962), pp. 155–57.

fixed, (b) the sovereign authority is determined, (c) and the nature of the end to be preserved by the association and all its members prescribed.[8] Further on, he enlarges this definition and asserts that a constitution broadly conceived is tantamount to the way of life of its people.

In addition, Aristotle developed a sixfold classification of constitutions—three good constitutions and a perverted form of each. The distinguishing characteristic of a good constitution is that it strives for the well-being of the whole community; the perverted form, on the other hand, is only concerned with the good of the ruler. Thus, in a monarchy, the rule by one man, the good of the community is the end of the state; in its perversion, tyranny, only the good of the tyrant is served. In an aristocracy, rule by the few, the good of the whole society is served, while in its perversion, oligarchy, only the good of the wealthy few is served. And in a polity, rule by the many, the interest of the whole is the consideration, while in its perversion, democracy, the majority rather than the community as a whole benefits.

Aristotle acknowledges that, theoretically, monarchy is the best constitution. If you could find a man who was all-wise and all-good, then he should certainly rule. Aristotle is quick to add, however, that such a person would be a god and not a man. This leads him to a discussion of which constitution is generally appropriate to most civic bodies.

Aristotle concludes that polity is the best, practical constitution —that is, it is not the best possible constitution but the best constitution possible.[9] It is a constitution distinguished by rule of law; even the officers of government are subject to rather than above the law. Furthermore, it is a mixed constitution combining the virtues of wisdom and good breeding characteristic of aristocracy, with the virtues of democracy, for it actively involves the mass of the citizenry in its rule. It works best when there is a large middle class and an absence of extremes of wealth and poverty. Democracy has two virtues that the polity can appropriate. First, the collective opinion that emerges from discussion among many men will often

[8] Ibid., pp. 156–58.

[9] The term "polity" is used in two different senses by Aristotle—in its generic sense, as synonymous with state or political community, and in its specific sense, referring to one of the six forms of government.

be more competent than that of the few. Even though individually the few may be wiser, they do not possess the experience of the many.

Second, Aristotle concedes that there are some arts the user can judge better than the artisan; politics is one of these. The old adage that you do not need to be a shoemaker to know when the shoe pinches, nor a cook to know when the broth is spoiled, also applies to politics.

Although polity is the best form of government, from a practical standpoint, not all civic bodies are suited to it. Some barbarians may require a tyrant to instill discipline and maintain law and order. And, when most of the population is poor, democracy may be the most appropriate type of government—though, of course, there are many forms of democracy, such as agricultural, pastoral, and urban (the worst according to Aristotle). Democracy is characterized by liberty, freedom from government interference, where everyone lives as he pleases. Its main problem is combining popular power with intelligent administration; its philosophical weakness is that it has an arithmetic rather than a proportional sense of justice. According to democratic principles, everyone should be treated alike. But Aristotle considers this a fallacious view of justice; on the contrary, people should be treated differently according to their individual differences and according to their contributions to the general welfare.

Both Plato and Aristotle believe that the good of the whole takes precedence over the happiness of the individual. Although Aristotle may liken Platonic unity to a single note rather than an orchestral unity that creates harmony out of variety,[10] both regard the state's chief function as promoting the good and virtuous life of its citizens. A continually rising standard of living is not enough; in fact, an excess of wealth and luxuries may undermine the well-being of the community.

Plato and Aristotle both addressed themselves to questions raised by the existence of democracy. Despite their differing analyses of democracy, they both viewed it with disdain. This often comes as a shock to students. Today, democracy is so popular in theory—if not in practice—that every country claims to be one. Furthermore, we have always been told that democracy is by far the best form of

[10] Barker, ed., *The Politics of Aristotle,* p. 51.

government possible. But people should not accept everything they are told, especially about politics. We hope they will examine all doctrine skeptically, no matter how pervasive. Yet from where is the challenge of this popular idea to come? Students who wish to learn more about democracy may well turn to Plato and Aristotle— not because they were antidemocratic, but because they were intelligent, indeed brilliant, in their analyses. It is not necessary to agree with their conclusions about democracy to profit from an attempt to deal with their objections.

Consider the sense of order in the works of Plato and Aristotle. In their conception of the world, that which is stable is best, and that which changes rapidly is worst. Order is a primary value in much classical political philosophy, but a true democracy is not likely to be stable. Since people gain and lose power on the basis of ability rather than family connections, political leadership tends to fluctuate from generation to generation. Furthermore, policies change with public opinion, thus the policies of the political system are in a constant state of flux. In all this flux, people may begin to desire order and become less committed to democracy. Everyone is attracted to order at some time or another. How can the desire for order be reconciled with the disorder of democracy? This is one of the questions presented by Greek philosophy. As we indicated in Part I, democratic theory itself has been strongly influenced by the classical value of political order.

Much has been written about the concept of justice. Our own confusion about it is indicated by the contradictory ways different people use the term. Imagine a situation in which a man robbed a bank because he was mentally unstable. If the court shows leniency and finds him not guilty, many would consider the verdict just. If, on the other hand, he is found guilty and sentenced to forty years in prison, another group of people would conclude that justice had been served. We have yet to decide amongst ourselves what justice means. When we do, the approaches of both Plato and Aristotle will have to be considered. It is inconceivable to discuss justice without reference to their ideas.

One other example should help clarify the importance of Plato and Aristotle in the study of politics. (Of course, we are not compiling a comprehensive list of their contributions here but simply indicating a few areas where their ideas have been particularly influential.) Both writers reveal an unresolved tension between the contemplative life and the political life. Should one just think about politics, or should he attempt to do something about it? Aristotle remarked: "Goodness by itself is not enough: there must also be a capacity for being active in doing good." [11] Here is a brief but eloquent statement on the need to reconcile thinking and doing. While not characteristic of classical political philosophy, the theme is extremely significant to us, and it recurs often in this book (see Chapter 15).

POSTSCRIPT TO CLASSICAL POLITICAL PHILOSOPHY

Two philosophers who bridge the classical and the modern philosophic traditions are Saint Thomas Aquinas (1225?–1274) and Niccolò Machiavelli (1469–1527). Their ideas will pave the way for the themes that will be discussed in the remainder of Part III.

St. Thomas, who represents the culmination of scholastic philosophy in style and content, attempted to reconcile science, philosophy, and religion. But he was also a true figure of the Renaissance in that he reflected the rediscovery of the classical world of antiquity. His debt to Aristotle was great and explicit. Throughout Aquinas's writing Aristotle is simply but almost reverently referred to as the "Philosopher." We are not going to deal with his theology or political theory here. We shall confine ourselves to a brief description of his theory of law, which raised some questions that are highly relevant to the central concerns of this book.

Aquinas believed a hierarchy of law existed, descending from eternal law through divine law and natural law to human law. When each level is understood, he asserted, they would fit together as a harmonious whole.

Eternal law, the most abstract, is beyond man's comprehension, for it is God's will or reason. It covers knowledge of the cosmos and the relation of all things. It is remarkably similar to Plato's idea of the Good. Divine law is revealed law. It comes down to man through the word of God, as revealed in the Old and New Testaments and by the saints and the church. All who are in God's grace can know divine law.

Natural law is composed of those truths that all men can know

[11] Ibid., p. 289.

through reason and that are natural to man as a human being. Aquinas uses the term "natural" as Aristotle did, that is, in a teleological sense. Natural law includes philosophical and scientific truths that God, in giving man reason, provides the means to discover. But man discovers natural law; he does not make it. For example, while the law of gravity was discovered by Newton, it existed in St. Thomas's time, some four hundred years earlier.

St. Thomas gives an excellent summary of natural law precepts:

> Because in man there is first of all an inclination to good in accordance with the nature which he has in common with all substances, inasmuch as every substance seeks the preservation of its own being, according to its nature; and by reason of this inclination, whatever is a means of preserving human life and of warding off its obstacles belongs to the natural law. Secondly, there is in man an inclination to things that pertain to him more specially, according to that nature which he has in common with other animals; and in virtue of this inclination, those things are said to belong to the natural law "which nature has taught to all animals," such as sexual intercourse, education of offspring, and so forth. Thirdly, there is in man an inclination to good, according to the nature of his reason, which nature is proper to him: thus man has a natural inclination to know the truth about God and to live in society; and in this respect, whatever pertains to this inclination belongs to the natural law, for instance, to shun ignorance, to avoid offending those among whom one has to live, and other such things regarding the above inclination. . . .
>
> Although reason is one in itself, yet it directs all things regarding man, so that whatever can be ruled by reason is contained under the law of reason.[12]

Human law, those laws made by man for man's proper governance, is of greatest interest to us. Aquinas lists four standards or criteria that must be present for a human law to be in harmony with natural law, divine law, and eternal law. First, the law must be a product of reason. Thus, a law that denied a driver's license to a person with red hair would not be proper because it has no justifiable basis and is not a rational proposition.

---

[12] St. Thomas Aquinas, "Summa Theologica," in *The Political Ideas of St. Thomas Aquinas,* ed. Dino Bigongiari (New York: Hafner, 1953).

Second, it must be for the public good, not for a private benefit. Thus, taxation for the support of education must be justified on the grounds that education benefits the whole public, not just those receiving the education. Third, it must emanate from the community or from the authorized spokesman of the community. In modern parlance, it must come from a legitimate source and be enacted in a legitimate way. Fourth, it must be promulgated. This means that someone who wants to comply with the law must have a reasonable way of knowing what it is. There must, for example, be "No Parking" signs posted on a street before one can be prosecuted for parking there.

Now, according to St. Thomas, laws that meet these criteria are valid and carry a moral as well as legal obligation for obedience. Natural law criteria of this sort are much more useful as standards than substantive criteria, such as property rights, advocated by later proponents of natural rights. Defining rights in a substantive fashion, inviolable regardless of time, place, or circumstance, eventually leads to indefensible dogmatism.

It is possible to argue, for example, that capital punishment in the United States in the 1970s violates natural law criteria, that it is not in the public interest, nor an act of reason. But the much more extreme proposition that capital punishment is, has always been, and always will be a violation of natural rights is more difficult to defend.

Many people believe that the contemporary Thomists are the only ones who are keeping alive the philosophical tradition of antiquity. At any rate, Thomas Aquinas still serves as a vital support for the role of reason in man's affairs.

NICCOLÒ MACHIAVELLI

Whereas Saint Thomas Aquinas turned to ancient philosophers for his inspiration, Niccolò Machiavelli drew heavily on the ancient Romans. His interpretation and outlook were so different from Aquinas's that he may be considered the first of the moderns. Machiavelli was the first political writer to question the proposition that the search for the right ruler was also a search for a good man. At certain times, he declared, a good ruler must be able to act like a bad man.

It is often assumed that Machiavelli was amoral, that he rejected the common religious and secular definitions of goodness.[13] Quite the contrary: he subscribed to the basic Christian views on good and evil. But he did maintain that a ruler who desires to remain in power must occasionally do evil things. And he was not hypocritical about this. When he advocated an evil act, he labeled it as such, and did not attempt by any shady logic to maintain that black was white. In a sense, his ruler was nobler because he jeopardized his own soul to be a successful ruler. For the ruler *raison d'état* must replace all other commandments; Christian morality was a luxury he could not afford.

The following excerpts from *The Prince* are probably the most frequently quoted passages on Machiavellianism.

> . . . A prince being thus obliged to know well how to act as a beast must imitate the fox and the lion, for the lion cannot protect himself from traps, and the fox cannot defend himself from wolves. One must therefore be a fox to recognise traps, and a lion to frighten wolves. Those that wish to be only lions do not understand this. Therefore, a prudent ruler ought not to keep faith when by so doing it would be against his interest, and when the reason which made him bind himself no longer exists.
>
> Nor have legitimate grounds ever failed a prince who wished to show colourable excuse for the non-fulfillment of his promise.
>
> Thus it is well to seem merciful, faithful, humane, sincere, religious, and also to be so; but you must have the mind so disposed that when it is needful to be otherwise you may be able to change to the opposite qualities.[14]

Machiavelli's use of the terms *virtu, necessita,* and *fortuna* provides a good basis for understanding his views. The virtu he admired was that of the courageous hero who had the strength to do what the situation demanded. It seemed to be Machiavelli's hope that virtu would be adopted as a code of values for rulers and citizens. He knew how powerful a force religion was in propagating

[13] It is true, however, that Machiavelli felt that Christianity made men weak, humble, and unmanly, and advocated, instead, the virtues of strength and virility, which he thought existed in pre-Christian times.

[14] Niccolò Machiavelli, *The Prince Including the Discourses,* trans. Luigi Ricci (New York: The Modern Library, 1950), p. 27.

a system of values among the people. Therefore he wanted to make religion an instrument of the state to inculcate his sense of virtu.

Necessita, or the requirements of the situation, were the overriding consideration for Machiavelli, and sufficient justification for any behavior. On the other hand, he regarded unnecessary cruelty as the epitome of foolishness. He did not mean that necessita should not be sought out, for necessita promotes virtu. For example, he advises a commander to place his troops in jeopardy deliberately to force them to be courageous and virtuous.

Both virtu and necessita are required if man is to overcome fortune. Friedrich Meinecke, a well-known German historian, describes Machiavelli's attitude toward fortune in a most illuminating passage:

> . . . *Fortuna* has got to be beaten and bruised like a woman one wants to possess, and boldness and barbarity will always be more successful there than coldness. But this boldness has got to be united with great cunning and calculation, for each situation of fate demands a method specially suited for dealing with it.[15]

It is this view of fortuna that sets modern political theorists apart from the ancients. From this time on, man's fate no longer seemed to depend on the will of the gods; rather it was something, like clay, that could be molded and shaped according to the requirements of the here and now, not the hereafter.

REALISTS AND IDEALISTS

The four writers discussed in this chapter were all concerned with various aspects of the study of politics. But in their approach to the subject matter, we can discern at least two different methods.

Aristotle and Machiavelli generally followed the descriptive approach to politics. Aristotle acknowledged that the most meaningful systems were not necessarily the best theoretically, but were those that would work best in this imperfect world. Machiavelli went even further when he declared that at times even the best for this world should be put aside for something less good. In short, Aristotle

[15] See Friedrich Meinecke, "Machiavelli," in *Essays in the History of Political Thought,* ed. Isaac Kramnick (Englewood Cliffs, N.J.: Prentice-Hall, 1969), pp. 111–26.

and Machiavelli are realists: they modify their theories to account for phenomena existing in the real world. Although Plato and Aquinas share some realist notions, they are more easily classified as idealists.[16] Their approach is to delineate the ideal, with the hope that the real world will try to emulate it.

These divergent positions introduce a tantalizing dilemma in the study of politics. Idealists have the advantage of freedom in their speculation. They are not constrained by existing empirical reality. As a result, idealist writers often produce more eloquent and intriguing political analyses than realists, since they can transcend this world and speak in theoretical terms. At the same time, because their ideas are speculative, one is bound to ask: What are they good for? Scintillating as the thoughts may be, unless they have some application to the present condition of the world, they are meaningless. Because of this lack of empirical concern, many idealists are either reactionary or revolutionary in their theories. They want to return to a world they consider more perfect or advance to a new state more in conformity with their theories. For this reason, idealists provide visions of future (and past) societies that often move people to action, simply on the strength of the vision.

The realist tradition also has its virtues. Realist writers try to understand contemporary problems to advance their individual goals. If idealists have provided the visions, the realists have demonstrated the gap between those visions and the present realities. Realists, therefore, tend not to be revolutionary or reactionary in their politics; they are usually firmly rooted in worldly concerns. One very real danger is that the realist will become skeptical of the possibility of fundamental social change. Political realists are often cynical, and even if they avoid cynicism (like Machiavelli), there is still the danger that cynical leaders will use their theories for personal ends. (See Chapters 12 and 14 for modern examples.)

Is there any way to combine the advantages of both traditions? Some writers, like Marx, have tried. When he analyzed capitalism in his economic writings, he was brutally realistic—there is not a

---

[16] Earlier in this chapter we described Plato as a realist in contrast to the Greek nominalists. Now we are calling him an idealist in contrast to realists. This linguistic confusion is difficult to avoid. But a word like idealist (or liberal, democrat, socialist, and so on) only has meaning in a specific context in contrast to its opposite. Thus, an idealist who is the opposite of a materialist is different from an idealist who is the opposite of a realist.

sentimental word in all of *Das Kapital*. But some of Marx's earliest works, despite his own denial, are full of idealism. Other writers have also tried, with varying success, to be both idealistic and realistic.

It is true that there are major differences between the political perspectives of Plato, Aristotle, Aquinas, and Machiavelli. But there is obviously no reason why political philosophers should share the same political views. Some have been monarchists, some democrats, some socialists, some reactionaries, and so on and so on. The one thing they have not been is apolitical. All the writers discussed here have been vitally concerned with the political issues of their times. The nature of the concern varies, but not the concern itself.

9 The Liberal Tradition

In one of their operettas, Gilbert and Sullivan remarked that every English child is born either a little Liberal or a little Conservative. Although they happened to use the word liberal first to complete a rhyme, there is some justice in asserting the primacy of the liberal tradition. For, in many ways, every American and English child is born a liberal, even if he calls himself a conservative. The reason is that there are so many meanings of the word liberal. An individual may drink a liberal amount of coffee, and at the same time take a liberal attitude toward those who prefer tea. Or, on the political side, a resident of New York State may decide to vote for the candidate of the Liberal party because the Democratic candidate is too "liberal." The possible meanings of the word liberal are so various that we shall confine our discussion to two common, and historically significant meanings.

Some people call themselves liberals in comparison with their opposites, the conservatives. This current meaning of liberalism is programmatic; it defines liberalism in terms of a certain political program. Thus the contemporary liberal believes in government intervention in the economy to insure economic stability, the extension of civil rights and liberties at a measured pace, and other specific items of public policy. The opposite of this form of liberal is the conservative, who generally holds the opposite point of view toward public policies.

The second meaning of liberalism, the one we shall use here, is more important historically. In this sense, liberalism refers to a general attitude toward politics, irrespective of specific public policies. The liberal is receptive to political change—generally at a slower rate than the revolutionary—while the conservative wants change to be gradual—but not as slow as the reactionary, who wants to keep things exactly the same or even turn them back. In this sense, the word "liberal" is synonymous with "progressive." This form of liberalism believes in constant progress toward a higher goal—which is why we said that every child born in England or America is a liberal. In the culture of both countries, progress is almost universally regarded as good. One American corporation even proclaims: "Progress is our most important product"—which is symbolic of the popularity of the idea of progress. Business corporations, unions, consumer organizations, and many others share, and to some extent shape, this belief. Consumer advocate Ralph Nader and the president of General Motors, antagonists on matters of public policy, both believe in progress and, therefore, are part of the liberal tradition.

The belief in progress distinguishes the liberal from the classical tradition. Few of the ideas discussed in the previous chapter were liberal. One could debate whether the ideal republic of Plato was a progressive development at the time or a primitive form of totalitarianism. In either case, Plato would not be a liberal; he did not consider progress a first priority. Neither did Aristotle, St. Thomas, and Machiavelli. This is why the classical world is unfamiliar to the American student. For clearly, the belief in progress pervades the modern world. If the skeptical reader analyzes the children's stories he has read or the tradition his parents have passed on to him, he will find, in most cases, the dominant theme to be progress. The universality of liberalism—its approval by all—has obscured its origins and some of its major tenets. Before he can understand and evaluate his own value system, the student must understand liberalism—not in its fuzzy and programmatic contemporary sense, but in its origins.

The term "liberal" did not appear in politics until the early nineteenth century. Yet the word had such a favorable connotation that the Whig party in Britain, the champion of parliamentary power, decided to change its name to the Liberal party in 1840. But long before liberal became a household word, the idea had appeared as philosophical concepts in the writings of Thomas Hobbes, who wrote in the seventeenth century.

For purposes of analysis, we may divide liberalism into two separate philosophical traditions. The earlier one, classical liberalism, is often referred to as contract or natural rights theory. The American Constitution and Declaration of Independence stand as monuments to the influence of this type of liberal theory. But liberalism today is at least equally influenced by the utilitarian tradition, especially by John Stuart Mill's ideas on freedom from his essay "On Liberty" (1859).

CLASSICAL LIBERALISM

It should not be assumed that these two traditions are connected in any logical way. In fact, contemporary liberalism is often an inconsistent mixture of values drawn from each—which adds to the definitional confusion over the word "liberal."

The major tenets of classical liberalism may be summarized under four headings:

Individualism. This is a highly atomistic conception of society, based on the absolute autonomy of individual will and worth. Classical liberalism viewed society as an aggregation of individuals who might choose by individual acts of will to act in concert.

Contract Theory. The legitimacy of government rests upon the free consent of the governed. Therefore, the only legitimate and enduring means of securing domestic tranquillity is by law based upon reason and representation rather than force. This may be interpreted as perhaps unwarranted faith in constitutions and constitutionalism.

Liberty. Certain inalienable rights are vested in individual man by his very nature; without them he would be dehumanized. Commonly referred to as natural rights, these were thought to be best protected by constitutional guarantees much as a bill of rights. This also led to the belief that the government that governs least governs best.

Liberal Epistemology. A transcendental order exists in the universe, which ordinary mortals can understand without the help of divine revelation. However, both reason and will are required before an individual can translate this universal order into a practical guide for moral conduct. Therefore, the choice between liberty and license, order and anarchy, is an individual one. In liberalism, the theory of knowledge, as well as the theory of politics, departs from the classical tradition.

To understand these tenets, we must explore their origins. A number of writers, ranging from Grotius in the seventeenth century to Thomas Paine in the late eighteenth, contributed to the liberal tradition. But the two men who had the greatest influence on classical liberalism were Thomas Hobbes (1588–1679) and John Locke (1632–1704).

THOMAS HOBBES

The first half of the seventeenth century was a period of great turmoil and discontent. The Thirty Years' War lasted from 1618 to 1648. It is not surprising that Hobbes, a thoughtful Englishman, became alarmed about the spread of religious conflicts from the Continent. The great civil wars of the Puritan revolution seemed likely to bring only ruin and despair. To Thomas Hobbes, a civil war that divides a nation, and families within that nation, was the worst of all wars; and a civil war fought on religious grounds was the worst of all civil wars. There were three major issues involved in the strife: religious liberty, the constitutional question of whether supremacy lay with the Parliament or the monarch, and the class question of what role should be played by the new commercial bourgeoisie in the affairs of state.

As companion and tutor to the eldest son of Lord Cavendish (later the earl of Devonshire), Thomas Hobbes was in a position to observe these developments. The Cavendish family, one of the most aristocratic in England, brought Hobbes into contact with the ferment of his era. He met scientists like Harvey, Descartes, and Galileo, and apparently Francis Bacon had quite an influence on him. He also had the opportunity to travel widely, sometimes in exile. Like the Greeks, he was a political man.

Hobbes wrote extensively on political matters; his important works include *Elements of Law* (1650), *De Cive* (1642), *Leviathan* (1651), *De Corpae* (1655), and *De Homine* (1658). We shall draw upon *Leviathan*, certainly his best known and most influential work.

Hobbes's central concern was to provide a philosophical basis for the maintenance of a strong sovereign, which he felt was essential for the preservation of law and order. He was aware that the divine right of kings theory was no longer a viable defense and, in fact, led to a challenge of authority. He felt a new theory was necessary to preserve the civilization that England had struggled so hard to build.

The main themes of Hobbes's argument—the state of nature and contract theories of the origin of civil society—dominated political thought for nearly two centuries. But, equally important, Hobbes was really the first modern political "scientist." He drew upon mathematics, especially geometry, for his analytical model.

Hobbes started with a few axioms that were generally accepted as self-evident truths and then proceeded to construct more complicated theories on the nature of politics, which would be as unassailable as the more complicated theorems of geometry. The first, and for Hobbes the most significant, axiom was that man preferred life over death. To Hobbes, it followed that a fundamental motivation of man was fear—especially fear of violent death. Hobbes developed his hypothesis by asking what life would be like in a state of nature. If sovereign authority were removed, if there were no longer any police, any courts, any prisons, any army, any laws, we would find ourselves in such a state (which, he pointed out, was an analytical device, not an historical fact).

In a state of nature men would be equal, for inequalities were artificial differences created by society.

> Nature has made men so equal in the faculties of the body and mind as that, though there be found one man sometimes manifestly stronger in body or of quicker mind than another, yet, when all is reckoned together, the difference between man and man is not so considerable as that one man can thereupon claim to himself any benefit to which another may not pretend as well as he. For as to the strength of the body, the weakest has strength enough to kill the strongest, either by secret machination or by confederacy with others that are in the same danger with himself. And, as to the faculties of the mind, setting aside the arts grounded upon words, and especially that skill of proceeding upon general and infallible rules called science—which very few have and but in a few things,

as being not a native faculty born with us, nor attained, as prudence, while we look after somewhat else—I find yet greater equality among men than that of strength. For prudence is but experience, which equal time equally bestows on all men in those things that equally apply themselves unto.[1]

Hobbes's view has been neatly summarized by one student: "that while individuals may differ in their individual capacities, nature was the great equalizer." Hobbes's own description of the human condition in the state of nature appears in a memorable passage:

> Whatever, therefore, is consequent to a time of war where every man is enemy to every man, the same is consequent to the time wherein men live with the other security than what their own strength and their own invention shall furnish them withal. In such condition there is no place for industry, because the fruit thereupon is uncertain, and consequently no culture of the earth; no navigation nor use of the commodities that may be imported by sea; no commodious building; no instruments of moving and removing such things as require much force; no knowledge of the face of the earth; no account of time; no arts; no letters; no society; and, which is worst of all, continual fear and danger of violent death; and the life of man solitary, poor, nasty, brutish, and short.[2]

So ingrained in man are the dangers that exist in the state of nature and so powerful is the fear of violent death that it creates "a general inclination of all mankind; a perpetual and restless desire of power after power that ceases only in death." [3] But, fortunately, man is also rational and his reason will show him the wisdom of entering into a covenant with a sovereign, investing him with supreme power to create the conditions of law and order that are essential to a commodious life, even to life itself.

Hobbes's state is not totalitarian but authoritarian, an important distinction. While Hobbes would not limit the power of the sovereign in any way, he assumed that the sovereign's sole function

---

[1] Thomas Hobbes, *Leviathan: Parts One and Two*, ed. Herbert W. Sneider (New York: Liberal Arts Press, 1958), pp. 104–5.

[2] Ibid., p. 106.

[3] Ibid., p. 86.

was to maintain law and order with whatever force was necessary. The sovereign, whether one man or an assembly of men, would oversee a state in which the citizens could pursue their own, largely private, certainly individual interests with the assurance that peace, the essential condition for such pursuits, would prevail.

As a matter of fact, Hobbes has given us an important, although negative concept of liberty. First of all, it is clear that man in the state of nature is free to do what he likes.

> A freeman is he that in those things which by his strength and wit he is able to do is not hindered to do what he has a will to do.[4]

In civil society, however, liberty consists in the silence of the sovereign. How often have we heard that we are free to do anything the law allows, and what is law but the commands of the sovereign authority?

Finally, Hobbes had a keen understanding of the foundation upon which civil society rests. As one commentator, John Plamenatz, observed: "He understood that men are not born but are made sociable, that there is no justice without law, and no law without discipline, and no discipline without sanctions."[5]

With his emphasis on authority and his constant fear of death and anarchy, can we place Hobbes in the liberal tradition? Where, for example, is the belief in progress? Actually, Hobbes is very much in the liberal tradition; we must realize that his perspective was shaped by the situation he was reacting against. Hobbes's insight is that individual liberty is not synonymous with lack of government. Without government comes constant strife—which is not conducive to liberty. Hobbes, in short, was the first in the liberal tradition to show how liberty depends on the existence of government, just as Aristotle showed that justice was only possible in the state. This was indeed a progressive notion in terms of the turmoil of his era, and in that sense Hobbes was a liberal.

But another point should be reemphasized. According to classical liberalism, the function of the state—to maintain order—should not

[4] Ibid., p. 171.

[5] John Plamenatz, *Man and Society* (New York: McGraw-Hill, 1963), vol. 1, *Machiavelli through Rousseau*, p. 154.

be confused with something the state is prohibited from doing—interfering with the natural freedom of commerce. Hobbes's view of economics resembles the modern conservative approach in many ways. It is not the business of the state to engage in economic enterprise. The state should only regulate *in order to preserve* freedom of contract. Thus, for Hobbes, as for classical liberalism in general, freedom (or liberty) is an economic concept. Society is like the marketplace. Individual rights generally mean property rights. Freedom refers to the right to own property, not to say whatever one thinks. For free speech may lead to anarchy, while free enterprise will not. These notions, generally associated with liberalism, were progressive in the context of the times. They were part of the effort to supersede a mercantilistic system in which the state hindered economic progress by its artificial entry into the natural system of supply and demand. In this respect, too, Hobbes is part of the liberal tradition.

JOHN LOCKE

No name is more prominent in classical liberalism than that of John Locke. As long as liberal thought is influential, he will be remembered for phrases like "life, liberty and property," "consent of the governed," and "the majority have a right to act and conclude the rest." He was truly the father of constitutional government, as we comprehend it.

With his progressive scientific outlook, Locke was well attuned to the times. His close friends included Robert Boyle, the founder of modern chemistry, and Thomas Sydenham, England's leading physician and pioneer of the clinical method. He also had close connections in political and social affairs. Locke began his political career with the earl of Shaftesbury, later lord chancellor, and continued to be associated with Whig politics all his life.

Almost as important as Locke's contribution to political philosophy are his views on empiricism, on how reality is understood. In a frequently quoted passage, he outlines his empirical position.

All ideas come from sensation or reflection—Let us then suppose the mind to be, as we say, white paper, void of all characters, without any ideas: how comes it to be furnished? Whence

comes it by that vast store which the busy and boundless
fancy of man has painted on it with an almost endless variety?
Whence has it all the materials of reason and knowledge? To
this I answer, in one word, from experience.[6]

Both Hobbes and Locke rejected the possibility of innate ideas,
but Locke's approach was empirical and Hobbes's was not. Locke
relied on the observation of data and developed his theory by inductive reasoning; Hobbes, on the other hand, preferred to follow
a deductive method modeled after geometry. In spite of their different approaches, both developed contract theories of the state
based on a particular view of life in the state of nature.

Locke did not believe that life in the state of nature would be a
condition of war; on the contrary, men would live in harmony with
one another, governed by their individual rational, albeit not complete, understanding of the laws of nature. Certain inconveniences
in the state of nature, however, would lead men to establish a civil
society through a contract or, perhaps more accurately, a trust
agreement.

The major inconvenience of the state of nature was that every man
must interpret the laws of nature himself. To deal with this problem
we have legislative bodies composed of the enlightened citizens;
they are supposed to provide authoritative statements of law, end-
ing the ambiguity and confusion caused by many individual interpretations of the law. In Locke's view the legislator does not have
carte blanche, only the authority to operate within the confines of
natural law. His job is not to *make* the law but to *discover* it.

Another inconvenience of Locke's state of nature is that every
man must be the judge in his own case. Locke was nothing if not
practical; he knew how self-interest interferes with a rational assess-
ment of guilt or innocence. A third inconvenience was having to enforce any penalties or repayment of damages oneself. In other words,
the inconveniences Locke found in the state of nature—that each
man must determine the law for himself, judge his own case, and
execute his own decisions—were almost as bad as the state of war
in Hobbes's conception.

Both Locke and Hobbes see an end to the state of nature through
contract. Locke considers the contract between the governed and

[6] John Locke, *An Essay concerning Human Understanding* (New York: Dover,
1959), pp. 121–22.

the governing equally binding on both. The people are obliged to obey the law but only when it is in accord with the contract. And while the only legitimate government is one in which the people consent, Locke rejects Hobbes's view that the legitimacy of government rests on man's fear of violent death; he also rejects the idea that legitimacy is based on divine right or some other mysterious force. It rests, he contends, on the rational consent of naturally equal men.

But how do we know whether men consent or not? On this Locke is not very helpful. He says that legitimacy depends on the consent of the majority, but he does not suggest that the majority has any superior virtue. In fact, his answer is highly mechanistic and amoral.

> For that which acts any community being only the consent of the individuals in it, and it being one body must move one way, it is necessary the body should move that way whither the greatest force carries it, which is the consent of the majority; or else it is impossible it should act or continue one body, one community.[7]

As occasions for explicit consent are very rare in political life, Locke was forced to recognize tacit consent as well as express consent. He asserted that an individual who is of age and chooses to remain within society, reaping its benefits of protection to life and property, tacitly consents. It would seem that, according to Locke, the people of any state not engaged in violent insurrection were giving their consent. If this is the case, it is not a very useful device in identifying different kinds of states. Certainly Locke's view of consent would not distinguish between Britain and the United States on one hand, and Stalin's Russia or Mao's China, on the other —so long as each was at peace internally.

One other facet of Locke's political theory, his views on property, needs elaboration. He has been instrumental in raising property rights almost to the status of a sacred natural right in liberal theory. He starts out reasonably enough:

> 1. In the original state of nature property belonged to no one and everyone; it was there for the taking.

---

[7] John Locke, *The Second Treatise of Government* (New York: Liberal Arts Press, 1922), p. 55.

2. Man has an absolute right to his own person, including his labor.

3. When man mixes his labor with property he establishes a right to that property.

4. There is a natural limit, however, to the amount of property man can hold, and his natural right only extends to the property he can use. For example, if a man picks apples from a natural orchard in the state of nature, he makes those apples his, but he has no right to pick more apples than he can use or trade before they spoil.

5. The problem is that Locke believed that the invention of money ended the natural limitations on the accumulation of wealth; there was no longer a restriction on how much a man could acquire.

Thus, the introduction of a complex economic system—represented by the use of money—complicates Locke's theories on property, as he himself recognized. After the natural limits are removed, the freedom to obtain property may create such inequalities that some may be denied their natural rights. In other words, if a small group of people obtains all the property, everyone else is denied that right. Locke was aware of this problem, but he never resolved it satisfactorily—nor has any liberal thinker since.

Both Hobbes and Locke considered property a basic freedom and the system of supply and demand a necessity. Political freedom would be impossible without some form of capitalism, which kept the most essential economic units in private hands. This view, emphasizing the dependence of political freedom on capitalism, has been extremely influential in the United States. For years it was revered constitutional doctrine. For example, in *Lochner* v. *New York* (1905), the Supreme Court held that a law that prohibited bakery workers from working more than sixty hours a week was unconstitutional. Their reasoning was that it interfered with freedom of contract, and therefore it struck a blow at political freedom. Because of this, bakery workers who wished to retain their jobs were obliged to work as many hours as their employers demanded. Significantly, elements of the philosophy of Hobbes and Locke were used to justify the power of employers. It raises the question of the relationship between the origins of liberalism and modern capitalism. Some have suggested that Hobbes and Locke were not paragons of democratic virtue, but apologists for a new industrial order.[8] Liberalism is seen as the ideology of the newly emerging bourgeoisie, which was to replace the older landed aristocracy as a ruling elite. Locke's reputation as a political theorist depends more on the usefulness of his views to this new elite than on his style, the consistency of his logic, or the validity of his ideas.

UTILITARIANISM

The British empirical tradition, which originated with Thomas Hobbes and John Locke, reached maturity with the philosophical radicals known as utilitarians. These men added to or departed from the liberal position in a number of areas. For one thing, they abandoned the metaphysical speculation, whether explicit or implicit, of classical liberalism. For example, the utilitarians referred to natural law as "nonsense upon stilts." Second, they believed the apparent conflict between the "is" and the "ought" could be resolved by the pleasure-pain principle. Whatever gave pleasure would be adhered to; painful things would be avoided.

Third, reason applied to government and social institution would eliminate superstition, tradition, and mystique, so that a new era of progress would ensue. This is a reassertion of the liberal tradition.

Fourth, liberty was defended on the grounds of social utility, not as an essential ingredient of humanity.

Fifth, the legitimate end of government was not the promotion of the good life, justice, or the protection of the natural rights of man, but governmental response to the desires of the people. Finally, the concept of a social contract was abandoned. It was too speculative to suit the empirical bent of the utilitarians. They preferred to defend political systems on their merits, not on the basis of a logical construct. The trouble with the social contract was that you could not read it anywhere.

The utilitarian movement, which was to inherit the liberal mantle from the classical liberals, had two leading exponents—Jeremy Bentham (1748–1832) and John Stuart Mill (1806–1873). Rarely have two philosophers been so similar, and yet made such distinct

[8] This point is elaborated and brilliantly defended in C. B. MacPherson, *The Political Theory of Possessive Individualism: Hobbes to Locke* (New York: Oxford University Press, 1962).

contributions. The precociousness of both has been well noted.
Bentham was writing Latin at five and reading Voltaire in French at
six, and Mill was reading Plato and Demosthenes in the original
Greek at ten. Perhaps the exceptional intellectual abilities of the
two men explain why they both believed that all politics and political institutions could be made completely rational.

Both, however, subscribed to David Hume's dictum: "Reason is,
and ought only to be, the slave of the passions." Reason, therefore,
could not tell us what was desirable but only serve as an efficient
means of satisfying our desires.

JEREMY BENTHAM

Bentham states his agreement with Hume's proposition very force-
fully on the first page of *Introduction to the Principles of Morals and
Legislation.*

> Nature has placed mankind under the governance of two
> sovereign masters, pain and pleasure. It is for them alone to
> point out what we ought to do, as well as to determine what
> we shall do. On the one hand the standard of right and wrong,
> on the other the chain of causes and effects, are fastened to
> their throne. They govern us in all we do, in all we say, in all
> we think: every effort we can make to throw off our subjec-
> tion will serve but to demonstrate and confirm it.[9]

He also developed what has become known as the Benthamite
Calculus. Each man is like a computer; when faced with a choice,
he makes his decision on the basis of which alternative will give
him either the most pleasure or the least pain. Bentham tells us that
there are fourteen single pleasures, such as sense, wealth, and skill,
and twelve single pains, such as privation and awkwardness. Each
in turn is subdivided into components, for example, sense into touch,
ear, eye, and sex. These single pains and pleasures may be combined to produce complex pains or pleasures. We not only record
these pleasures and pains, but we also weigh them quantitatively ac-

[9] Jeremy Bentham, *The Collected Works of Jeremy Bentham, Section Two:
Principles of Legislation* (New York: Oxford University Press, 1970), vol. 1,
An Introduction to the Principles of Morals and Legislation, eds. J. M. Burns
and H. L. Hart, p. 1.

cording to seven criteria—intensity, duration, certainty or uncertainty, propinquity or remoteness, fecundity (the chance of its being repetitious), purity, and the number of people affected (which is not, strictly speaking, an individual calculation).

Obviously Bentham does not mean that each individual actually draws up a ledger of the alternatives before making a decision. But, in a crude fashion, he does program these factors through his computerlike brain and makes a decision on that basis. For Bentham, there are no qualitative differences: "Pushpin is the same as poetry if it gives the same pleasure." [10] This is the exact opposite of the Greek concept of justice.

In terms of public policy, it would seem to follow that if what we call right, just, moral, or good is merely that which gives us pleasure, then government ought to follow those policies that give the greatest happiness to the greatest number. While logically this might lead—in fact, has led—to a welfare state that seems dedicated to meeting the demands of the people, the result was not so obvious to Bentham. He shared the atomized individualism of his predecessors, believing that no one could determine for another what would bring him pleasure. The state might act to prevent pain (for instance, stop the slave trade), but should not attempt to promote happiness except by providing the conditions of security in which individuals could seek their own pleasures (as long as these pleasures did not interfere with others in their search for pleasure).

It seems that the primary function of the state would be the same as in classical liberalism: to mediate between conflicting claims in a highly competitive and individualistic society.

JOHN STUART MILL

John Stuart Mill's amendments to Benthamite utilitarianism are significant. His famous remark, that it is better to be a "Socrates dissatisfied than a pig satisfied," leaves little of Bentham's simple pleasure-pain thesis.[11] While Mill asserted that some pleasures, such as pleasures of the intellect, were inherently better than other

---

[10] Pushpin, a children's game, perhaps could be compared to pinball.

[11] John Stuart Mill, "Utilitarianism," in *John Stuart Mill: A Selection of His Works,* ed. J. M. Robson (New York: Macmillan, 1966), p. 161.

pleasures, he was unable to tell us why. He did, however, argue that this is a consequence of man's subtle and complex nature. Those who prefer the baser pleasures have not experienced the higher ones; for those who have are not content with the baser pleasures. He did not realize that he had, in fact, abandoned Bentham's basic utilitarian concept.

However, Mill's place in the liberal tradition rests not on his critique of the pleasure-pain principle but on his defense of free speech in "On Liberty." The assumption, sometimes more implicit than explicit, underlying this essay is that progress depends on the ideas put forth by the intelligentsia. Mill believed that the tyranny of the majority presented a new danger in democratic society. And the intelligentsia, because they were innovators, constantly challenging the status quo in politics, economics, and social mores, became particular targets for the wrath of the masses.

To ensure the creative freedom needed by this elite, Mill argued for the social utility of freedom of expression on four grounds.

> We have now recognized the necessity to the mental well-being of mankind (on which all their other well-being depends) of freedom of opinion, and freedom of expression of opinion, on four distinct grounds; which we will now briefly recapitulate.
>
> First, if any opinion is compelled to silence, that opinion may for aught we can certainly know, be true. To deny this is to assume our own infallibility.
>
> Second, though the silenced opinion be an error, it may, and very commonly does, contain a portion of truth; and since the general or prevailing opinion on any subject is rarely or never the whole truth, it is only by the collision of adverse opinions that the remainder of the truth has any chance of being supplied.
>
> Thirdly, even if the received opinion be not only true, but the whole truth, unless it is suffered to be, and actually is, vigorously and earnestly contested, it will, by most of those who receive it, be held in the manner of a prejudice, with little comprehension or feeling of its rational grounds, and not only this, but, fourthly, the meaning of the doctrine itself will be in danger of being lost, or enfeebled, and deprived of its vital effect on the character and conduct: the dogma becoming a

mere formal profession, inefficacious for good, but cumbering the ground, and preventing the growth of any real and heart-felt conviction, from reason or personal experience.[12]

We have quoted these principles at length because they illustrate the major characteristic of utilitarianism. Unlike Aquinas, whose standards were based on divine or at least idealistic criteria, Mill's arguments for freedom of expression are not even based on human-istic grounds. They all rely on the social utility of freedom of ex-pression. There is, therefore, a practical, or pragmatic character to utilitarianism, and this has been very influential in the United States. It is summarized by the question, Does it work? If it does, it passes. If not, it is abandoned. This pragmatism is one of the legacies of the utilitarian strain in the liberal tradition.

CONCLUSION

The basis of the capitalist system of property relationships is a practical one. Economic man was forced to confront economic man, not in terms of traditional superstition or religion, but in terms of profit and loss. There was no room for the impractical. The utili-tarianism point of view was quite hospitable to the economic sys-tem of nineteenth-century England. It justified human activity on the basis of rational calculation. It taught that ethics and morals, if impractical, could not be right and should be avoided. It advo-cated pleasure (and what could be more pleasurable than the ac-cumulation of riches?) and warned against pain (and what could be more harmful than poverty?). Just as classical liberalism was the philosophy of the origins of private property, utilitarianism was the theoretical basis for the development of property relationships. Thus, in many ways, it is the logical outgrowth of classical liberal-ism.

In a sense, it is difficult for us to evaluate the liberal tradition, because we are so much a part of it. While we have been critical of liberalism in this chapter, we believe in progress, and therefore elements of liberalism are incorporated in our point of view as well. Furthermore, few would deny that liberalism has made some fundamental contributions to the present world. The idea of liberty

[12] John Stuart Mill, "On Liberty," in *John Stuart Mill: A Selection of His Works,* ed. J. M. Robson (New York: Macmillan, 1966), pp. 68–69.

is basic to all contemporary peoples—although the meaning may differ from nation to nation. And the idea of liberty developed with liberalism; both words have the same root. In addition, liberalism emphasizes the importance of democracy, defined as the alternative to absolutist rule. This, too, is an important value. So there is much that is worthwhile and important in liberalism, and we recognize our debt to it.

Yet certain problems have always been associated with the liberal tradition. Earlier we pointed out that freedom of property for the few could interfere with freedom of property for the many. This is symptomatic of one basic difficulty: many liberal ideals are statements of what *ought* to be. Mill's "On Liberty," for example, champions free speech, asserting that political systems should guarantee free speech because it is socially advantageous. But we need more than "oughts." Why is it that free speech is so often denied?

The ability of liberalism to deal with the world's problems is frequently debated these days. In the socialist countries, as well as in much of the so-called Third World of Asia, Africa, and Latin America, liberalism has been challenged and found inadequate to cope with poverty and economic development. Similarly, within the United States—the bastion of liberalism and progress—many, including the writers of this book, have begun to question the relevance of the liberal tradition. It has become clear that liberal ideas are not so much valid laws for all time as an expression of the need of a particular historical era. However, new historical eras have created different needs, which should be reflected by the ideologies. A recent book by Theodore Lowi has the title: *The End of Liberalism.*[13] The burial may be slightly premature, but the direction seems certain. We can expect the development of a postliberal ideology shortly, but its content is hard to predict.

In fact, it is the profusion of competing ideologies that makes prediction so difficult. We are in a period of transition, and our society is groping for new values. The extraordinary success of books like Charles Reich's *The Greening of America* and Theodore Roszak's *The Making of a Counter-Culture*—which deal with the new lifestyle emerging among youth—indicates this search. It is significant that these works are being widely read outside of the academic community. It is also significant that Daniel Bell's *The*

[13] *The End of Liberalism* (New York: Norton, 1969).

End of Ideology, which celebrated the absence of ideology in America, should rise and fall like a meteor in the sky. For, obviously, "ideologies are alive and well in the United States." [14] The resurgence of a left-wing movement in the United States shows that. But utilitarianism, defining public policy in terms of pleasure rather than needs, will die or is already dead. The new social philosophy will seek criteria of the just political system; the question is not whether the philosophy meets the requirements of industrial capitalism, but whether it serves humane goals. In a sense this will be progress and, therefore, liberal. But the liberal tradition as represented by Hobbes, Locke, Mill, and Bentham will have to be seriously altered if progress is to be maintained. Once again, the nature of liberalism has been expressed paradoxically.

[14] A recent study describes in some detail seven American ideologies competing for dominance in the 1970s: Kenneth Dolbeare, *American Ideologies: The Competing Political Beliefs of the 1970s* (Chicago: Markom, 1971); see also Kenneth A. Megill, *The New Democratic Theory* (New York: Free Press, 1970).

10 The Conservative Tradition

CONCURRENT WITH THE individualist liberalism there is a conservative philosophy, which, though never as explicitly developed, presents a clear alternative. In a very significant article, Samuel Huntington proposes a useful typology of conservatism.[1] The following three-part definition is drawn from his article.

First, there is the historical, situational definition of conservatism —the Marxist definition. This views conservatism as an ideology that is permanently linked to the *ancien régime,* with the value system of the landed aristocracy. Its influence has been on the wane since the French Revolution, for in the Marxist conception (to be examined in more detail in the next chapter), as the mode of production changed from the feudal or agrarian to the capitalistic, the bourgeoisie replaced the landed aristocracy and liberal ideology replaced conservatism. Thus, conservatism is no more than a cultural lag doomed to disappear. Although this view of conservatism is important, it is of limited use since it refers only to one historical situation.

The second definition of conservatism is situational also, but it

[1] The following discussion of types of conservatism is based, in part, on Samuel P. Huntington, "Conservatism as an Ideology," *The American Political Science Review,* 51, no. 2 (June 1957):454–73.

#3 certain values &
principles that are above
circumstances.

#2 Conservatism
defense of status quo
in any situation.

refers to a recurring, rather than a specific historical situation. It
views conservatism as the defense of the status quo in any particular
situation. But a conservative in this sense need not be opposed to
all change; he may, in fact, seek some reforms that will strengthen
the status quo. He is likely to favor the general direction public
policy has been taking and would prefer that things continue along
the same line. Under this definition, any defense of the status quo is
conservative. Thus, even a revolutionary can be a conservative,
when, for example, he is consolidating the revolution (which was
the case with Stalin). As a general definition of conservatism, this
one is helpful, and it parallels the definition of liberalism used in the
previous chapter.

The third, more autonomous, definition maintains that there are
certain long-established conservative values or principles which
are not contingent upon particular circumstances. This is the most
significant and enduring definition. For that reason, we will examine the conservative tradition by discussing seminal writers who
represented its principles best.

Conservative principles can best be understood in comparison
with liberal principles in three basic areas. In the first place, the
conservative tradition places a much stronger emphasis on community than the liberal tradition, and a corresponding lack of emphasis on individualism. Conservatism, historically, has been concerned with people living together in communities, with eliminating
conflict, and with establishing harmonious social relationships. Com-
monalty can come from a monarch, nationalism, a rural way of life,
social class, ethnic group, religion, and so on. But individualism of
the sort advocated by Hobbes, Locke, Bentham, and Mill is definitely opposed.

Second, conservatives reject the rationalism of liberal thought.
The conservative tradition, as we are defining it, is receptive to
speculative reason, intuition, even mysticism, but highly skeptical
of scientific reason and empiricism. In the last two chapters, we
noted that each tradition of political philosophy has a corresponding epistemology, or conception of knowledge. This is true of conservatism as well. Since science is often associated with progress
and progress is related to liberalism, conservatism has often taken
a hostile attitude toward scientific thought. This hostility may be
expressed in religion or in other forms. The conservative tradition
rejects the idea that everything which appears real is real. Some

constructivism receptive to intuition, etc

feelings cannot be measured by the Benthamite calculus and some political forces cannot be understood by man.

Finally, there is a sense of tradition. Because conservatism values the continuity of human civilization, it explicitly rejects Locke's view that every individual is born with a clean slate upon which experience writes its lessons. On the contrary, each person enters a world dominated by the past. One must study and understand the past to realize its virtues. It has generally been good and has much to offer us. Thus, while the liberal looks forward to more and more progress, the conservative looks back to the progress that has been made and savors that.

With these principles in mind, we can now examine the conservative tradition by considering the contributions of two political philosophers, Jean Jacques Rousseau (1712–1778) and Edmund Burke (1729–1797). Despite the fact that Rousseau's ideas were a major influence in the French Revolution, while Burke was its most articulate and passionate opponent, the two have much in common. They share an antithetical attitude toward the liberal tradition and generally agree on the conservative principles just listed. Rousseau and Burke indicate the diversity and range of the conservative tradition.

JEAN JACQUES ROUSSEAU

Rousseau was an early antiestablishment hero. He gained sudden fame in 1749, when he won an essay contest on the topic: "Has the Progress of Science and the Arts Contributed to Corrupt or Purify Morals?" With a perversity typical of his later career, Rousseau's "First Discourse" took the very radical position that scientific progress corrupts man. In both this and his second discourse, "On the Origins of Inequality," he advocates the simple life and stresses the natural goodness and innocence of man before civilization corrupted him. His views parallel those expressed in Genesis, dealing with the Garden of Eden and man's loss of innocence after eating the fruit from the tree of knowledge. Although his essays attacked the ultrasophisticated, artificial, and effete Parisian society, its leading figures began to shower him with attention. Rousseau responded with disdain, and he tried to shock them by wearing soiled clothes, dressing in quaint Armenian style, and giving away his watch as a symbol of contempt for time and regularity.

Rousseau's private and public quarrels with everyone of note, particularly with those who had befriended him, have become legend. His sexual adventures began at an early age and continued through most of his life. However, these aspects of his personality are best left to Freudian scholars to analyze. It is his political philosophy that we are interested in. No less controversial today than when he lived, Rousseau is regarded by some as the founder of totalitarianism and by others as the father of participatory democracy. Although our primary concern is his concept of the general will, we will also touch on his view of nature and natural man, as well as the practical problems of majority rule he was never able to resolve.

Rousseau's conception of the state of nature is almost diametrically opposed to that of Thomas Hobbes. In Rousseau's view, man was naturally good and in harmony with his environment in the state of nature. But although good, he was also uninformed. In harmony with nature and so much a part of it, man neither examined his place there nor his relations with his fellow man. He was motivated by love, but one could hardly call him moral, for he was an unreflecting creature, a good, kind, but dumb beast. In contrast to most political philosophers, Rousseau regards passion as a virtue. Strong passion is natural, and by protecting us from weakness and vanity, it preserves our freedom. Love, reinforced by strong passion, keeps us free.[2] Rousseau's view has been aptly summarized by John Plamenatz, a twentieth-century interpreter:

> . . . Our primitive passions keep us alive and healthy, and do not move us to harm one another. In the state of nature they are strong enough to maintain life and health. But in society we find more obstacles in our way, and our natural passions, being weak, are diverted from their objects. We are frustrated, and we become more concerned to get rid of the obstacles than to satisfy our natural passions; we become angry, fretful, and malevolent. It is then that self-love gives birth to vanity, to the comparison of self with others, and to the desire

---

[2] By self-love Rousseau does not mean infatuation with oneself, but rather the natural desires of an individual to satisfy his true needs. Self-love gives birth to other passions, including the love of others, as one's desires are satisfied or frustrated. Proper love and care during infancy leads to a genuine love of others which grows out of self-love. For a more thorough treatment see Rousseau's *Emile*, especially Book II.

to avenge and dominate. . . . If their natural passions had been stronger, men would have surmounted or removed the obstacles in their way, or would have had the courage to resign themselves to the inevitable, and would not have wasted their energies in bitterness, ostentation, or revenge.[3]

However, men do succumb to vanity; and after acquiring knowledge, they turn to their reason rather than their feelings for guidance. They become thoroughly corrupted by society. "Man is born free, and yet we see him everywhere in chains. Those who believe themselves the master of others cease not to be even greater slaves than the people they govern." [4]

In *The Social Contract*, Rousseau attempts to show how man can organize his collective life to be as free, in fact freer, than in his natural state. He makes it clear that there can be no return to the state of nature.

My design in this treatise is to enquire whether, taking men such as they are, and laws such as they may be made, it is not possible to establish some just and certain rule for the administration of the civil order. In the course of my research I shall endeavour to unite what right permits with what interest prescribes, that justice and utility may not be separated. . . .[5]

Rousseau believes that justice and utility will be one when the aggregation of men, united only by force and territory, becomes instead an association. This occurs when men are united by a common purpose, a public interest, or as Rousseau would call it, a "general will." This elusive concept of the general will is the key to Rousseau.

According to Rousseau, individuals have a common or general will, which can unite them to all others and which transcends their particular will. Only when they act in accordance with the general

---

[3] John Plamenatz, *Man and Society* (New York: McGraw-Hill, 1963), vol. 1, *Machiavelli through Rousseau*, p. 377.

[4] Jean Jacques Rousseau, *The Social Contract*, ed. Charles Frankell (New York: Hafner, 1947), p. 5.

[5] Ibid., p. 5.

will do people become free. Then they realize what is in their true interest. However, people often ignore their true interest and pursue their particular desires instead because these are immediate and do not require unity of purpose with the rest of the community. But this is self-deception, which only leads to subservience to narrow interests, rather than to freedom and moral excellence.

To illustrate the concepts of general will and popular will, we will turn to the writings of British economist Lord Keynes. His description of a deflationary situation makes Rousseau's concepts much clearer. As Keynes observed, in a period of recession when individual employers are faced with a declining market and profits, it is certainly in each entrepreneur's interest to cut costs and expenditures. If he were to do otherwise, while his competitors reduced their expenditures, he would be the first to go bankrupt. However, if all employers acted in terms of their individual will, which Rousseau would characterize as the will of all in contrast to the general will, the recession would get worse, the deflationary spiral would increase, the number of bankruptcies would multiply. The general will requires that they cooperate to increase expenditures rather than decrease them. Government, says Lord Keynes, can do what individuals acting independently cannot do; it can increase total expenditure and thus revise the deflationary spiral. The action, which follows the general will rather than the sum of the particular wills, produces the results the individual truly desires.

The same principle applies to cases of full employment and inflation. If the state rejects the workers' demands for higher wages and the employers' demands for higher profits and instead imposes taxes and other monetary restraints to check inflation, then the state is acting for the public good or the general will rather than responding to the pressure of many individual wills. (It rarely, however, happens that fairly as President Nixon's troubles indicate.)

Here are Rousseau's own words on the advantages man reaps by being placed under the authority of the general will.

> . . . whoever refused to obey the general will shall be compelled to it by the whole body: this in fact only forces him to be free; for this is the condition which, by giving each citizen to his country, guarantees his absolute personal inde-

pendence, a condition which gives motion and effect to the political machine. . . .

. . . The passing from the state of nature to the civil state produces in man a very remarkable change, by substituting justice for instinct in his conduct, and giving to his actions a moral character which they lacked before. It is then only that the voice of duty succeeds to physical impulse, and a sense of what is right, to the incitements of appetite. Man, who had till then regarded none but himself, perceives that he must act on other principles, and learns to consult his reason before he listens to his inclinations. Although he is deprived in this new state of many advantages which he enjoyed from nature, he gains in return others so great, his faculties so unfold themselves by being exercised, his ideas are so extended, his sentiments so exalted, and his whole being so enlarged and refined. . . . he ought to bless continually the happy moment that snatched him forever from it, and transformed him from a circumscribed and stupid animal to an intelligent being and a man.[6]

Even if one accepts the existence and authority of the general will, how is it possible to know when the commands of the state are a reflection of the general will, the will of all, or the particular will of some persons or groups? Rousseau never really resolves this problem. At times he seems to say that the general will can operate only in a small homogenous community—like the Greek city-state or his romanticized Geneva, or perhaps in the ideal Quaker town meeting. Yet he was reluctant to restrict his views to such a community, because they are so rare.

He is, therefore, forced to resort to reliance on the legislator, the leader who knows the general will better than the people, especially in large nations, and who can articulate it and receive a response from the populace. However, for every Lincoln who articulates the general will, there has been a modern dictator who also claimed to speak for the will of the nation. As human beings seldom achieve perfection, they cannot ordinarily be entrusted with interpreting the general will. Thus, theory comes into conflict with mundane reality. Partially realizing these difficulties, Rousseau at

[6] Ibid., pp. 18, 19.

other times places his confidence in the majority of the people.[7] He was motivated in part by his distrust of representative assemblies, for he recognized they developed a will of their own all too quickly, and the assembly's will was a particular will rather than the general will of the state. However, going from the leader to the people only shifts the problem from one person to many; it does not solve it.

Finally, Rousseau gave us an alternative to the liberal definition of freedom. To replace the liberal view of freedom as the absence of external restraints, there is moral freedom; only a person who lives by common rules can be morally free. Someone who obeys rules from force of habit or from fear is not really moral. But by willing the rules he thinks ought to be obeyed, by everyone including himself, a man becomes doubly free: he obeys himself and thereby possesses full freedom of choice, and he is also free of all the petty ties of self-interest, narrow clannish loyalties, and mean calculation. To achieve this freedom, a person must identify with the good of the community. If all citizens do this, the general will can be achieved.

This, however, is not achieved without any loss; in fact many would judge the loss greater than the gain. Rousseau's community overcomes the alienation of the large impersonal aggregations of people, so exemplified by the modern city where a man can live for years in an apartment building without knowing his neighbors, or, worse still, can lie dying or be assaulted on the streets without anyone coming to his aid. In Rousseau's community, on the other hand, individual anonymity disappears, but so does the right to eccentricity, nonconformity, even perversity—as anyone who has lived in a small town knows. For with all its drawbacks, the large impersonal metropolis does permit its members a freedom of thought and action not possible in the small community. (Of course, Rousseau would regard this condition as slavery rather than freedom.) In Rousseau's community, the tyranny of the majority, which J. S. Mill feared, becomes a reality. It is not Rousseau's political philosophy that has totalitarian implications, but his psychology, which so ruthlessly stamps out individualism. Once again one is struck by

[7] "This is indeed supposing that all characteristics which mark the general will still reside in the most votes; when that ceases to be the case, whatever measures may be adopted, it means the end of liberty." Ibid., p. 95.

the contradiction between his life, characterized by deviant behavior, and his concept of the well-ordered society. Could Rousseau have lived such a creative life if his own model had been realized? In all likelihood, he would have been ground down to mediocrity and conformity, or been confined to an asylum for the insane.

Although the liberals were willing, indeed quite anxious, to develop ideas that would be compatible with the world around them, writers like Rousseau preferred the serenity of an earlier time; conservatives tend to look backward to a golden age, free from contemporary ills. Certainly there are evils in the present world. The conservative tradition, so disheartened by these evils, has a tendency to glorify the past and romanticize it to an unwarranted extent. For the past, too, was once the present. Then, as now, people looked back to an even more remote past, which also had its conservatives. The problem with the conservative tradition, therefore, is that it often fails to account for the values of the present and the traditions that created those values. After all, our present evils originated in the past. Because they overlook this fact, writers like Rousseau are more important for the questions they ask than the solutions they develop. Rousseau—as much as any political philosopher—is concerned with the difficulties of the human condition. But, unfortunately, he does not provide a realistic solution.

EDMUND BURKE

Edmund Burke, who is generally regarded as the father of conservatism, stands midway between Rousseau, the spontaneous romantic, and Hegel, the most complex of philosophical system builders.

In our characterization of Burke as the arch conservative, we must not forget that only on one of the major issues of his day, the French Revolution, can he be considered a conservative. In other areas he was well ahead of prevailing opinion and even demonstrated his courage by speaking out on behalf of the Americans during the Revolutionary War:

> In order to prove that the Americans have no right to their liberties, we are every day endeavoring to subvert the maxims which preserve the whole spirit of our own. To prove that the Americans ought not to be free, we are obliged to deprecate

the value of freedom itself and we never seem to gain a paltry advantage over them in debate without attacking some of the principles or deriding some of those feelings for which our ancestors have shed their own blood.[8]

Although Burke never wrote a treatise on political theory comparable to Hobbes's *Leviathan* or Locke's *Second Essay on Civil Government,* his writings and parliamentary speeches reveal certain principles of conservatism sharply opposed to those of liberalism. These include a distrust of abstract, *a priori* reasoning, opposition to social contract as the basis of the state, and a theory of virtual, rather than actual, representation. Parliament is regarded as a deliberative body, not one in which the will of the people is merely mandated. Burke expresses these views with the rhetoric of a politician, rather than the subtleties and qualifications of a philosopher. Disregarding the passionate appeal of his oratory, Burke is perfectly able to speak for himself; he seldom needs clarification or elaboration, and he speaks to all who will listen.

Burke did not object to abstract reasoning because it was ineffective, but because it was too effective. He understood that there were reasons behind tradition that could not be analyzed. For example, if you try to find rational grounds for those things that matter most in life, you are likely to destroy them. Do not, Burke warned, try to analyze faith and religion rationally—or love or beauty, or anything that is highly cherished, like those customs and traditions that affect the well-being of government and the state. A dispassionate study might persuade the English to do away with wigs on judges and barristers, but, Burke would ask, at what a cost to the dignity, even the majesty of the law and judiciary.

For the abstract reason of the liberal, Burke would substitute the wisdom of the practitioner who realizes that politics is not a matter for science but one for judgment and prudential wisdom.

> The lines of morality are not like ideal lines of mathematics. They are broad and deep as well as long. They admit of exceptions; they demand modifications. These exceptions and modifications are not made by the process of logic, but by the rules of prudence. Prudence is not only first in rank of the

---

[8] Edmund Burke, "Speech on Moving his Resolutions for Concilliation with the Colonies," *The Works of Edmund Burke,* vol. 1 (London: Bohn, 1896), pp. 450ff.

virtues political and moral, she is the director, the regulator, the standard of them all.[9]

It is especially in applying the principles of morality to the practical problems facing the statesman that prudential wisdom rather than abstract reason is needed.

> The science of constructing a commonwealth, or renovating it, or reforming it, is, like every other experimental science, not to be taught *a priori*. Nor is it a short experience that can instruct us in that practical science; because the real effects of moral causes are not always immediate, but that which in the first instance is prejudicial may be excellent in its remoter operation, and its excellence may arise even from the ill effects it produces in the beginning. The reverse also happens; and very plausible schemes, with very pleasing commencements, have often shameful and lamentable conclusions. . . . The science of government being therefore, so practical in itself, and intended for such practical purposes, a matter which requires . . . even more experience than any person can gain in his whole life, however sagacious and observing he may be, it is with infinite caution that any man ought to venture upon pulling down an edifice which has answered in any tolerable degree for ages the common purposes of society, or on building it up again without having models and patterns of approved utility before his eyes.[10]

Burke considered the liberal notion of a social contract a fiction that obscures the whole foundation of civilization:

> Society is, indeed, a contract . . . but the state ought not to be considered as nothing better than a partnership agreement in a trade of pepper and coffee, calico or tobacco, or some other such low concern, to be taken up for a little temporary interest, and to be dissolved by the fancy of the parties. It is to be looked on with other reverence; because it is not a partnership in things subservient only to the gross animal existence of a temporary and perishable nature. It is a partnership in all

[9] Edmund Burke, "An Appeal from the New to the Old Whigs," in *The Works of Edmund Burke,* vol. 3 (London: Bohn, 1896), p. 16.

[10] Edmund Burke, "Reflections on the Revolution in France," in *The Writings and Speeches of Edmund Burke,* vol. 3 (Boston: Little, Brown, 1901), p. 358.

science, a partnership in all art, a partnership in every virtue and in all perfection. As the ends of such a partnership cannot be obtained in many generations, it becomes a partnership not only between those who are living, but between those who are living, those who are dead, and those who are to be born.[11]

In Burke's view, the greatness of England lay in her deliberative assembly, where the educated and well-born, representing the great fixed interests of the realm, could and would legislate for the public good after constructive debate. It was not necessary that all should be represented, in fact it was not desirable. In that case the legislature might become a place for registering the will of the people, rather than a place for deliberation on national policy. In his best rhetoric, Burke describes the role of the member of Parliament in a manner that still inspires respect:

My worthy colleague says his will ought to be subservient to yours. If that be all, the thing is innocent. If government were a matter of will upon any side, yours, without question, ought to be superior. But government and legislation are matters of reason and judgment, and not of inclination: and what sort of reason is that, in which the determination precedes the discussion; in which one set of men deliberate, and another decide; and where those who form the conclusion are perhaps three hundred miles distant from those who hear the arguments.

Parliament is not a *congress* of ambassadors from different and hostile interests; which interests each must maintain, as an agent and advocate, against other agents and advocates; but Parliament is a *deliberative* assembly of *one* nation, with *one* interest, that of the whole; where, not local purpose, not local prejudices, ought to guide, but the general good, resulting from the general reason of the whole.

Your representative owes you, not his industry only, but his judgment; and he betrays instead of serving you, if he sacrifices it to your opinion.[12]

Burke opposed the Reform Act of 1832, the first genuine extension of the franchise in Britain, because he feared that it would lead to

[11] Ibid., pp. 359–60.

[12] Edmund Burke, "Speech to the Electorate at Bristol," *The Works of Edmund Burke,* vol. 1 (London: Bohn, 1896), pp. 446–47.

actual rather than virtual representation. In his view, Parliament should be composed of able representatives of all the fixed and permanent interests of Britain, the various estates, ranks, and orders. The landed aristocracy, the great overseas trading companies, the new commercial and industrial interests, the clergy, and the no-bility—these, not individuals, were the interests which must be represented. When these interests met together in Parliament to deliberate on matters of national policy with the nation's welfare foremost in their thoughts, it was the best system of government that could be devised. Burke saw no reason why he, as representa-tive from Bristol, could not also represent other places that had common concerns but no representative in Parliament. To insist on actual rather than virtual representation would destroy the de-liberate nature of Parliament and make the members mere delegates subject to all the evils of pressure politics. No longer would men of character and ability be attracted to careers in Parliament, but only hirelings willing to do someone else's bidding.[13]

While few today would agree with Burke's contention that the employer knows the interests of his employee best, we have not abandoned Burke's theories of representation altogether. In fact, what he feared has come to pass. We now have actual rather than virtual representation, the franchise has become almost universal, and the legislature has declined as a deliberative assembly. In its place, the pluralistic model of the modern industrial society has emerged. On the other hand, virtual representation—even less repre-sentative and certainly less responsible than Burke's Parliament—has become the dominant mode of interest articulation on the numerous boards, agencies, and committees of the modern bureau-cratic state. And pressure-group politics, which excludes the poor, blacks, youth, in other words the mass of the people, makes a mockery of democracy.

Contemporary attempts to put into practice the complex ideas of Burke and Rousseau indicate the false understanding and appli-cation of the modern liberal's approach to the subtleties of political philosophy. Such steps toward direct democracy as the direct pri-mary, the initiative, and the referendum have been unsuccessful attempts to translate Rousseau's concept of the general will.

[13] For a more detailed treatment see Samuel Beer, "The Representation of Interests in British Government," *The American Political Science Review,* 51, no. 3 (September 1957):635–45.

The conservative quest on behalf of the public welfare has been at best a rear guard action against the dominant liberal (utilitarian) emphasis of giving the people what they desire—provided their group organization is strong enough. The old laissez-faire confidence in the unseen hand seems still to prevail. There it is assumed, in an anti-Rousseau fashion, that the will of all is identical with the general will, that there is no public good but only the demands of the various organized and powerful groups.

CONCLUSIONS

There is no doubt that the conservative tradition has made some genuine contributions to political discourse. Anyone who has ever felt isolated, lonely, or alienated should appreciate the virtues of community. Indeed, the concept of community has dominated political thinking in various periods. It can be seen in Plato's *Republic,* where all the levels of society shared enough interests to be considered communal. The idea is strong in Rousseau, and in others who are not usually regarded as conservatives. Many socialists, for example, understand the necessity of communal life. The communes that are springing up today are a curious mixture of Rousseau's ruralism and Marxist socialism. Many who realize the dangers and frustrations of extreme individualism see an alternative in the conservative tradition.

Reactions against reason also occur periodically, often among the same people who are attracted to community. Of course, overemphasis on rationality has dangerous implications.[14] Relentless logic starting from inhumane premises can lead to genocide and the destruction of civilization. Especially in an age when science has provided the means for total world destruction, it is healthy to question the utilitarian calculus. Such questioning will generally lead to the third principle of conservatism, tradition. Some traditions—like that of love and concern for others—are worth preserving. Others—like war and oppression—are not. But in this, as in challenges to individualism and rationalism, one has the conservative tradition itself to fall back upon.

In spite of its contributions, the values of conservatism often come under attack. To many, the thought of holding onto the present

[14] For insight into an advocate of total reason, see Herman Kahn, *Thinking About the Unthinkable* (New York: Horizon Press, 1962).

when evils are so apparent becomes an evil itself. Conservatives are considered even more irrelevant than liberals in the task of improving the world. There is some truth in this charge, for conservatives, as we pointed out with respect to Rousseau, do frequently lose contact with the immediate reality and its problems. If liberalism is support for an order which is bad, conservatism too often is support for a previous order which was even worse. For example, Burke viewed the pragmatic wisdom of the politician as a major asset to a political system. Politicians dealing with concrete interests, working in a very practical fashion, were more likely to further the public good than theoretically oriented intellectuals and philosophers without a sense of politics. But, it would seem that this practicality is sometimes the worst thing for a system. In periods of crisis—like the one the United States is going through now in Southeast Asia and at home—it may be better to seek the man of theory who can make sense out of events than the practical man who lacks the long view.

In short, the major defect of the conservative tradition—and of the liberal tradition—is its failure to examine the power relationships in society to see who actually benefits from the high-sounding principles. Liberals spoke of freedom, but did not face the fact that only those with economic means benefited from the freedom; those without were enslaved by it. Conservatives speak of community, of people living together under common rules. It is a healthy vision, but the real question is, Whose rules do they live under? In this world, people generally live under rules established by the most powerful, since they are the only ones with the means to enforce their rules. Consequently, conservatism is used by those in power to gain acceptance of their decisions: the people are told they have an obligation to the community to obey them; they are told, the decision of the few is actually that of the many. This is why it is so hard for those who feel they must break the rules. They are viewed, not as disobeying the rules of a few, but the will of many. Conservatism, in short, serves the dominant group in a society all too well.

Liberalism, the ideology of the new order, will probably become more conservative as the new order becomes more firmly established. This is why *liberalism*, at the present time, is a *conservative* force.

11 Idealism and Materialism

NEARLY ALL THE writers discussed in the last two chapters were English or French. But during the same period, other traditions of political philosophy were emerging elsewhere, and these came to rival the French and the English schools. For the most part, the alternative traditions developed in Germany, which meant that they were built on a different philosophical system. The methodology behind German philosophy was much more difficult and abstract than the English system. For that reason, we must begin our discussion of the German philosophical tradition by examining its methodology.

It is necessary, first, to redefine certain terms. For example, in the German philosophical tradition, idealism is not the same as utopianism, nor does it mean ideal in the sense of not real or non-utilitarian. In the Germanic tradition, idealism refers to a belief in the primacy of ideas, spirit, and will in shaping man's existence. Similarly, materialism is not synonymous with the desire for material comforts and luxuries. It instead affirms the primacy of material, concrete things rather than ideals. Accordingly, a person who already possesses a reasonable amount of worldly goods and comforts is more likely to be an idealist, than someone living in abject poverty, who will probably be very conscious of his material environment.

The story of the relationship between idealism and materialism is the story of how Marxism—certainly one of the most complicated and powerful political philosophies ever to appear—originated. For this reason, we will be concerned here with the ideas of revolutionary socialism, the main tradition opposing liberalism and, to a lesser extent, conservatism.[1] We will start with Hegel, the idealist philosopher who influenced Marx in unique ways. Then we will turn to the two philosophical strains that developed from Hegel— one, primarily British, retained the idealist character of Hegelian thought and became essentially liberal; the other, associated with Karl Marx and his collaborator Friedrich Engels, changed idealism into materialism and became revolutionary. We will conclude by examining some key ideas of other Marxists, particularly V. I. Lenin.

HEGEL

Like most philosophers, Georg Wilhelm Friedrich von Hegel (1770–1831) was concerned with the nature of reality. A theological student in his youth, Hegel found religion's answers inadequate. He therefore devoted himself to developing a system that he believed would explain the true nature of reality.

The first task was to develop an approach to reality; this led Hegel to something called the dialectic. He focused on one specific thing in reality: change, observing that everything is in a process of change, that nothing is as it appears to be but is constantly becoming something other than what it seems to be. In some things this process of change is readily discernible—we are either growing up or we are in the process of dying, in fact we are reaching maturity and dying at the same time. In other objects, such as tables, rocks, and so forth, the process of change is much less apparent but no less real. Everything is subject to change; nothing is permanent. Therefore, the key to understanding the real world must lie in the process of change. Two assumptions are possible about this ever-changing world: that it is in a state of flux, chaos, and therefore meaningless and beyond comprehension; or, the opposite, that it is rational. Hegel takes the second approach (as we

[1] The material in this chapter reflects our indebtedness to the works of Herbert Marcuse and John Plamenatz.

all do to some extent): *the real is rational and the rational is real.* It follows, then, that reason which comprehends the process is more real than the substantive things that make it up. Hegel reveals his unbounded faith in reason in the following passage:

> The only Thought which Philosophy brings with it to the contemplation of History, is the simple conception of Reason; that Reason is the Sovereign of the World; that the history of the world, therefore, presents us with a rational process. . . . On the one hand, Reason is the *substance* of the Universe; viz., that by which and in which all reality has its being and subsistence. On the other hand, it is the *Infinite Energy* of the Universe; since Reason is not so powerless as to be incapable of producing anything but a mere ideal, a mere intention—having its place outside reality, nobody knows where. . . . It is the *infinite complex of things*, their entire Essence and Truth. It is its own material which it commits to its own Active Energy to work up. . . . It supplies its own nourishment, and is the object of its own operations. While it is exclusively its own basis of existence, and absolute final aim, it is also the energising power realizing this aim; developing it not only in the phenomena of the Natural, but also of the Spiritual Universe—the History of the World. That this "Idea" or "reason" is the *True*, the *Eternal*, the absolutely *powerful* essence; that it reveals itself in the World, and that in the World nothing else is revealed but this and its honour and glory—is the thesis which . . . has been proved in Philosophy, and is here regarded as demonstrated.[2]

This process which is real, Hegel calls the dialectic, a process by which truth is reached through the interpenetration and sublation of concepts. In other words, a person has an idea but that idea contains its own negation. The idea and its negation together produce a synthesis, which is closer to the truth than either the original idea or its negation but which, in turn, becomes its own thesis with its own negation. This is the dialectical process.

The most common illustration of the dialectical process revolves around the concept of being. Hegel maintains that the concept being is self-contradictory, in that if a thing has only being (no

[2] Georg W. Hegel, "Philosophy of History," in *Hegel: Selections*, ed. Jacob Loewenberg (New York: Scribner's, 1963), pp. 348–49.

other attribute) then it is nothing, which is nonbeing or the antithesis of the thesis, being. Hegel would even say that these two
concepts are identical or pass into one another, which introduces
the third concept—becoming, which reconciles the two concepts
and thus is their synthesis. This is an example of the operation of
the dialectic, albeit in a rather pure, abstract form.

Perhaps an illustration from nature would make this illusive concept clearer. Take the process of a seed becoming a flower. The
bud of the plant is the negation of the seed, the blossom is the
negation of the bud. However, a plant does not act on knowledge
or fulfill its potentiality on the basis of its own comprehending
power. A plant merely "endures the process of fulfillment pas-
sively." [3] Man, however, sees the bud as potentially the blossom.
Through his understanding of the reality of the process, he can
even direct and, to an extent, control its development, while the
objective world is blind and contingent. Our understanding enables us to see that everything (persons included) is essentially
different from what it could be if its potentialities were realized.
Finite things are negative. They never are what they can and ought
to be; they always exist in a state that does not fully express their
potentialities. The finite thing has as its essence this absolute unrest, this striving not to be what it is. It is never being or nothing
but always becoming; its reality is in its becoming, which is reason
making itself manifest. Thought that comprehends this process is
more real than its object.

Because of his commitment to the dialectical process Hegel saw
it operating in all things, and he often spoke of one thing negating
another when it would have been more precise to say that they
were related but different. The following are Hegelian triads (the
relationship between a thing, its opposite, and a new synthesis)
related to politics.

Hegel's concept of social class, for instance, might well be considered a vertical rather than a horizontal concept. He believed that
everyone engaged in agricultural vocations belonged to one class
that included both the wealthy landowner and the poor farm
laborer. The antithetical category was the industrial class, which
included both the factory owner and the employee. This division
parallels a rural-urban division in society, and the dialectical con-

---

[3] Herbert Marcuse, *Reason and Revolution: Hegel and the Rise of Social Theory*,
2d ed. (New York: Humanities Press, 1963), pp. 64–65.

frontation between the two groups is obvious. The third class, the higher more noble one, is the universal class. Composed of the bureaucrats and civil servants, its function is to maintain order, do justice, and look after the public interest—which is why it is called the universal class.

Hegel's division of government also reflects his dialectic. Like the English and French, he divided government into three branches— the legislative, the executive (primarily the state bureaucracies but the judiciary as well), and the sovereignty. The function of the legislative branch was to determine the universal will; the executive's function was to apply the universal will in particular cases; and the function of sovereignty, vested in the monarchy, was to express the unity of the state—one is tempted to say, safeguard the constitution and integrity of the state. Here, too, the synthesis transcends and universalizes the other two.

A third example refers to the greatest triad of them all—the family, civil society, and the state. Except for Hegel's abstract style, his discussion of this is reminiscent of Aristotle. Hegel's observations on the family are rather commonplace, reflecting the solid middle-class conventions of his day. But his comments on the family function of developing a moral will, a conscience in its children, rise above the commonplace. Children are punished because they need to be made moral, not just because they have done wrong. While they cannot reason, they must, nevertheless, be taught to act reasonably. A child's feeling of inferiority and immaturity is not bad, for it is temporary and encourages him to grow up and be accepted as an adult. If children are reasoned with when they are incapable of reasoning, are treated as adults when they are still children, it will only prolong their childhood. The family's chief concern is moral, but moral within a limited sphere and only partaking of the absolute will of reason, which is the ultimate source of all morality and reality itself, to a small extent.

Hegel's writing on the nature of civil society is difficult for us to understand, partly because we generally view society as the larger whole, synonymous with community itself, and the state and government as particular aspects of society's many functions. Hegel reverses this: society is less than the state—less moral, less universal, and less rational. All the same, civil society performs many functions that we usually consider state functions. For Hegel, civil society is the whole system of economic and political relations concerned with satisfying individual needs. It follows, therefore, that law, courts, police, and the whole administrative bureaucracy are as much organs of the civil society as the state. When they are concerned with reconciling and promoting private or personal interests, they are organs of civil society; when they serve to unite a society in service to its highest rational order, they are agencies of the state. What then is the state?

> The state is the actuality of the ethical Idea. It is ethical mind *qua* the substantial will manifest and revealed to itself, knowing and thinking itself, accomplishing what it knows and in so far as it knows it. The state exists immediately in custom, mediately in individual self-consciousness, knowledge, and activity, while self-consciousness in virtue of its sentiment towards the state finds in the state, as its essence and the end and product of its activity, its substantive freedom. . . .
>
> The state in and by itself is the ethical whole, the actualization of freedom; and it is an absolute end of reason that freedom should be actual. The state is mind on earth and consciously realizing itself there. . . .
>
> The march of God in the world, that is what the state is. The basis of the state is the power of reason actualizing itself as will. In considering the Idea of the state, we must not have our eyes on particular states or on particular institutions. Instead we must consider the Idea, this actual God, by itself. On some principle or Other, any state may be shown to be bad, this or that defect may be found in it. . . . But since it is easier to find defects than to understand the affirmative we may readily fall into the mistake of looking at isolated aspects of the state and so forgetting its inward organic life. The state is no ideal work of art; it stands on earth and so in the sphere of caprice, chance, and error, and bad behaviour may disfigure it in many respects. But the ugliest of men, or a criminal, or an invalid, or a cripple, is still always a living man. The affirmative, life, subsists despite his defects, and it is this affirmative factor which is our theme here.[4]

[4] T. M. Knox, trans., *Hegel's Philosophy of Right* (Oxford: Oxford University Press, 1967), pp. 155, 156, 279.

It is through the state that the absolute spirit, universal reason, makes itself manifest to man. We mentioned at the beginning of this discussion that, for Hegel, the sole purpose of life was to make reason, the true reality, actual. What then is the role of man? It is, Hegel believes, to join his will to the will of the state, which is the most rational, the most universal, and the most moral. This, however, does not make Hegel a totalitarian, for it is only to the ideal state—that state in which the absolute spirit has made itself completely manifest—that man owes absolute obedience. Such a state, by definition, would be completely rational, completely just, and completely moral. In such a state, and only in such a state, would man find true freedom.

Hegel's definition of freedom is closer to the notions of Rousseau than to the individualism of liberalism. Freedom cannot exist in a situation where each man follows his own interests. Extreme individualism leads to irrationality. Freedom only evolves when people act with reason. Since the state is the embodiment of reason, it follows that true freedom comes about only through the state.

Up to this point, our discussion has been highly abstract and undoubtedly difficult to follow. Perhaps demonstrating the way Hegel applied his dialectical reasoning to history will make things clearer. Not only did Hegel see the dialectic as the operation of the logical here and now, he also believed that history reveals a grand dialectical pattern. He viewed the process of history as the means by which reason revealed itself to the world. It is a history of progress as man moves from superstition and slavery to rational comprehension and control over his environment and over himself, from slavery to freedom.[5] But, man cannot be more rational than the reason of his epoch, and reason advances through the progress of mankind. Ethical life must be communal. This is what Hegel means when he speaks of the state as the embodiment of reason and individuals as its accidents.

If the whole of history is not mere happenstance, but the unfolding of a rational plan, of the absolute spirit, then all that occurs must be a part of that plan and contain its rational elements.

It is the duty of every man to bring his life into accord with the

[5] It should be noted that while Hegel's anti-individualism placed him in the conservative tradition, his concept of progress in history is liberal. In fact, Hegel is difficult to classify in terms of liberal and conservative traditions.

spirit of the age; all is measured in terms of the spirit of the age. In the Middle Ages the saint was the ideal man, and while all could not be saints, all could serve the absolute in terms of their own station in life. But now the absolute spirit is manifest in the nation-state, the statesman replaces the saint as the ideal man, and patriotism replaces religiosity as the highest virtue.

One may not like what Hegel has to say. Philosophy, however, is not an apology for belief but a search for truth. His ideas should provide an insight into reality and new perspectives, so that we can see things that were not previously visible. Taking Hegel's writings metaphorically, rather than literally, their accuracy, novelty, and insight is undeniable. For example, the primacy of the state in the modern epoch is all too obvious. To a larger extent than we may wish, the state determines whether we shall live or die, prosper or suffer, be free or enslaved. While it may be argued that Jefferson's agricultural society is preferable to our modern technological state, that alternative has been foreclosed. History restricts our options; we can only choose from the choices history has left open to us. In Hegel's words, it is the "history of the world which is the world's court of judgment." [6]

In spite of his complexity, or perhaps because of it, Hegel's impact on later writers has been staggering. For over a century, it was impossible to be a philosopher in Germany without dealing with the Hegelian thought system. That system has had two major influences, and the contrast between them suggests the paradoxical nature of the Hegelian legacy. There are both reactionary and revolutionary strains in Hegel's thought, and writers influenced by him have tended to be one or the other.

Hegel's emphasis on the state as the very definition of reason has reactionary implications if applied to the states that existed in his day. For example, some Hegelians, and Hegel himself in his later life, thought that the early nineteenth-century Prussian state fitted the Hegelian definition. Since it was the ultimate in reason, since freedom was only possible within it, state supremacy could be asserted. Therefore, many Hegelians associated themselves with the Prussian nobility and became apologists for a strong state. Their political ideas shifted far to the right as they defined Prussia as the only rational state; everything else was attacked—England,

[6] Georg W. Hegel, "Philosophy of Law," in *Hegel: Selections*, ed. Jacob Loewenberg (New York: Scribner's, 1963), p. 468.

France, socialists, Jews, anything perceived as a threat to the glory of the Prussian state. If the notion sounds familiar, it is because many of Hitler's theorists were attracted by this aspect of Hegelian thought.

But those who derived reactionary ideas from Hegel were really misreading him. They focused only on the end of the dialectical process, the synthesis, ignoring how it occurred. They appreciated the substance of Hegel's work, the conclusions he came to, but not the method that produced them. Those who emphasize the Hegelian process, on the other hand, end up with quite revolutionary ideas. This is the importance of the dialectic, and the reason we tried to explain it. Dialectical reasoning is subversive; it constantly leads to an undermining of what exists. If everything is in a process of change, then nothing is permanent—including all the values conservatives hold dear, like love of country and state. One could easily get the impression from Hegel that all was in a state of flux, that all social reality, including the newly emerging capitalism, would eventually pass on to a newer form. The dialectic is important because it is a way of looking at reality that can lead to revolutionary conclusions. And before long, some of Hegel's students began to apply his ideas to society with just that result.

Those who leaned toward revolution were called "left Hegelians." They formed tight little circles in various German cities, where they developed their ideas further. Soon it became apparent that there were two different schools of thought within the left Hegelian camp: both stressed process rather than substance, but they disagreed about the nature of the process.

One group believed in the idealistic aspects of Hegelian thought. Since ideas contained their own opposites within them, new ideas would constantly be appearing. These new ideas had revolutionary implications, since they were always undermining the old ideas. The best-known left Hegelian idealists, Bruno Bauer and Max Stirner, are familiar because they were so heavily criticized by another Hegelian, Karl Marx. But instead of dealing with the ideas of Bauer and Stirner, which are not that historically important, we shall examine the development of idealism in Britain, for it is closer to the American experience. First, however, we must go back to the other group of left Hegelians.

Some of Hegel's followers gradually came to the conclusion that the mere study of ideas was not enough. Where, after all do ideas come from? Granted that ideas are constantly changing, but what makes them change? Questions like these bothered German philosopher Ludwig Feuerbach, who questioned the relevance of a purely idealist approach in a theological treatise, *The Essence of Christianity* (1841). Others, like Karl Marx and Friedrich Engels, felt that Feuerbach was headed in the right direction, but had not gone far enough. They began to view the origin of ideas in material relationships, an approach that led in time to Marxism. The contrast between British idealism and Marxist materialism is indicative of the many and diverse philosophical strains that started with Hegel.

BRITISH IDEALISM

Idealism in England was less nationalistic and more concerned with individual self-realization. In short, it became associated with the liberal tradition. Although the name seems to imply a dependence on Hegel, the British idealists actually owe more to another German philosopher, quite different from Hegel, Immanuel Kant (1724–1804). In the manner of Plato, Kant returned to a distinction between the world of appearances, which he called *phenomena,* and the real world, *noumena.*

Kant maintains that we gain knowledge in three ways—through the senses, through the intellect, and through the moral will. Knowledge gained through the senses and intellect is knowledge of the world of appearances or phenomena. As creatures of desire, we belong to the phenomenal world; this is our empirical self. But man, and man alone, can have contact with the real world through the exercise of his moral will; this is our moral self, our transcendental self, our truly human self. This is the self that is free. We are all conscious of the conflict between "what is" and "what ought to be." It is by exercising our moral will, and acting in accordance with it, that we are free. For example, the sex drive in men and animals is a reflection of the empirical self and can be investigated empirically; but love, while no less real, is brought into being by an act of will and thus cannot be verified empirically.

In the early years of the twentieth century, renewed interest in idealism appeared in Britain. Prominent in this movement were Thomas Hill Green, Francis H. Bradley, and Bernard Bosanquet. In accord with Kant, these British idealists recognized that freedom consists in the pursuit of the good will, not just the absence of restraint, and human freedom is achieved, not by alienating our natural impulses, but in uniting them with a higher goal, self-perfection. Self-realization is the object of the moral will.

However, self-perfection can never be achieved in isolation. How far an individual progresses toward his potential is closely related to the level of civilization in which he lives. Someone born in the ghetto, for example, has less opportunity for self-realization than someone born in the suburbs. The idealists would speak, and properly so, of deprived persons as being less free.

While not as committed to the state as Hegel, the British idealists nevertheless regard it as a necessary and positive force for human freedom. The state is not created by the general will, as Rousseau believed, but the reverse: the state creates the general will. It teaches us what we ought to prefer. The basis of the state is neither consent (that is, contract), nor the fear of force, but will—the recognition that the state embodies the highest reason and serves the common good. Only the state can insure collective well-being as a precondition of individual freedom and responsibility.

Rights, including property rights, are desirable as security for individual personal development. But, in addition, they must always be justified as consonant with the public good.

This form of idealistic philosophy represents an attempt to provide a new foundation for contemporary liberalism. Its major advantage is that it is not anchored in egotistical self-interest based on a mechanistic concept of the state as the arbitrator of private interests and desires, in the manner of Bentham and the utilitarian liberals. Instead, it tries to show that politics and the state ought to be concerned with the public good. In effect, the British idealists attached a condition to the Hegelian view of the state as the embodiment of reason. They believed that freedom can only be realized through the state when the public good is also realized through the state. Thus, British idealism provides the philosophical justification for the welfare state; which is seen as a positive force that removes obstacles to the public good, like ignorance, illness, and discrimination. Only then is individual self-realization possible.

British idealism thus brings Hegel and Kant into twentieth-century liberalism. But we observed earlier that perhaps liberalism, including the idealist version, is an anachronism. Those who say it is often base their contention on Marxism, our next topic.

MARXISM

If Hegel is correct that history may be understood as a series of dialectical clashes between a thesis and its antithesis, then what we are witnessing today is the resolution on the world stage of the clash between idealism and its antithesis, materialism. The belief that material forces, rather than ideas, determine man's destiny has existed since ancient times; but Marxism, a materialist philosophy conceived in reaction to the ills of the expanding industrial and technological order, did not appear until the middle of the nineteenth century. This new philosophy inspired both fear and hope among many. The final synthesis of the dialectic between idealism and Marxism has not yet been resolved.

Karl Marx (1818–1883) is certainly Hegel's best-known student. Many contend that he far surpasses his master. In terms of immediate political effect, this is certainly true. But there is little question that the philosophical depth Marxism possesses is due to the Hegelian influence.

Marxist theory revolves around the concept of dialectical materialism, which has two intimately related aspects: the dynamic or historical dialectic (differing from Hegel in that the root cause is material, not idea) and the static aspect. In the latter, the structure of society during any historical epoch is analyzed in terms of its relation to its material substructure.

Marx explains dialectical materialism most clearly in his Preface to *A Contribution to the Critique of Political Economy*. The following paragraph from the work describes the static relationships that exist between the economic substructure of society and its superstructure:

> My investigation led to the result that legal relations as well as forms of state are to be grasped neither from themselves nor from the so-called general development of the human mind, but rather have their roots in the material conditions of life, . . .
> In the social production of their life, men enter into definite relations that are indispensable and independent of their will, relations of production which correspond to a definite stage of

development of their material productive forces. The sum total of these relations of production constitutes the economic structure of society, the real foundation, on which rises a legal and political superstructure and to which correspond definite forms of social consciousness. The mode of production of material life conditions the social, political and intellectual life processes in general. It is not the consciousness of men that determines their being, but, on the contrary, their social being that determines their consciousness.[7]

The following diagram illustrates this aspect of Marx's dialectic. While in theory such a structure exists in any historical epoch, it is with capitalism, the dominant system of his day, that Marx is most concerned.

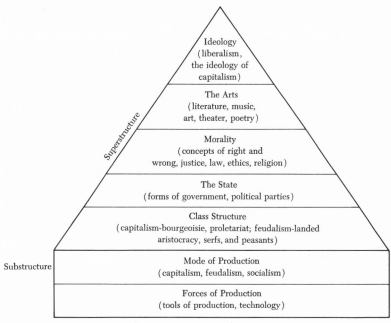

Superstructure

Ideology
(liberalism,
the ideology of
capitalism)

The Arts
(literature, music,
art, theater, poetry)

Morality
(concepts of right and
wrong, justice, law, ethics, religion)

The State
(forms of government, political parties)

Class Structure
(capitalism-bourgeoisie, proletariat; feudalism-landed
aristocracy, serfs, and peasants)

Substructure

Mode of Production
(capitalism, feudalism, socialism)

Forces of Production
(tools of production, technology)

THE STRUCTURE OF SOCIETY

It is the substructure which is all-important in Marxist thought. It determines the general (not, it should be noted, the specific)

[7] Karl Marx, Preface to *A Contribution to the Critique of Political Economy*, in *Karl Marx and Frederick Engels: Selected Works in One Volume* (New York: International Publishers, 1968), p. 182.

character of the social, political, and spiritual processes of life. This means that before any fundamental change can occur in society, the substructure of that society must first be changed. Moreover, the initial changes in the superstructure are going to be relatively insignificant.

In his analysis of substructure, Marx included both the "mode of production" and the "forces" or tools of production. The distinction between the two is not very clear, however. Sometimes he focuses almost exclusively on technological advance, a sophistication of the forces of production. More frequently, he emphasizes the manner in which the production forces are organized, the mode of production, whether capitalism, feudalism, or socialism. We will examine the relationship of the substructure to the superstructure, considering, in turn, the various parts in the "Structure of Society" chart.

Marx contends that throughout history there have always been two classes—the ruling class and the ruled class. The ruling class controls the mode of production; all others belong to the ruled class. In capitalism, the ruling class is the bourgeoisie, those who own the capital, and the ruled class is the unpropertied class, the proletariat. In feudal times, the ruling class was comprised of landowners. Despite the significance of class structure in his analysis, Marx does not develop his theories very far. Concepts like objective class and subjective class, false class consciousness, and the necessity to develop true class consciousness are introduced but not elaborated.

Marx's view of the state is particularly important. Unless we recognize his limited construction of the notion of state, we are likely to misunderstand him. Marx defines the state as an instrument of the ruling class; its function is to utilize its monopoly of legitimate power to maintain the ruling class in power, that is, in control of the mode of production. This explains the special concern of the state and its agencies—the police and the courts—for the protection of property in a capitalistic society. Other institutions, like parliaments and political parties, are tolerated in capitalistic society as long as they do not threaten to alter the mode of production. But any party that advocates changing the production system, the only kind of change that is meaningful, will be viciously attacked, even outlawed.

Similarly, religion, codes of conduct, and the arts reflect and help to maintain the existing production system. For example, Marx today might well call television the "opiate of the people," as he once did religion. Thus, there is bourgeois art, literature, and morals, and proletarian art, literature, and morals.

At the pinnacle of the pyramid is ideology. This term, which Marx used with derision, refers to the overarching ideal that serves as the ultimate rationalization of the ruling class. According to Marx, liberalism has no external validity but only serves the class interest of the bourgeoisie. Marxism, on the other hand, is not an ideology because it is scientific, rather than a normative myth designed to aid the ruling class exploit the ruled.

In the Preface to *A Contribution to the Critique of Political Economy,* Marx gives a succinct description of dialectical materialism as a historical process that will inevitably lead to the downfall of capitalism by revolutionary means and the emergence of communism.

At a certain stage of their development, the material productive forces of society come in conflict with the existing relations of production, or—what is but a legal expression for the same thing—with the property relations within which they have been at work hitherto. From forms of development of the productive forces these relations turn into their fetters. Then begins an epoch of social revolution. With the change of the economic foundation the entire immense superstructure is more or less rapidly transformed. . . . a distinction should always be made between the material transformation of the economic conditions of production, which can be determined with the precision of natural science, and the legal, political, religious, aesthetic or philosophic—in short, ideological forms in which men become conscious of this conflict and fight it out. Just as our opinion of an individual is not based on what he thinks of himself, so can we not judge of such a period of transformation by its own consciousness; on the contrary, this consciousness must be explained rather from the contradictions of material life, from the existing conflict between the social productive forces and the relations of production. No social order ever perishes before all the productive forces for which there is room in it have developed; and new, higher relations of production never appear before the material conditions of their existence have matured in the womb of the old society itself. Therefore mankind always sets itself only such tasks as it can solve; since, looking at the matter more closely, it will always be found that the task itself arises only when the material conditions for its solution already exist or are at least in the process of formation.[8]

The following diagram illustrates the process of dialectical materialism from feudalism through capitalism to the socialist revolution, to the final and lasting thesis, communism. ("Final" here does not mean an end to conflict and flux, but a final social form.)

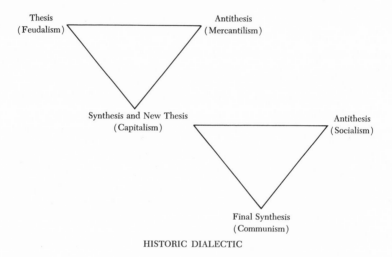

Thesis (Feudalism)　　　　Antithesis (Mercantilism)

Synthesis and New Thesis (Capitalism)　　　　Antithesis (Socialism)

Final Synthesis (Communism)

HISTORIC DIALECTIC

This theory of the dialectical movement of history and revolution is what Marx is generally remembered for—and feared and worshipped for. His assertion that the class division and the gulf between the classes will become deeper and more antagonistic as capitalism becomes more mature is equally familiar. The time will eventually come, Marx declared in the *Manifesto*, when "The proletarians have nothing to lose but their chains. They have a world to win. WORKING MEN OF ALL COUNTRIES, UNITE!" [9]

However, socialism is not communism. Socialism, according to

[8] Ibid., pp. 182–83.

[9] Karl Marx and Friedrich Engels, "Manifesto of the Communist Party," in Ibid., p. 63.

Marx, is a temporary phase in which the state still exists but is for the first time an instrument in the hands of the majority, that is, the proletariat. This transitional period is characterized by the dictatorship of the proletariat.

> . . . no credit is due to me for discovering the existence of classes in modern society, nor yet the struggle between them. . . . What I did that was new was to prove: (1) that the *existence of classes* is only bound up with *particular, historic phases* in the development of production; (2) that the class struggle necessarily leads to the *dictatorship of the proletariat;* (3) that this dictatorship itself only constitutes the transition to the *abolition of all classes* and to a *classless society.*[10]

And in the following passage, Engels succinctly describes a Communist order:

> *The proletariat seizes the State power, and transforms the means of production in the first instance into State property.* But in doing this, it puts an end to itself as the proletariat, it puts an end to all class differences and class antagonisms, it puts an end also to the State as the State. Former society, moving in class antagonisms, had need of the State. . . . (Now) The interference of State power in social relations becomes superfluous in one sphere after another, and then ceases of itself. The government of persons is replaced by the administration of things and the direction of the process of production. The State is not "abolished," *it withers away.*[11]

Marx and Engels did not describe the new society in detail because they felt that would be unscientific. Since the material conditions of socialism had not been produced, no one could guess what the new society would look like. To try to describe it would be an un-Marxist thing to do; the time for such description had not yet arrived. Nonetheless, they make it clear that communism will bring forth a new man, an individual who for the first time in history will be free—free from oppressive class tyranny and subjugation

---

[10] Karl Marx, "Letter of Georg Wydemeyer," March 5, 1852, trans. Dona Torr, *Selected Correspondence of Marx and Engels 1846–1895* (New York: International Publishers, 1942), p. 57. Italics in original.

[11] Friedrich Engels, "Anti-Duhring," in A *Handbook of Marxism*, ed. Emile Burns (New York: Random House, 1935), pp. 295–96. Italics in original.

of the state. He will be free to realize his true and good human nature.

We can do no better than to end our discussion of Marxist theory with Marx's remark: "The Philosophers have only *interpreted* the world, in various ways; the point, however, is to *change* it." [12] And it is to Lenin that we must turn when the emphasis shifts to change.[13]

More than any other figure in history, Lenin combined the roles of theorist and activist. The sole preoccupation of this serious student of Marx was to apply his theories to the practical problems of revolution and government. Lenin's contributions to Marxist thought were so great that the whole body of theory is now accurately called Marxism-Leninism.

One of Lenin's major contributions was to the theory of revolution. Troubled by Marx's description of spontaneous revolution growing out of the dialectical process of history, Lenin conceived the notion of the Communist party as the vanguard of the revolutionary movement. It was to be a dedicated, disciplined party, flexible in tactics but anchored in theory. Thus the Bolshevik party was born—a party small in numbers, disavowing parliamentarianism as a bourgeois trap to snare the ignorant worker and peasant, but dedicated to seizing power in the name of the proletariat when objective social conditions warrant it. From the concept of the party as the vanguard of the revolution, Lenin went on (in *State and Revolution*) to expand Marx's ideas on the dictatorship of the proletariat that was to hold power during the extended period of socialist transition between capitalism and communism.

Lenin's other major contribution to Marxist theory appears in his *Imperialism, the Highest Stage of Capitalism* (1916). In this work, Lenin sets out to prove that capitalism leads to imperialism in its continuing search for more raw materials, which in turn leads to conflict and war between the capitalistic nations. But, more significantly, he maintained that class divisions exist not only within states, but also between states. Some nations, with less than 10 percent of the world's population, can be considered bourgeois states, while the other underdeveloped countries are proletarian states. Lenin felt that early twentieth-century Russia was a prole-

[12] Karl Marx, "Theses on Feuerbach," XI, trans. Foreign Languages Publishing House, Moscow, in Feuer, ed., *Marx and Engels: Basic Writings,* p. 245.

[13] Even the title of his most significant monograph, *What Is to Be Done?* (1902), expresses this activist concern.

tarian country that experienced the contradictions of capitalism so strongly that revolution was a real possibility. At the same time, he foreshadowed later developments in Asia, Africa, and Latin America.

CONCLUSIONS

It is not coincidental that most Americans find Marx totally simplistic and easy to refute, while people who live in socialist countries see capitalist ideas as contradictory and doomed to fail. Because much of the world is engaged in a struggle between liberalism and Marxism, people who live in that world become part of the struggle, whether they want to or not. Soon it is impossible to tell whether one's evaluations of liberalism and Marxism are really objective or are a subjective phenomenon growing out of world conditions. For this reason, we shall not go into the positive and negative aspects of Marxism but simply note its importance.

Marx's writings have been so influential in the development of our ideas about society that we are devoting the next chapter to a closer analysis. Suffice it to say that anyone who relates economic conditions to social phenomena—as the American historian Charles Beard did in his book *An Economic Interpretation of the Constitution*—will be operating under the spell of a principal Marxist hypothesis. And since economic conditions obviously play a major role in history, Marx made a major intellectual contribution by emphasizing them.

Marxism has had a major impact on the practice as well as the theory of politics. To a greater and greater extent, the whole phenomenon of revolution has become a Marxist phenomenon. Countries trying to free themselves from the economy of the United States find that only with socialism can they achieve this. Thus, they increasingly turn to Marxism for answers to their dilemmas. Fidel Castro, for example, went through many stages in his political development before concluding that Cuba needed socialism to achieve a true revolution. In many other countries, the same process is being followed. Obviously there is something powerful in Marxism, something which speaks to people in many parts of the world. The appeal of Marxism is not only that it is a revolutionary doctrine directed to oppressed people, but also that it contains the possibility of realizing a revolution. It suggests the inevitability of a new order, and to those opposed to the old order, this is a meaningful message.

To those, on the other hand, who are satisfied with the status quo, Marxism is regarded as a major threat. Intellectually, this means showing that there are alternatives to the socialist approach to change. Thus, one American foreign policy official wrote a book on economic development, subtitled A Non-Communist Manifesto.[14] Practically, this means the creation of a foreign policy that can shape the revolutionary forces in the world into non-Communist developments. Seldom in the history of the world has ideological agitation been so closely intertwined with the realities of world politics.

[14] W. W. Rostow, The Stages of Economic Growth: A Non-Communist Manifesto (Cambridge: Cambridge University Press, 1960).

IV CONTEMPORARY ANALYSES OF POLITICS

THE TRADITIONS DISCUSSED in the previous section have not come to an end. All ages have their political philosophies, and we will discuss some that have been particularly influential in the modern world. The modern theories may not be as grandiose as some of the earlier ones, but then brilliant political thinking does not occur every century, only at certain crucial points in history. And if the material talked about here does not seem like philosophy, that is the nature of contemporary political theory. Nonetheless, every student of politics needs to find an identity in the present political theories to help him understand and, perhaps, even change the world.

12 The Anti-Marxist Reaction

MARX'S STATURE AS a social thinker can be measured not only by his ideas, but also by the prodigious efforts others have made to refute them. In some ways, the entire history of twentieth-century political thought can be seen as the struggle between those who wanted to save Marx and those who wanted to bury him. Even areas which seem remote from Marxist questions, like the behavioral revolution in social science, are part of the anti-Marxist reaction. For example, studies that show which percentage of which sociological category votes for which candidate can be regarded as an affirmation of the electoral process, designed to refute Marx's allegations that Western democracies do not allow the least powerful elements a voice in government. In other words, a basic motive for studying voting patterns in Western societies is to disprove a Marxist hypothesis.

Similarly, some concepts in social science belong to the anti-Marxist reaction. Sociologists prefer to speak of social stratification rather than class because of the Marxist connotation of class. Even the *Encyclopedia of the Social Sciences,* supposedly the most up-to-date summary of important concepts in the social sciences, omits an entry under class, instructing the reader to "See Social Stratification." Though a negative tribute to Marx's role in the history of social science, it is a tribute nonetheless.

This chapter will follow the development of various ideas and concepts that were advanced to refute some of Marx's basic propositions. There are two general approaches; one challenges Marx's methods, the other takes issue with the substance of his work. Since, in many cases, the same people used both arguments, some repetition of names is bound to occur in the following discussion. But the basic distinction between substance and method is helpful in unraveling the argument of Marx's critics.

MARXIST METHODOLOGY

Marx's views of method are most accessible in his commentary on other writers. Like most other political thinkers, Karl Marx began by criticizing other political writers. He was extremely distressed by the vacuity of his contemporaries; he felt they were asking the wrong questions in the wrong ways. But Marx found a kindred spirit in Friedrich Engels, and together they wrote *The German Ideology*. It is in this work that Marx's most significant statement on problems of methodology appears.

The political thinkers of Marx's time were followers of Hegel in one way or another. Marx felt that anyone who was basically attuned to "pure," "logical," or "metaphysical" categories was missing the real world, no matter what his Hegelian orientation. One school of Hegelian thought, represented by Ludwig Feuerbach, held that the body politic could be changed if men learned how to change their consciousness—if they could remove parochial blinders on their own minds, by opening themselves to many cultures and ideas, and rise to a new consciousness. Marx's scathing attack upon this point of view indicates the first premise of his methodology:

> The ideas of the ruling class are in every epoch the ruling ideas: i.e., the class which is the ruling material force of society is at the same time its ruling intellectual force. The class which has the means of material production at its disposal, has control at the same time over the means of mental production, so that thereby, generally speaking, the ideas of those who lack the means of mental production are subject to it. The ruling ideas are nothing more than the ideal expression of the dominant material relationships grasped as ideas. . . .[1]

[1] Karl Marx and Friedrich Engels, *The German Ideology* (New York: International Publishers, 1947), p. 39.

It was no surprise to Marx and Engels that the Young Hegelians' ideas eventually became conservative and supportive of the status quo. They were middle-class people, so their ideas would be middle class. Of course, Marx and Engels were also middle class. Engels, in fact, inherited enough money from his father's business to support his intellectual activity. But Marx and Engels regarded the connection between material relationships and intellectual ideas as more of a tendency than a law. Other things being equal, a political theorist would reflect his class position. But by being aware of the problem, a political theorist could avoid automatic identification. He must be a partisan; he must identify himself with the proletariat struggle and not hide behind any neutrality or objectivity because such characteristics were actually an expression of commitment to the bourgeoisie. Truth emerges by adopting the viewpoint of a revolutionary class and seeing it fulfilled as a revolutionary force.

THE ATTACK ON MARX'S METHOD

The first significant attack on Marxist methodology comes at this point. In developing a world view opposed to the Marxist one, the importance of objectivity and the ultimate bias of partisanship had to be reasserted. This is clear in the works of Max Weber and another German social theorist Karl Mannheim (1893–1947).

Marx had claimed the mantle of science. He repeatedly emphasized that his methodology would result in empirical findings about the real world, which would constitute science because they were true. Max Weber had another conception of science. For him, ideas were not the product of economic relationships but were independent phenomena. Ideas can occur at strange times, "when smoking a cigar on the sofa," or "taking a walk on a slowly ascending street." [2] But regardless of the circumstances, scientific ideas have certain things in common. For one thing, the scientist is specialized: "A really definitive and good accomplishment is today always a specialized accomplishment." [3] Furthermore, science is constantly relative:

[2] Max Weber, "Science as a Vocation," in *From Max Weber: Essays in Sociology*, eds. Hans Gerth and C. Wright Mills (New York: Oxford University Press, 1958), p. 136.

[3] Ibid., p. 135.

In science each of us knows that what he has accomplished will be antiquated in ten, twenty, fifty years. That is the fate to which science is subjected; it is the very *meaning* of *scientific* work, . . . Every scientific "fulfillment" raises new questions; it *asks* to be surpassed and outdated. Whoever wishes to serve science has to resign himself to this fact.[4]

Finally, science is not a glorious activity, but slow and reasonable. Weber noted that in his time (just as in ours) there were those, "especially among youth," who advocated "personality" and "personal experience" as a path to understanding.[5] Such introspection, however, is not science; science is objective rather than subjective, and dispassionate rather than passionate.

The disagreements between Weber and Marx, then, begin at the beginning, with different conceptions of scientific activity. Marx, a committed generalist, viewed science accordingly. He believed that by identifying with a revolutionary cause and studying society as a whole, one could gain insights into political processes. Weber, on the other hand, maintained that scientific insight was the product of specialization and detachment. To him, the essential characteristic of scientific activity was its freedom from values.

To paraphrase the title of one of Weber's essays, "Objectivity" should be a basic goal of "social science and social policy." German society after the turn of the century was characterized by extensive political polemic. Marxists were calling other Marxists "reactionary," while right-wing groups (which later became powerful in the Hitler movement) dismissed them both as traitors. Polemic was so pervasive that, according to Weber, reason was being sacrificed. Political debate assumed a religious quality, the conflict between totally divergent world views. In such an atmosphere, each system of thought closed in on itself, changing only in self-defense, never critically examining the world beyond. To get around this situation, Weber suggested shedding dogmatism for the pursuit of a value-free science.

There is and always will be—and this is the reason that it concerns us—an unbridgeable distinction among (1) those arguments which appeal to our capacity to become enthusiastic

---

[4] Ibid., p. 138.
[5] Ibid., pp. 137, 143.

about and our feeling for concrete practical aims or cultural forms and values, (2) those arguments in which once it is a question of the validity of ethical norms, the appeal is directed to our conscience, and finally (3) those arguments which appeal to our capacity and need for *analytically ordering* empirical reality in a manner which lays claim to *validity* as empirical truth.[6]

Weber did not say that all values should be dismissed, that the social scientist should avoid judgments on public issues. He only suggested that such judgments not be accepted as science. Although science can help evaluate different types of value judgments, it cannot prove the truth or falsity of any particular series of judgments. Weber was obviously thinking about Marx when he declared: "An empirical science cannot tell anyone what he *should* do—but rather what he *can* do—and under certain circumstances—what he wishes to do." [7]

This objectivity has many consequences. Weber argues that politics is out of place in the classroom: ". . . the true teacher will beware of imposing from the platform any political position upon the student, whether it is expressed or suggested. 'To let the facts speak for themselves' is the most unfair way of putting over a political position to the student." [8] Again, Weber's attitude was influenced by the political atmosphere in Germany, where students were known to harass professors whose political opinions they disliked. Besides, German professors were more authoritarian than their American counterparts. The German lecture hall was so imposing that the professor seemed more like a god than an ordinary instructor. Maintaining neutrality and avoiding partisanship, then, were ways of calling a truce to vituperative political debates.

Karl Mannheim's methodology took up where Weber's left off.[9] He began by noting how much of what was sociological could be characterized as "ideological." Ideology has to do with being par-

---

[6] Max Weber, " 'Objectivity' in Social Science and Social Policy," in Weber, *The Methodology of the Social Sciences,* trans. Shils and Finch (New York: Free Press, 1949), p. 58.

[7] Ibid., p. 54.

[8] Weber, "Science as a Vocation," p. 146.

[9] This discussion is based upon Mannheim's book, *Ideology and Utopia: An Introduction to the Sociology of Knowledge* (New York: Harvest Books, n.d.).

tisan; a priori distrust of an opponent's point of view indicates an ideological mentality. Thus Marxism is an ideology because Marxists are so loathe to accept the arguments of bourgeois thinkers. But Marxism does not have a monopoly on the ideological mentality: there is also bureaucratic conservatism, historical conservatism, liberal-democratic bourgeois thought, and fascism.

All these ideologies are partisan, designed to promote specific programs and points of view. But to do so, they must explain reality. Events that seem to contradict the world view are explained by resorting to a theory of false consciousness. An example of this is provided by Marxism. Marx had predicted that workers would reject the capitalistic state. When presented with evidence that workers regularly vote for candidates who uphold capitalism, sometimes vehemently, the Marxist replies that a false consciousness has been forced upon the workers so that they are unaware of their true class interests. In this way, the original theory is saved.

Mannheim was critical of false consciousness arguments because he felt that they substituted unprovable mythology for provable fact. As such, it is an absolutist, and inherently unscientific, way of thinking. In an interesting paradox, Mannheim points out that absolutist ways of thinking are very limited: "Only when we are thoroughly aware of the limited scope of every point of view are we on the road to the sought-for comprehension of the whole." [10] Since nearly all social thought was originally ideological and since all ideologies are absolutists, there would seem to be little chance of a general awareness of our limited perspectives—making the prospects for a scientific study of political and social events seem remote. But Mannheim remains optimistic. He thinks that ideological thought may decline in significance, making a scientific study of politics more likely.

Two things work for a more scientific social science. First there are insights of a new field of sociological inquiry, which Mannheim calls "the sociology of knowledge." The job of the sociologist of knowledge is to explore the ideological basis of thought, to explain the context in which statements about society are made. Because this can be done, social investigators no longer need to worry about creeping ideologism:

[10] Ibid., p. 105.

Just because today we are in a position to see with increasing clarity that mutually opposing views and theories are not infinite in number and are not products of arbitrary will but are mutually complementary and derive from specific social situations, politics as a science is for the first time possible. The present structure of society makes possible a political science which will not be merely a party science, but a science of the whole. Political sociology, as the science which comprehends the whole political sphere, thus attains the stage of realization.[11]

The second factor favoring a nonideological science of society is the development of a new group to carry out the science, a group Alfred Weber calls the "socially unattached intellectuals."[12] Contrary to Marx's assertion that intellectuals nearly always reflect the interests of the ruling class, Mannheim argues that intellectuals are the most classless element in modern society and therefore the one element that could describe objective reality. After analyzing the education of intellectuals and their roles in previous ideological questions, Mannheim concludes that unattached, socially unstable, deliberative intellectuals, trained in methods of sociology, could develop a procedure "which is not closed and finished, but which is rather dynamic, elastic, in a constant state of flux, and perpetually confronted by new problems."[13]

We can see now that Mannheim was somewhat premature. If all social thought is the product of its era, this applies to Mannheim's thought as well, despite his beliefs to the contrary. After Mannheim, many writers developed an ideology of no ideology, that is, they were so obsessed with avoiding absolutes that they made an absolute out of the doctrine of no absolutes, with statements like "There should be no absolutes." This is not just a problem of semantics; some of Mannheim's followers, in their pursuit of nonideology, developed all the characteristics that Mannheim had described as ideological in nature—rigidity, false consciousness, and parochialism.

Those intellectuals who Mannheim felt would carry forward the tradition of sociology of knowledge did so, but without becoming

[11] Ibid., p. 149.
[12] Ibid., p. 155.
[13] Ibid., p. 156.

independent of classes or countries. The best example of this was the Congress for Cultural Freedom, founded by several of Mannheim's students as a place where all ideological thinking might be avoided.[14] The CCF, however, turned into an institution so closely identified with the interests of the United States and its allies that when its connections with the Central Intelligence Agency were revealed, few people who knew the organization were surprised. This is not to suggest that intellectuals cannot be independent of partisan attachments, only that it is much more difficult than Mannheim anticipated.

The disagreements among Marx, Weber, and Mannheim on the way to pursue truth can lead to confusion. These three brilliant men espouse contradictory views that all sound reasonable. Whose views on the truth are closer to the truth? It is no simple question. However, all three writers agree that there is a relationship between a theorist's methodology and the content of his thought, that assumptions about the nature of truth play a role in discovering truth. Therefore, if we compare the content of Marx's thought with that of his critics, perhaps we will be able to see who was right on the questions of method.

THE ATTACK ON MARX'S SUBSTANCE

The substantive critique of Marx, like the methodological critique, begins with Max Weber, whose entire body of work was devoted to refuting key Marxist hypotheses. For example, one reason that Weber developed his highly influential sociology of religion was to disprove the Marxist notion that everything is determined by economics.[15] Weber contended that economic activity was important, but not all-important. Some things can be explained by other forces, like religion. Thus, in *The Protestant Ethic and the Spirit of Capitalism,* Weber set out to demonstrate that one important factor in the rise of capitalism was the idea of accumulation found in Protestant thought. Weber contended that this idea led to an economic condition, while the Marxists held that economic conditions produce

[14] See Christopher Lasch, *The Agony of the American Left* (New York: Vintage, 1969), Chapter 3, for an account of the Congress for Cultural Freedom.

[15] Max Weber, *The Protestant Ethic and the Spirit of Capitalism* (London: George Allen and Unwin, 1930).

ideas. This is just one example of the anti-Marxist emphasis in Weber's work.

When it came to politics, Weber began with a definition of the state that was not too different from the Marxist one: ". . . a state is a human community that (successfully) claims the monopoly of the legitimate use of physical force within a given territory." [16] But while Marx's state claims its force from its closeness to powerful economic forces, Weber's is independent of economic classes and applies simply to those in control at any given time, presumably even in a Communist state where the lower classes hold power. Power, argued Weber, is misunderstood if explained exclusively in economic terms. Nations, for example, command the loyalty of their citizens for other than economic reasons. Furthermore, power is not necessarily bad; it does not automatically mean exploitation, as Marx would lead us to believe. In fact, Weber noticed that people are very often willing to obey those in power, sometimes more willing to obey than the people in power are willing to enforce. When people do obey the powerful, power can be said to be "legitimate," or acceptable. Since it is acceptable, it can hardly be considered an example of class exploitation. Legitimacy, which he divided into three different categories, occupied a very important place in Weber's thought.

One kind of legitimacy derives from tradition. This is the case where people obey powerful individuals because people always have. This is ". . . the authority of the 'eternal yesteryear,' i.e., of the mores sanctified through the unimaginable ancient recognition and habitual orientation to conform." [17] Traditional authority is characteristic of societies with histories that go back for some time and are continuous up to the point at which they are being examined, in which the past has a major impact upon the present. Two other types of authority are the charismatic and the legal:

> There is the authority of the extraordinary and personal gift of grace (charisma), the absolutely personal devotion and personal confidence in revelation, heroism, or other qualities of individual leadership. This is charismatic domination, as exercized by the prophet—in the field of politics—by the elected

[16] Max Weber, "Politics as a Vocation," p. 78.
[17] Ibid., pp. 78, 79.

war lord, the plebiscitarian ruler, the great demagogue, or the political party leader.

Finally, there is domination by virtue of "legality," by virtue of the belief in the validity of legal statute and functional competence based on rationally created *rules*. In this case, obedience is expected in discharging statutory obligations. This is domination as exercised by the modern servant of the state and by those bearers of power who in this respect resemble him.[18]

Which type of legitimacy produces the best kind of political system? Weber does not answer this explicitly, for that would be making a value judgment. Yet it is not hard to guess which he prefers. Since Weber believes that legal authority maximizes rationality (Weber's supreme value), it is the most likely choice.

Legal authority is more rational than charismatic authority because it is more predictable. Charismatic authority is highly unstable, arising out of crisis conditions and depending totally on one man. Since one man cannot live and rule forever, Weber felt that charismatic authority would eventually be "routinized" and come to resemble legal authority. The respect given to the charismatic figure would turn into respect for his heirs, then respect for the state, and finally respect for the administrative apparatus. And legal authority is more rational than traditional authority—though the latter is theoretically more "predictable"—because legal authority is fairer. In an authority system regulated by law, there is more chance that some form of equality will emerge. Traditional authority is unstable because it is so stable; it will stay the same, even when the conditions of life change. Then, its stability would be out of line and lead to instability. Legal authority, on the other hand, is more capable of changing and hence more rational.[19]

A system of legal authority ultimately turns into a bureaucracy, which is essentially what Weber called "functional competence based upon rationally created rules." [20] (See Chapter 7.) But bureaucratic authority, as Weber defines it, poses a number of problems for the Marxist analysis of politics and society. First, it terminates

[18] Ibid., p. 79.

[19] Ibid., p. 78.

[20] Max Weber, "Bureaucracy," in eds. Gerth and Mills, *From Max Weber*, p. 221.

the purely economic determination of political relationships. Weber maintained that bureaucratic power becomes an end in itself, divorced from the economic relationships that caused it. Second, bureaucratic power is not as oppressive or exploitative as naked economic power. People obey bureaucratic decision makers because they accept the bureaucratic model as the only available alternative, no matter how much they complain. According to Weber, a bureaucracy is more likely to be neutral in the struggle between the classes than Marx would admit. Government intervention on behalf of the poor in the class struggle would follow from Weber's analysis, but the failure of such a program would follow from Marx's analysis.

Perhaps the most important consequences of bureaucracy have not yet been considered. "The bureaucratic structure goes hand in hand with the concentration of the material means of management in the hands of the master." [21] Thus, instead of a few capitalists controlling the means of administration, we have the bureaucrats controlling the means of administration. There is a great difference between these two forms of concentration. Whereas capitalists rise to power on hereditary factors or economic daring, bureaucrats gain power on the basis of their own technical skills. As a result, the bureaucratic class will be more rational than the capitalist class, so its regime will be more stable. In Weber's words: ". . . the demand for legal guarantees against arbitrariness demand a formal and rational 'objectivity' of administration, as opposed to the personally free discretion flowing from the 'grace' of the old patrimonial domination." [22] In addition to its rationality, the bureaucratic class is also recruited more evenly from all classes in society than the capitalist class. Because "the advance of the bureaucratic structure rests upon technical superiority," people have to be recruited to fill the structure from all parts of society. This leads to a "leveling" of social differences, which mitigates the class struggle, making it less important.

The vital role of bureaucracy in preventing a Marxist revolution is now apparent in Weber's thought. Rather than withering away, as Marx predicted, the state becomes more and more permanent. This is probably the most important social consequence of bureauc-

[21] Ibid., p. 220.
[22] Ibid., p. 228.

racy—to the extent that it exists, it will tend to continue to exist, making revolution impossible. As Weber stated, "And where the bureaucratization of administration has been completely carried through, a form of power relation is established that is practically unshatterable." [23] Since every segment of society will develop an interest in having bureaucracy continue, it will continue. No social revolution can occur in such circumstances.

We have discussed Weber's theory on the permanence of the state, but have not examined the character of its existence. This was done by many critics of Marx, particularly Karl Mannheim, Gaetano Mosca (1858–1941), Vilfredo Pareto (1848–1923), and Robert Michels (1876–1936). These writers all agreed that political equality was an impossible goal, that a few would rule and everyone else would obey in all societies. Because they believed that an elite would always be present—contrary to the Marxist hypothesis that a classless society was possible—this group of writers is often called the elitist school. This does not mean they all favored elitism—some did more than others—but that they considered it inevitable. To prove this inevitability, they developed extensive critiques of key Marxist propositions.

In his substantive critique of Marx, Mannheim followed the same reasoning he used in his methodological critique. His book *Man and Society in an Age of Reconstruction* advocates certain changes in society while trying to avoid absolutes in thought. He warns against the dangers of complete and total democracy, on the one hand, and of unrestrained dictatorship, on the other. Neither alternative is particularly rational. In mass democracy, ". . . irrationalities which have not been integrated into the social structure may force their way into political life." [24] In other words, so long as people are in a state of deprivation, their mass entry into the political process will produce irrationalisms, "suggestions, uncontrolled outbursts of impulses, and psychic regressions. . . ." [25] A rational and stable political system must be able to control the masses and their impulses, without going to the opposite extreme of dictatorship. Mannheim was too close to the Nazi experience to find any hope

[23] Ibid., p. 228.

[24] Karl Mannheim, *Man and Society in an Age of Reconstruction* (New York: Harvest Books, 1940), p. 63.

[25] Ibid., p. 61.

for rationality in rule by one man. His search for an alternative to these extremes is the underlying theme in much of his political writings.

In his search for a segment of society that was not prone to either mass democracy or to one-man dictatorship, Mannheim turned again to the intellectuals. The ideal society, according to Mannheim, would combine the freedom found in a democracy with the planning of dictatorships. Unlike many of his era, he did not feel these goals were contradictory. "Planning in this sense means planning for freedom, mastering those spheres of social progress on which the smooth working of society depends, but at the same time making no attempt to regulate the fields which offer the greatest opportunities for creative evolution and individuality." [26] This was to be brought about by the intellectuals, a group that often pursues both freedom and rational planning. And of all intellectuals, behavioral scientists would be best suited to take on this task, because they, more than most, depend on rationality in their explanations of social events.

Mannheim, then, seems to envision a society in which class conflict would diminish because behavioral scientists studying the causes of conflicts would provide immediate solutions that would prevent full-scale revolution. In this sense, Mannheim was prophetic. Much of behavioral science is currently used as a way of regulating behavior. Unfortunately, as they become involved in social control, intellectuals lose their neutrality. The question is always who is controlling whom, and when intellectuals enter the struggle on the side of the controllers, they are indicating their own partisanship and ideology.

This brings us to the central question of control: Who actually runs a political system? This is the question that Mosca, Pareto, and Michels tried to answer. Mosca observed:

> Among the constant facts and tendencies that are to be found in all political organisms, one is so obvious that it is apparent to the most casual eye. In all societies, . . . two classes of people appear—a class that rules and a class that is ruled. The first class, always the less numerous, performs all political functions, monopolizes power, and enjoys the advantages that power brings, whereas the second, the more numerous class, is directed and controlled by the first, in a manner that is

[26] Ibid., p. 264.

now more or less legal, now more or less arbitrary and violent. . . .[27]

There is nothing particularly startling in this passage. Its significance lies in its contrast to Marx's view. While Mosca considered
the division between elite and mass the most crucial in society,
Marx emphasized the bourgeois-proletariat distinction. Elite is a
political concept but class is an economic one, and someone who
views the world in political terms is likely to underrate economic
factors. For Mosca, the elite-mass division characterized all societies,
so even if classes disappeared, something else would produce political inequality. In this basic sense, the ideas of Mosca and Marx
are antithetical.

Another difference between Marx and the elitist school emerges
in the work of Vilfredo Pareto. Pareto, like Mosca, believed that a
few would always rule, but he paid more attention to the composition of the elite. Any group that excelled in any particular respect
he called an elite. Thus, there could be a military elite, a commercial elite, even an artistic or musical elite. In Pareto, this
phenomenon is caused by psychological and physiological, rather
than political factors. Some will always be better than others, he
seems to be saying. No matter what the political system, these
elites will still emerge. To Pareto, democracy was a sham because
the elites would never permit it to occur. However, one society does
differ from another in the composition of elites. In some, military
elites may predominate, while in others it may be the landed aristocracy. In other societies, the leading elites may rotate in top
position. The anti-Marxist nature of Pareto's concept of continually
varying elites is noted by T. B. Bottomore. He observes that Pareto's
purpose is ". . . to show that the Marxist conception of a 'ruling
class' is erroneous, by demonstrating the continual circulation of
elites, which prevents in most societies, and especially in modern
industrial societies, the formation of a stable and closed ruling
class." [28]

Robert Michels added an empirical element to the philosophical
ideas of Mosca and Pareto. If one wanted to prove to everyone's
satisfaction that an elite will always emerge in any social organism,

[27] Gaetano Mosca, *The Ruling Class* (New York: McGraw-Hill, 1939), p. 50.
[28] T. B. Bottomore, *Elites and Society* (Baltimore: Penguin Books, 1964),
pp. 17–18.

where should one turn? This is the question Michels asked. He thought immediately of the German Social Democratic party (comprised of Marx's followers), an organization that denies the inevitability of an elite. If an elite does exist there, it would seem that an elite would exist anywhere. What distinguished Michels's analysis was that it depended more on factual material than the hypotheses of Mosca and Pareto. Michels examined financial records, editorial boards, membership lists, social and economic backgrounds, and voting patterns to support his contention that the party which believed in the withering away of the state was dominated by a small elite who made the major decisions and used all sorts of devices to perpetuate its leadership.

Michels generalized from the situation he found in the German Social Democratic party. In any institution or state, "the majority is thus permanently incapable of self-government." [29] Consequently, ". . . the majority of human beings, in a condition of eternal tutelage, are predestined by tragic necessity to submit to the dominion of a small minority, and must be content to constitute the pedestal of an oligarchy." [30] This conclusion, summarized by Michels's famous phrase, "Iron Law of Oligarchy," is an empirical proposition, that is, it attempts to make a generalization about the way social events occur. And the experience of most people would tend to confirm it, though not in all places at all times. But is oligarchy inevitable? Perhaps rule by a few is caused by the nature of specific social organizations, like capitalism, rather than by irresistible forces in all organizations. In any case, that is how a Marxist would respond.

The important point is that Michels formulated his law to refute some key Marxist propositions. He felt that no change in society would affect the emergence of oligarchy. In other words, no state would ever wither away. As for the future, Michels contends that the basic social changes envisioned by the Marxist revolution cannot occur because people and their institutions are incapable of bringing them about. Michels concluded, pessimistically:

> History seems to teach us that no popular movement, however energetic and vigorous, is capable of producing profound and

[29] Robert Michels, *Political Parties* (New York: Macmillan, 1962), p. 353.
[30] Ibid., p. 354.

permanent changes in the social organism of the civilized world.[31]

From Marxist revolution to antirevolutionary cynicism—this is the path of the anti-Marxists.

ANTI-MARXISM TODAY

The basic anti-Marxist themes have dominated American social thinking up to the present, just as Marxist themes predominate in socialist countries. It is now generally accepted that class conflict need not lead to revolution, that economic factors do not cause everything, that the state is not likely to wither away in the near future, that the working classes are "satisfied" and the nonworking classes "fair," that some elite is inevitable, that a relatively "objective" social science is not only possible but present, and that democracy is a type of state which is different (fairer, more representative) than any other. These points constitute an anti-Marxist perspective and consensus, and their strength indicates the influence anti-Marxist writers exert on American thought. Not only do most American social scientists trace their ideas to Weber, Mannheim, and Michels, but, in addition, the two schools of political philosophy into which Americans divide themselves—liberalism and conservatism—compete to prove which is more anti-Marxist. (Those who claim that liberals are suspiciously close to communism do not know a thing about their liberals.)

Few people realize that anti-Marxism has been just as strong on the left as on the right in the United States. For years, the liberals and socialists in the United States have tacitly agreed on the horrors of communism. The American Socialist party has spent about equal time denouncing people on its left and on its right. A group of writers known as Social Democrats profess a belief in rapid change, but condemn Marxism in the strongest possible language. Social Democrats range from Sidney Hook and Lewis Feuer on one side—people who, in the name of anticommunism, have accepted America almost exactly as it is—to the less conservative group of writers around the magazine *Dissent*.[32] As Michels studied the

[31] Ibid., p. 355.

[32] Representative of the writers from *Dissent* are Irving Howe and Lewis Coser. See also *The New Leader* for strong expressions of anticommunism.

German Social Democrats to test his hypothesis on organization, we can examine to see how far the anti-Marxist reaction has gone.

The anti-Marxist tradition has paralleled social democracy in the domination of American social science. Contrary to the assertion of Social Democrat Lewis Coser, that "Marxian modes of analysis, certain strands of Marxist doctrine and of Marxist method have become an enduring component of . . . American social science," [33] it seems that nearly all the great books of contemporary social science are attempts to disprove key Marxist notions about man and society empirically. The most outstanding example is Seymour Martin Lipset's influential work *Political Man.*

In his book, Lipset tries to show through the discipline of sociology that democracy does exist in many countries because the necessary preconditions are present, that the working classes in those democracies are satisfied and happy, hence unrevolutionary or even counterrevolutionary, that the class struggle has been replaced by the voting machine in those countries, that upper classes are more prone to change than lower classes, that bureaucracy is a permanent force to be reckoned with, and that attempts radically to alter democratic societies are doomed to failure.[34] We evaluated Lipset's views in Part I. What we want to reemphasize here is the important role the anti-Marxist reaction played in framing Lipset's questions. Lipset represents a pattern of American thinking which is liberal in politics and sociological in discipline, but which shares with social democracy a distaste for revolution.

The anti-Marxist tradition has naturally dominated the conservative, as well as the liberal and socialist, tradition in America. By conservative, we mean people who view order and stability as basic goals, such as John Adams (1735–1826), Alexis de Tocqueville (1805–1859), the contemporary writer Hannah Arendt, and of course the philosophers discussed in Chapter 10. We do not mean those who have developed political philosophies designed to keep one group, businessmen, in a privileged position, or to keep another group, the current enemies of America, outside the pale. Of course, since Burke, Rousseau, Adams, and de Tocqueville wrote before

[33] Lewis Coser, "USA: Marxists at Bay," in *Revisionism*, ed. Leopold Labedz (New York: Praeger, 1962), p. 362. Quoted in Seymour Martin Lipset, *Political Man: The Social Bases of Politics* (Garden City, N.Y.: Doubleday Anchor, 1959), p. xx.

[34] Lipset, *Political Man*, passim.

Marx, they can hardly be called anti-Marxist. But some contemporary writers have taken ideas from these men and combined them with the insights of the anti-Marxists, to produce some new conclusions of their own.

Hannah Arendt is one example of this mixture. To her, there is a clear separation between a political goal like maximizing freedom and an economic goal like eliminating poverty. The former is defined essentially by civil liberty, freedom of speech and thought. It is all right for a group of people to try to obtain freedom through political means, according to Arendt, for that is what the Americans did in their revolution. But no one should ever try to obtain abundance through politics, that is, through revolution, because it will lead to disaster. "Nothing, we might say today, could be more obsolete than to attempt to liberate mankind from poverty by political means; nothing could be more futile and dangerous." [35]

Why? Poverty arises out of economic conditions—scarcity—and can only be solved by economic conditions—abundance—through technology. All the poor can do, according to Arendt, is wait for a technology that will free them from their poverty. However, many of the poor are unwilling to wait, a condition that can be directly attributed to Karl Marx. For Marx told the poor they could obtain relief through politics—which makes his doctrines among the most pernicious in the history of man. The terror and totalitarianism of the twentieth century, including that practiced by Hitler, can be blamed on Marx because he suggested revolution.

> Every attempt to solve the social question [poverty] with political means leads into terror, and . . . it is terror which sends revolutions to their doom. . . . Freedom has been better preserved in countries where no revolution ever broke out, no matter how outrageous the circumstances of the powers that be, and . . . there exists more civil liberties even in countries where the revolution was defeated than in those where revolutions have been victorious.[36]

A more complete synthesis of the basic ideas of American conservatism and the anti-Marxist tradition would be hard to find. The separation of politics and economics and the cynical attitude toward revolution are both crucial aspects of anti-Marxism.

[35] Hannah Arendt, *On Revolution* (New York: Viking, 1963), p. 110.
[36] Ibid., pp. 108, 111.

In this hasty sketch, we can see the influence of the Marxist and the anti-Marxist tradition in much of contemporary thought. The former stresses conflict, particularly class conflict, injustice, and political revolution to achieve redress. In spite of its short-term pessimism that gradual change will produce no significant improvements, it is actually extremely optimistic since it believes a revolution will lead to the perfectibility of people. The anti-Marxist tradition, on the other hand, stresses mutual interest. Statism and bureaucracy are as inevitable in this school of thought as revolution is in the Marxist. Anti-Marxists are optimistic in the short run because they believe that things are really working out fairly well in the Western world. But toward long-term fundamental change, they are quite cynical. The anti-Marxists seem to feel that the basic nature of man will never be altered. While Marx regards greed, hierarchy, and other evils as aspects of one type of economic system, his critics are convinced that these characteristics will appear in every form of society. It is in their expectations for the future that Marx and his critics go their separate ways.

Nearly every contemporary writer who is concerned with politics fits into one of these two traditions. Some have belonged to both traditions, changing from one to the other as times changed. Others have anticipated a time when the intellectual world would no longer be divided into Marxist and anti-Marxist, when all intellectuals would be able to agree on fundamentals. That vision seems premature. A more realistic conclusion would be that no one can be in both traditions at the same time. Most twentieth-century American social scientists have belonged to the anti-Marxist tradition, but a few have remained apart.

The next chapter, which deals with the development of the concept of alienation (a key aspect of the writings of Marx and Hegel), will show how those who write about alienation are usually optimistic. They have the hope that the alienation they uncover can be made to disappear. In that sense they are very much like Marx and very unlike his critics.

13 Alienation and the Human Condition

In the previous chapter, we discussed how a fear of Marxism led writers like Weber and Mannheim to a very pessimistic world outlook, or if not pessimistic, then to what is more corrosive, cynicism. Sidney Hook once wrote that the greatest evil facing men was naïveté, but, clearly, cynicism is worse for the body politic.

Primarily, this is so because the cynic allows the worst faults of political systems to perpetuate themselves. Assume that a considerable amount of exploitation exists in a political system. In this situation, there are three general groups. First, there are those who do the exploiting, people in positions of power who use their power irresponsibly for their own ends. They should be identified and their methods analyzed. Then there are those who are exploited. They live in poverty, stripped of their identities, with their culture determined by others. In the struggle between the first group and the second, both often turn to a third—those people who are not directly exploiters or exploited. If these people are active, aware, and politically conscious, they may well side with the powerless group, adding weight to their demands for a better life. If, on the other hand, they are passive and cynical, they have inadvertently, or advertently, sided with those who exploit—whether they know it or like it or not—for their cynicism is what permits the exploita-

232

tion to continue. Those who say that human nature cannot be changed, that people are always going to exploit each other, are the people who are substantially responsible for the fact that human nature often does not change. For people do not change in a vacuum. A better life has to be considered a possibility, but cynicism is an excellent device for avoiding that consideration.

For this reason, we should recognize cynicism as a political phenomenon with real political consequences. Although it has intellectual roots in the anti-Marxist reaction, cynicism is not simply an intellectual movement. It is an attitude commonly found in many types of political systems. Since cynicism helps those in power, people who rule political systems have a vested interest in keeping the populations of their countries cynical. In the United States, as elsewhere, cynicism is a product of the learning process. In the schools and in the family, children are told, "since you can't beat them, join them," or "you can't fight city hall." Regardless of the formal commitment to democratic goals, the real life experience of every young person in America tends to teach him or her the futility of trying to alter the status quo in any basic way. The fact that teachers who say (and students who hear) that the system is unresponsive to demands for change do not realize what they are teaching (or learning) only makes the socialization process more pervasive and difficult to alter. In short, while the words American students read suggest hope and optimism, their experiences conspire to make them cynical.

We should all ask ourselves a few questions. Am I skeptical about the possibility of fundamental political change? If so, is it in my own interest to be cynical, that is, whom does my cynicism serve? Do I belong to that third group which neither exploits nor is exploited? In other words, does my cynicism make me at least partially responsible for the evils around me? If the answers to these questions are affirmative, then two basic options exist. One can continue in the same fashion, with the attitude that that's just the way things are. Many undoubtedly will take such a position, and there is not much we can do about it. But some will opt for the other alternative. They will want to know more about their cynical attitude and to find alternative paths of action to alleviate the cynicism. This is the concern of this chapter. We will begin by tracing cynicism to its ultimate—despair; then we will show how the same human condition that led to despair can, when faced with courage and faith, lead to a new sense of freedom; finally, we will try to show how what today is called the "revolution" is an attempt to break out of passivity and cynicism.

Cynicism turns to despair in the writings of men like Nietzsche and some of the followers of existentialism. Nonetheless, there are differences between the cynicism of their work and that of the anti-Marxists discussed in the previous chapter. Weber and Mannheim possessed a very rational cynicism. They developed an explicit focus on politics for a specific purpose—to show how the pursuit of revolution was futile. The writers discussed in the present chapter, on the other hand, have developed, out of a phenomenon called "alienation," a vision that encourages hope for the future of mankind.

There have always been people for whom existing reality was a horror. Recognizing the evils of the world around them, they became "turned off." They no longer considered themselves part of the system which produced the evils. Alienation is the result. Thus, if one arrives at a cynical position through alienation, rather than conscious rationality, the result is different. Cynicism through alienation is a necessary part of a dialectical process leading to a new beginning with an optimistic outlook. Alienated intellectuals may at first appear to be just as cynical as the writers discussed in the previous chapter. But their cynicism is a response to their political impotence. It is a cynicism from which faith in political change may arise if a concrete alternative to alienation can be found. It is important, therefore, to examine those intellectual traditions which try to come to grips with alienation in order to understand the contemporary world.

NIETZSCHE

Friedrich Wilhelm Nietzsche (1844–1900), the classicist, philologist, poet, and apolitical madman, added an important ingredient to the dimensions of contemporary alienation. Much has already been written about his bizarre life. His chances for normality seem to have ended in infancy, when his father died and he was brought up by his grandmother, mother, sister, and two aunts. His absurd attempt to be one of the boys in college was at best misspent time; at worst he may have contracted syphilis that led to paresis in later life.

Nietzsche's attraction to Richard Wagner, whom he regarded as the one living superman, was marred by his revulsion to Wagner's anti-Semitism. Undoubtedly one of the most pervasive influences on Nietzsche was his sister. With great personal courage he broke with her over her overt anti-Semitism, but unfortunately she gained control over Nietzsche's manuscripts after his death and attempted to portray him as an anti-Semite.[1] This charge and its accompanying link to Naziism should be decisively refuted.

In summary, this is Nietzsche's philosophy: God is dead, but while modern man knows this to be true, he hasn't the courage to act accordingly. He is still a prisoner of his superstitious beliefs in God. Instead of glorifying the true and heroic virtues of man, Christianity teaches man to be meek and submissive; it makes man effeminate rather than virile. Modern society is decadent and needs a new principle to live by. You cannot give up God and retain the moral system that is sustained by a belief in God. You must have the courage of your convictions.

What should replace God? For Nietzsche the answer was clear: a new creative force, the Will to Power. One must free oneself from all previous restraints, traditions, codes of conduct, and so forth. One must act upon his will to be the master. In this way, man can surpass himself, he can become a superman or *Übermensch* (literally, "overman"), which can be translated as "higher than," as well as "ruling over."

Nietzsche explains this in his best-known work, *Thus Spake Zarathustra:*

> *I teach you the Superman.* Man is something that is to be surpassed. What have ye done to surpass man? All beings hitherto have created something beyond themselves; and ye want to be the ebb of that great tide, and would rather go back to the beast than to surpass man? . . . Lo, I teach you the Superman! The Superman is the meaning of the earth. Let your will say: The Superman *shall be* the meaning of the earth! I conjure you, my brethren, *remain true to the earth* and believe not those who speak unto you of superearthly hopes! Prisoners are they, whether they know it or not.[2]

[1] See Lee Cameron McDonald, *Western Political Theory: From Its Origins to the Present* (New York: Harcourt, Brace, 1968), p. 507.

[2] Friedrich Wilhelm Nietzsche, *Thus Spake Zarathustra,* trans. Thomas Common (London: Allen and Unwin, n.d.), pp. 6–7, as quoted in McDonald, *Western Political Theory,* p. 510.

Nietzsche did not mean just the "political man," but probably the artist as well, the creative person who becomes immortal because he surpasses the traditional modes of expression. For every Caesar or Napoleon there is a Michelangelo or Picasso. But paradoxically, in spite of his will, the superman is no God, only a mortal like the rest of us.

> Ah, man returneth eternally! The small man returneth eternally!
> Naked had I once seen both of them, the greatest man and the smallest man: all too like one another—all too human, even the greatest man! Ah, Disgust! Disgust! Disgust! [3]

> Somewhere there are still peoples and herds, but not with us, my brethren: here there are states . . . the coldest of all cold monsters. Coldly lieth it also; and this lie creepeth from its mouth: "I, the state, am the people."
> It is a lie! . . .
> There, where the state ceaseth—there only commenceth the man who is not superfluous.[4]

Despite everything, Nietzsche retains the will to go on, to do one's best even without faith in God. Nietzsche concludes on this slightly optimistic note:

> . . . The ascetic ideal arose to give it [suffering] meaning—its only meaning, so far. But any meaning is better than none and in fact, the ascetic ideal has been the best stopgap that ever existed. . . . It signifies, let us have the courage to face it, a will to nothingness, a revulsion from life, a rebellion against the principal conditions of living. And yet, despite everything, it is and remains a *will*. Let me repeat, now that I have reached the end, what I said at the beginning: *man would sooner have the void for his purpose than be void of purpose.*[5]

While many have regarded Nietzsche as the end of philosophy,

[3] Ibid., p. 511.

[4] Ibid., p. 510.

[5] Friedrich Nietzsche, *The Birth of Tragedy and On the Genealogy of Morals*, trans. Francis Golffing (Garden City, N.Y.: Doubleday Anchor, 1956), as quoted in McDonald, *Western Political Theory*, p. 515 (italics added).

the existentialist sees not the end of philosophy, but rather a new beginning.

> The contemporary philosophical situation is determined by the fact that two philosophers, Kierkegaard and Nietzsche, who did not count in their times and for a long time remained without influence in the history of philosophy, have continually grown in significance. . . . They stand today as the authentically great thinkers of their age. . . . Their thinking created a new atmosphere. They passed beyond all of the limits then regarded as obvious. It is as if they no longer shrank back from anything in thought.[6]

EXISTENTIALISM

What is today called "existentialism" developed directly from Nietzsche. Existentialism is a complicated system of beliefs, which cannot really be summarized in a few words. Basically, though, existentialism, like Marxism, reverses Hegel's order of priorities. Hegel believed rational spirit should be the essence of existence: man would be free only so long as his ideas were rational. Existentialism, however, asks what comes before reason. To reason, a person must be alive, that is, he must exist. In that sense, existence precedes reason, and the focus upon man's existence becomes the basis of existentialism. Existence defies reason, for so long as man has been on earth he has existed, yet little is known about the nature of his existence. Thus, existentialism rejects Hegel's belief in reason and stresses the irrational character of existence.

Certain common themes run through the works of the leading existentialist writers—Kierkegaard, Jaspers, Heidegger, Sartre, and Camus.[7] Their central concern is the "human condition." This is something which becomes clearest in times of great personal crisis. At such times, all man's abstract categories, his learned responses, become irrelevant, meaningless, and unreal. Under traumatic ex-

---

[6] Karl Jaspers, *Reason and Existenz,* trans. William Earle (New York: Noonday Press, 1955), pp. 23–24, as quoted in McDonald, *Western Political Theory,* p. 508.

[7] Fictional works, such as Sartre's *Roads to Freedom* and *The Respectful Prostitute* and Camus's *The Rebel* and *The Stranger,* are probably better sources for an introduction to existentialism than philosophic works such as Sartre's *Being and Nothingness.*

perience we come to the sudden realization that we are alone and life is absurd. When we confront this reality of existence, we experience great fear and anxiety. We come to know our, and mankind's, fallibility, uniqueness, and loneliness. We come face to face with, and can no longer avoid the recognition of, the great void of nothingness that confronts us. Most of us lack the courage to face reality and bury ourselves again in preoccupation with jobs and success, or take escape in our ideologies, or in a futile search for happiness in physical pleasures. Karl Jaspers describes this futile search very well:

> Essential humanity is reduced to the general; to vitality as a functional corporeality, to the triviality of enjoyment. The divorce of labour from pleasure deprives life of its possible gravity: public affairs become mere entertainment; private affairs, the alternation of stimulation and fatigue, and a craving for novelty whose inexhaustible current flows swiftly into the waters of oblivion. . . . Youth as the period of highest vital efficiency and of erotic exaltation becomes the desired type of life in general. Where the human being is regarded only as a function, he must be young; and if youth is over he will try to show its semblance. . . . Great men pass into the background as contrasted with the efficient. . . . Without the support of the mass will he [the human being] is of no account. What he can be is not measured by an ideal, is not related to a genuinely present Transcendence, but is based upon his conception of the fundamental qualities of mankind as manifested in the majority. . . . Now the result of "leadership" of this kind is inextricable confusion. . . .
>
> With the unification of our planet there has begun a process of levelling-down which people contemplate with horror. That which has today become general to our species is always the most superficial, the most trivial, and the most indifferent of human possibilities. Yet men strive to effect this levelling-down as if, in that way, the unification of mankind could be brought about. . . . People dress alike. . . . [do] the same dances, [have] the same types of thought, and the same catchwords.[8]

[8] Karl Jaspers, *Man in the Modern Age*, trans. Eden and Edy Paul (Garden City, N.Y.: Doubleday Anchor, 1957), pp. 48, 55, and 85, as quoted in McDonald, *Western Political Theory*, p. 534.

There is, however, another way for man to react when he encounters the absurdity of existence. He can realize that he is absolutely free, and this sense of freedom provides a renewed basis for hope. Man in his being is not predetermined by anything. He is what he is by the choices he makes, by the attitudes he adopts. While it is true that a man does not choose, for example, to be black, nevertheless he is free to choose what attitude he shall take toward his blackness—resignation, defiance, humiliation, pride, inferiority. He is still free to choose, and what he chooses is what he is. We all choose the crosses we have to bear. There is no escape from freedom; only "bad faith," the pretense that we did not choose, is to be avoided. The "authentic man" is conscious of his freedom, knows he is responsible for what he is, and transcends his absurdity by facing it with dignity and compassion. He recognizes that when he chooses he chooses for all mankind. He may be an "absurd hero," but he is no coward.

People who assert that existential behavior and thought are irrational and anti-intellectual do not understand them. Let us, for a moment, compare the "scientific" with the "existential" attitude. The "scientific" attitude is characterized by objectivity and non-involvement, exemplified by the surgeon removing an appendix. The surgeon views the patient on the operating table in the same way that the jeweler views a timepiece he is repairing. Not that detachment is an inappropriate attitude for the surgeon; in fact, this is why surgeons do not operate on members of their own families.

The existential attitude, on the other hand, is characterized by total involvement and commitment. Whatever a person does, he does with his whole being, holding nothing back in reserve. He is not a manipulator of things or persons for his own ends. The meaning for him is in the process, not in some ulterior end. It is in this ability to break through, to transcend the human condition of loneliness and isolation by an act of will, that one discovers true dignity and communications with other human beings. Although this existential attitude may not be appropriate to all requirements of life (such as the surgeon's work), it is essential to the attainment of authentic human existence.

Both Nietzsche and the existentialists have paradoxical attitudes toward cynicism. To be sure, there is an element of despair in these writings. The world seems to be on the brink of its final catastrophe, as the meaning of the human condition goes unrealized. But at the same time, the despair produces cause for hope. Moments of great despair often bring insight into the nature of existence, which leads to a more positive attitude. This is best illustrated in an essay by Albert Camus, a much misunderstood existentialist. Camus relates the myth of Sisyphus, condemned by the Greek gods eternally to push a stone up a hill, only to have it roll back, so he pushes it further, only to have it roll back again.[9] Sisyphus's life is generally regarded as the essence of futility, spending eternity in an activity that never produces any results. But to Camus, the labor of Sisyphus is symbolic of the human condition, the meaning of all our lives. Instead of despairing over this fact, Camus suggests that we understand it, and thus free ourselves. This freedom would come from an awareness of the conditions of our own lives. Sisyphus, to Camus, was not an unhappy man. He was an existential man who had come to grips with his existence—a man with understanding.

The story of Sisyphus is helpful in interpreting existentialism. Camus, for example, would hardly be considered a revolutionary, for he does not urge Sisyphus to stop his labors and seek revenge on the gods. In fact, Camus's plea for us to recognize the Sisyphus in our lives is a politically conservative one, for it suggests that we should no longer attempt to alter oppressive conditions. In this way, much of existentialism, like the anti-Marxist reaction, discourages those who would use politics to change the human condition.[10] Although existentialism recognizes some rays of hope, these are not political rays. The existentialist does not think that political action can ever really alter the human condition. On the other hand, existentialism is eloquent in describing the human condition. It is quite possible to accept the existentialist description of a contemporary problem while rejecting the cynicism and despair of their conclusions.

MARX AND ALIENATION

Alienation does not always lead to despair. After recognizing alienation, one could make suggestions about dealing with it. Thus,

[9] Albert Camus, *The Myth of Sisyphus and Other Essays* (New York: Knopf, 1955).

[10] The one exception to this generalization is Sartre, who retained his belief in social change. Since the world was absurd, a "leap of faith" was needed to correct it.

even the most revolutionary of writers, Karl Marx, began his intellectual development with an investigation of the concept of alienation.

Much of the contemporary preoccupation with alienation stems from renewed interest in the early writings of Karl Marx. In his *Economic and Philosophic Manuscripts,* written in Paris in 1844, but not published until 1927 (and in English not until 1961), Marx developed his concept of alienation.

Earlier, Hegel, in *Phenomenology of Spirit,* had emphasized self-alienation, or alienation from self, as part of the human condition. According to Hegel, a necessary condition of man's developing consciousness, is that his subjective spirit, his individual consciousness, be in a dialectical relationship with the objective spirit of the external world. Therefore man is alienated because man's essence, his spirit, conflicts with the absolute spirit. It should be clear that Hegel "believed more in man's ontological essence, in his spirituality, than in his humanity." [11]

It is with this spirituality that Marx takes exception. His opening sentence in *The Holy Family* clearly indicates his objection: "Real humanism has in Germany no more dangerous enemy than spiritualism or speculative idealism, which puts 'self-consciousness' or 'spirit' in place of the real individual man. . . ." [12]

Marx seeks to understand and to free man as man, not man as spirit, laborer, or capitalist, or any of the other roles society has forced upon him. But, Marx asserts, because of the division of labor and the mode of production, man is alienated from himself and can never be seen, even by himself, as a whole man, only as a particularized man, only in a role, never as a human being.

There is one great fact characterizing the nineteenth century which cannot be denied by any part: on one side, industrial and scientific powers have developed which no former period of history could have fancied; on the other side, there are symptoms of disintegration surpassing even the well-known terrors of the late Roman Empire. In our time everything seems to be pregnant with its contrast. The machine is endowed with the marvelous power to shorten labor and to make it

[11] Karl Lowith, "Man's Self Alienation in the Early Writings of Marx," *Social Research,* no. 21 (1954), p. 207.

[12] Quoted in loc. cit.

more profitable; and yet we see how it produces hunger and overwork. The newly emancipated powers of wealth become, through a strange play of destiny, sources of privation. . . . Mankind becomes master of nature, but man the slave of man or of his own baseness. The result of all our inventions and progress seems to be that material powers become invested with spiritual life, while human life deteriorates into a material force. We know that the new form of social production, to achieve the good life, needs only new men.[13]

For Marx it is not only the proletariat that is alienated, but also the bourgeoisie. In fact, in some respects, the proletariat is less alienated than the bourgeoisie. Since the proletarian's dehumanization, his existence as a commodity is so obvious, he need only develop class consciousness to become aware of the situation. He need only reflect on and examine his surroundings. But the bourgeois is even more alienated because his dehumanization is totally unconscious and spiritualized. He does not realize that his being has been abstracted as an object; he is only aware of his wants and his needs.

No doubt, the humanistic concern found in Marx's early writings remained an inspiration and goal in his later "scientific" writings (see Chapter 11). To free man and remove alienating social conditions was the human meaning of the socialist revolution.

Self-reliance of man, his freedom, has still to be reawakened in the hearts of modern men. Only this feeling, which disappeared from this world with the Greeks, and into the blue haze of the skies with the Christians, can once more create from society a community of men dedicated to their highest aims, a democratic state.[14]

The concept of alienation differs considerably in Marx and in the writings of the existentialists. In the Marxist tradition, alienation is a material condition, something that oppresses people as they work and try to relate to each other and to their world. Alienation

[13] Karl Marx, "Die Revolution von 1848 und das Proletariat," as quoted in Karl Lowith, *Social Research*, pp. 214–15.

[14] Karl Marx, *Mensch und Revolutionar* (Berlin, 1928), p. 41, as quoted in Karl Lowith, *Social Research*, p. 226.

is another term for the oppression people feel under a capitalist system. In existentialism, on the other hand, alienation is the general condition of modern man. While the existentialists see alienation as an internal condition that calls for an act of will, resolute courage, to transcend the "human condition," others, including the Marxists, believe that alienation is caused by external environment—capitalism. Therefore, the external world must be changed, through the political act of revolution.

ALIENATION IN THE UNITED STATES

This brings us directly to the alienation that has been apparent in the United States since the mid-1960s. There is no denying that young people in the United States today are alienated from their culture, and that many adults share their sentiments. They recognize all too clearly the hypocrisy of the institutions that attempt to shape people's lives.[15] They are revolting against a system that preaches one set of values, yet practices another. It is this schism that upsets and incites so many people of various ages and races in the United States.

This hypocrisy is considered so pervasive, so all-encompassing, that enumeration of the discrepancies is almost impossible. A few examples will have to suffice. These examples are not arranged according to significance, for many are alienated from the totality of

---

[15] To those who protest that it is wrong to speak of today's youth as being in revolt when only a minority of the college youth are actually in revolt, the following is addressed: First, the proportion of today's college generation that is alienated from their culture is much greater than is generally recognized. It is certainly not limited to members of SDS who have received all too much credit. The search for meaning, the discontent, almost despair, on the part of students today with the way things are is very great, even though often unexpressed. The demand for relevancy and participation is being voiced by all segments of the campus. Second, it should be remembered that those taking the lead in the students' protests, both violent and nonviolent, are usually the most able students. They are, or would have been, future leaders of society. We ignore them at our peril. Third, it should also be kept in mind that a much higher percentage of youth are in college today than ever before. Finally, the feelings of alienation shared by young people are no longer shared only by young people. Many adults have come to question the war in Vietnam and other things the students have criticized. Nor is alienation only something that young people feel. Many "minority groups," like blacks and chicanos of all ages, have their own reasons for being alienated from American democracy.

their culture (though many more are perfectly happy with it). For this reason they cannot provide a list of ordered priorities to be dealt with by reformers. This alienation considers reform impossible; only total change will end the problem.

Clearly the war in Vietnam is one cause of alienation. It is not simply that a war is being fought, for many Americans found involvement in World War II a unifying and fulfilling, positive experience. In Vietnam, however, alienation is produced by the conflict between professed goals and the reality of everyday experience. An invasion of a new country is called a reduction of the war. Villages are destroyed so that they may be saved. People are slaughtered in the name of freedom. Elections are held, but only a few can vote. Self-determination is the professed goal, but the most populous elements in the country are not permitted to take part in that determination. Killing is bad, but it is alleged that Asians value life less than Americans, so it is not so bad. These are some aspects of the Vietnamese war that alienate citizens of the country that is doing the major part of the fighting. In war, it has been said, truth is the first casualty, but in this one, authenticity has been the victim. Because of the duplicity, many Americans will no longer trust the United States long after the last soldier has been killed in Vietnam.

Drugs is another area that leads to alienation. Society's whole approach to the "drug question" seems hypocritical. Although marijuana smoking is dealt with severely by the police and the courts, even mild attempts to alert persons to the dangers of cigarette smoking face formidable opposition. Furthermore, hardly any concern is voiced over the widespread use of alcohol and tranquilizers by the "mature," "responsible" adults of the community. The martini or two the businessman has at his expense-account lunch and the tranquilizer his wife takes, in the form of a pill or a soap opera on television, are now as American as the proverbial apple pie.

Recent elections indicate another strain. Although the great "silent majority" is concerned about the increase in crime in our nation, it is unwilling to deal with the urban social problems that foster crime. Moreover, these advocates of "law and order" fail to see the contradiction in their opposition to the Supreme Court's decisions on school desegregation, open housing, and the rights of the accused.

The American education system is yet another source of alienation. Today, the professed role of the university is to search for truth. It has abandoned its traditional role as a social critic and its expertise is for sale to the highest bidder, whether private industry or government. Even its primary function, teaching, is often overwhelmed by the needs of a society for technically trained people who do not think systematically about the conditions of their lives. At all levels, education is more interested in promoting conformity, than in teaching people to be "liberal." Not many students would describe their education as a wholesome and unalienating experience.

Finally, the phenomenon of racism turns people away from their own political system. Again, it is not the existence of racism, but the continual hypocrisy that surrounds it, which is so alienating. Civil rights advocates who live in segregated suburbs are particularly scorned, but the nature of the problem is such that nearly every white person is vulnerable to the charge of racism in some form (see Chapter 5). The worst part is the persistent refusal to deal with this problem, to admit to racist feelings and try to overcome them. Instead there is the plea of friendship for the cause of blacks—if only they were less shrill in their demands. Once again, the discrepancy between reality and what people want to believe produces feelings of alienation in those who—for whatever reason —are already dissatisfied.

In short, alienation has become a fundamental fact of political life for a great many Americans. People are reading Camus, Kierkegaard, Marx, and others who foreshadowed the present awareness of the human plight because they want to understand what has produced this feeling of alienation. For alienation is disquieting and difficult. There are few people who do not want to relate to others in warm and meaningful ways. To most of us, an alienated state is an unhappy state, but it motivates us to understand and to find out how to get out of it.

The intellectual tradition growing out of alienation has been divided between those who seek to understand it philosophically and those who want to change the world to eliminate it. In the United States this distinction would produce at least three variations— though these are neither mutually exclusive, nor all inclusive. They are simply tendencies which have appeared, and many individuals manifest more than one tendency. Groups illustrative of these categories are the "drop-outs," the "hippies," and the "heads," the "religionists," and the "activists."

It may seem strange in a discussion of politics to deal at all with those who reject politics, but this rejection is itself a political act. Those who have "dropped out," who spend their lives in a drug culture, are an example of the psychedelic response. Its style— the language, music, books, food, habits—represents an explicit rejection of the conformity and selfishness of much of American society. By adhering to a new life style (which, it should be pointed out, shares certain characteristics with the culture they are rejecting: "doing your own thing" is both a drug-oriented slogan and the ideology of American business), they implicitly confront the old. Are they challenging the very foundation of social order? Are they questioning the basic Aristotelian concept that to be human is to be political? Or is it that society has denied the Aristotelian primacy of politics by making politics subservient to private interest? Has contemporary society and contemporary political science disregarded the existence of a public philosophy, a general will, a common good? By exposing our emphasis of "the public" and "citizen," they are forcing us to confront our humanity or lack of it. This is the political message of the drug culture and the political question it is asking.

Nonetheless, the drug culture is existential in outlook. No matter how rebellious it may seem, it is essentially passive in its consequences. People who are "stoned" do not make good agents for systematic social change. Like the existentialists, drug-oriented, alienated youth know that things are wrong, but they have not taken positive steps to correct them. They look inward to a better life for themselves rather than outward to a better life for everyone.

Related to the drop-outs are the "religionists," those who express their alienation through the pursuit of the occult and the exotic. In recent years, the popularity of such things as Eastern religion, astrology, ancient myths, macrobiotic diets, mysticism, and other obscure phenomena has increased dramatically. The religionists seem to be affirming their agreement with Nietzsche that it is better to believe in a void than be void of belief. They do believe that God is dead, but it is the God of science and technology. What reflective person today, they ask, can have the blind faith in science and technology that American society requires? Has either made man moral? To the astonishment of their elders, many alienated young people say that of all of modern science only the "pill" has made life any more moral. And it would certainly be difficult to argue that the science of politics, as practiced in the United States, has led to a greater concern for man's humanity. Obviously, the religionist approach to alienation is an attempt to restore meaning and purpose to life in this world. Religionism, however, like the drug culture, is existential in direction and hence inward in consequence. The religionists have yet to constitute a challenge to the existing way of doing things in American society.

Third, the "activists"—often called the New Left or the Movement—are committed to overcoming alienation, to transcending the absurdity of the human condition. What distinguishes them from the other two categories is their commitment to the Aristotelian concept of man as a political animal. This leads many of them to agree with the Marxist concept that what we have to know about alienation is how to eliminate it.

The New Left combines the existential and the Marxist approaches to alienation, difficult as that may seem. The early character of the New Left was described by one of the authors of this book several years ago:

> Today's revolutionists have learned their history well, especially from Michels and Orwell, they distrust *all institutions*, regarding them as instruments of oppression and impediments to freedom, be it Public School 23, Columbia University, the U.S. Army, or the Communist party. They do not desire a revolution in the classical sense, i.e., "the displacement of the rulers by the ruled in order to redress an imbalance of power in the social system."
>
> Whether they know it or not, they are almost anti-Marxists, albeit not free of all the jargon. They certainly are not materialists. Their line of "dissent" is more closely tied to that of Hegel, Nietzsche, Freud, and Sartre than to Marx and Lenin. They recognize that it is *will* rather than *reason* which makes men free. They believe that if one has the will to be free, then he can be free in spite of laws, corporations, wars, or the state. Their activities may best be understood as an endeavor to find ways to sustain and to give concrete expression to this will to be free. [Their resolution] represents a revolution in life style,

the impact of which we have only begun to observe. But it is likely to be more revolutionary than the American, the French, or the Russian "revolutions." [16]

That judgment now needs modification. Much of the New Left clearly belongs to the Marxist tradition. In recent years, many have come to believe that it is not simply *will* that makes one free, but action, particularly political action directed against capitalism and imperialism. The most radical elements of the movement believe that a socialist revolution, along Marxist lines, is required. This means that those who are fighting against capitalism and imperialism—like the National Liberation Front and the Chinese Communist party—must be supported. These people desire a revolution in the classical sense. They have found the answer to alienation through political action.

CONCLUSIONS

Thus, the response to the alienating conditions of American life is varied indeed, touching on nearly all the writers discussed in this book. We have indicated our own preference for the tradition, spanning the range from Aristotle to Marx, that reaffirms the importance of the political. This tradition does not tell us which specific approach to social change is best. As a matter of fact, we disagree among ourselves. But we do believe that conditions which oppress people should be changed. The important point is that alienation need not stop with cynicism and despair, but can go beyond to the hope that appears when people try to regain control over their own lives. This is the meaning of the "revolution" we see around us.

[16] Charles A. McCoy, Letter to *New York Times Magazine*, December 8, 1968, p. 24.

14 Science and Scientific Theories

FOREMOST AMONG CONTEMPORARY approaches to political science is the scientific approach. The previous two chapters on cynicism and alienation examined politics from a normative point of view; that is, most of the writers discussed attempted to establish certain standards and to examine alternative procedures for realizing them. But this normative procedure involves all sorts of problems. What happens when people disagree about the norms? Who is to say that one person's norm is better than another's? How can we tell if the conditions necessary to establish a norm will ever exist? The first ones to raise these questions were a group of philosophers, generally called "logical positivists," who held that statements with normative values could never be proven; they could only be asserted. At first, the debate between normative and scientifically inclined writers only occurred on the intellectual level. But then came political leaders like Adolf Hitler and Joseph Stalin; both proclaimed normative values that led to a revealed "truth," and on the basis of this "truth," certain political acts, like genocide and terror, were justified. Many writers in England and America regarded the rise of dictatorships in the 1930s as the inevitable consequence of normative thought. This is what happens, they said, when normative judgments become the rule. Another way of thinking about political events was necessary—a scientific approach.

It was, however, difficult to agree on a definition of science. And, ironically, each definition tended to be based on a normative view of the world and the role of the scientists in that world. We have already seen how both Marx and Weber, with their contrasting ideologies and statements of scientific purpose, adopted the label "scientific." Marx claimed that he was a scientist because of his complete immersion in a particular method (dialectical materialism) and his identification with one group (the proletariat). Weber, on the contrary, maintained that the scientific observer must not be totally identified with any one group.

Clearly, it is the Weberian notion of science that has been adopted by the contemporary practitioners of a scientific political science. It attracted them because it saw a basic difference between fact and value: fact was provable, value was not. They liked the idea of "objectivity," not being identified with any historical group, but applying their critical insights to all groups. Finally, the image of science as moderate and temperate, rather than totalistic and cataclysmic, appealed to them. They preferred the quieter aspects of science, suggested in Weber's remark about scientific insights often occurring during a walk or when smoking a cigar. Stimulated by such considerations, the Weberian concept of science was adopted as the best method of analyzing political phenomena.

We can see this development in the works of three generations of American political scientists. The differences among them indicate how the scientific study of political phenomena evolved and suggest its implications.

The first generation of scientific political scientists was reacting against a field of study dominated by staid traditionalism. That approach depended on constitutions and procedures to describe political events. Treatises would be written on the rules of procedure in the various state legislatures, pointing out that in some states speakers of the lower house were instrumental in setting agendas, while in others their formal powers were highly circumscribed. No attempt was made to discover why it happened in some places and not others. No attempt was made to look beyond the formal powers to see who was the actual leader of a legislative body.

Scholarly discussions of this sort were often abstract and contained no analysis of the respective powers of the people, parties, groups, and states involved. Critics of this traditionalism noted that life, defined as real people and their political relationships, had to be poured into them. Arthur Bentley's *The Process of Government,* written in the early part of the twentieth century, made this point. But Bentley's voice went unheeded for almost thirty years, as traditional political science continued to dominate the discipline.

The first generation of scientific political scientists developed in the 1930s in the United States. Relying on earlier writers like Bentley, Charles Merriam, a professor at the University of Chicago, became the most outspoken critic of descriptive and legislative traditionalism. He and Harold Lasswell, first Merriam's student and later his colleague, wrote books, emphasizing that the process of politics was just as important, if not more important, as the institutions that made up the government.[1]

They believed that a completely scientific analysis of politics had to deal with such things as political leadership and its psychological aspects, which the traditionalists had often ignored. Furthermore, a process-oriented conception of politics would lead the analyst to many other items overlooked by traditionalists, such as the role of nongovernmental institutions (political parties, corporations, interest groups) in the making of public policy. Finally, Lasswell and Merriam showed how values and norms themselves were political phenomena that had to be explained. If people within a society believed their society to be democratic, the belief might be more important than the actual political status.

In short, Lasswell and Merriam invigorated a dying discipline. Their conception of science was a healthy one, challenging the sterility of technical and descriptive studies of isolated events. In focusing on the informal, the irrational, the not-so-obvious, they liberated the study of politics and began to concentrate on the real world of men and events.

Merriam and Lasswell trained a number of graduate students who became the second generation of scientific political scientists. The names sound like a "who's who" in recent political science. For example, three of the last five presidents of the American Political Science Association studied under Lasswell and Merriam at Chicago. V. O. Key, one of the earlier presidents of the association and also

---

[1] See Charles Merriam, *New Aspects of Politics,* 3d ed. (Chicago: University of Chicago Press, 1970); and Harold Lasswell, *Psychopathology and Politics* (New York: Viking Press, 1960).

one of their students, carried the scientific approach to the study of political parties, voting behavior, and interest groups. In Key's books, political phenomena were analyzed in a novel way. Key loved his subject, and he treated each political party as something to be cherished. At the same time, he sought to explain variations among them. In many ways, Key was the first political scientist to be interested in the infinite variation of political events.

A second student of Lasswell and Merriam, Herbert Simon, returned to focus on the formal institutions of politics, but with a new emphasis and style. Simon developed mathematical techniques to analyze and explain formal organizations and how they function. A third colleague, Gabriel Almond, revolutionized the comparative study of political systems by developing a framework (which will be discussed later in this chapter) for comparing different kinds of political systems. In nearly every area of political inquiry, one or another student of Merriam and Lasswell brought about a scientific revolution (called by yet another student, Robert A. Dahl, the behavioral revolution). But every revolution contains the seeds of a new orthodoxy, and just as Lasswell and Merriam had liberated political science from a traditional orthodoxy, their own students laid the groundwork for a new orthodoxy. These students evolved various models and methods, which, a few years later, their own students considered the only productive way to study political events.

The new orthodoxy of science was completed by the third generation of scientific political scientists, many of whom were students of men like Key, Dahl, Simon, and Almond. By this time, the University of Chicago no longer held the predominant position; Lasswell and Merriam's students were spread throughout the country. The newest generation of students generally isolated smaller phenomenon than whole countries or political parties and attempted to account for variation scientifically by developing more complicated mathematical and statistical techniques of analysis. Quantification, despite a warning by Merriam, became a basic tool of political analysis. As the method was increasingly refined, computer analyses, mathematical models, small-group experiments, intensive data collection, surveys, scaling techniques, and simulations all became part of the new science of politics. It soon became apparent that the new conception rivaled the old in its irrelevance. Modes of analysis took precedence over people and events. Once again, political science was in danger of squeezing life from its subject matter. Ironically, the scientific study of political science wound up resembling the traditional political science it had discredited and replaced.

Nonetheless, scientific political science still is the major approach to the study of political phenomenon. It is based on sophisticated philosophies of science that could not be summarized easily. Yet the approach is too important to pass over. Perhaps the best way to introduce the student to the scientific study of politics is by describing the procedure followed in one typical case. The research design outlined below is one way of studying a specific political problem in a generally "scientific" way. (The fact that this is the second time we have criticized material that we ourselves wrote in the past indicates how much both we and the field are in flux.)

RESEARCH DESIGN

Statement of the Problem.[2]   Descriptions of how politicians campaign for office are many and colorful, but little systematic information exists on the role of the campaign in the political process. To be sure, there are books by X and Y, and studies undertaken by Q, R, Z. But this literature is incomplete because it either lacks empirical evidence or is based on too few cases to formulate adequate generalizations. A review of the literature of political science reveals how little is understood about the role of this key aspect of the political process.

At the same time, politicians and the American public regard the campaign as crucial. Media coverage during campaigns increases. Many politicians use the campaign as a way of finding out what their constituents are thinking and also explaining their own ideas to the people. The campaign thus serves as a link between the politician and the office he holds. It is the arena in which, ideally, the representative accounts to the people. For that reason, understanding the campaign is important to understanding democracy.

Research Orientation.   As suggested above, most research on the campaign has consisted of single studies of single campaigns. While these provide insights and suggestive hypotheses, they do not lead to systematic generalization. A broad approach covering many campaigns is needed, even if it means sacrificing the depth and detail found in a case study. In the proposed study, then, a number of

[2] This research design is abstracted from Alan Wolfe, "The Senatorial Campaign" (Ph.D. diss., University of Pennsylvania, 1967).

campaigns will be analyzed in terms of a typology of campaigns based on certain key variables.

Hypotheses. The basic hypothesis of this study is that the campaign represents an important link between the politician's pre-office experience and the way he performs after he has been elected. To gain a better understanding of this link we will examine the first successful campaign of several politicians to a particular office.

More specific hypotheses follow from the general one. The first group of hypotheses relate the types of campaigns to characteristics of the politicians. For example, the better educated a politician, the more likely he is to use mass media in his campaign. And other predictions about his campaign could be made on the basis of his age, his occupation, his previous political experience, and the like. The second broad group of hypotheses relate the campaign to characteristics of his constituency. For instance, the more well-to-do a politician's constituency, the more likely he will be to use television extensively in his campaign. Other significant characteristics include population density, proximity to New York, and per capita expenditure on education. Finally, a third set of hypotheses would relate the campaign to the conduct of the politician after he was in office. What connection is there between the way a candidate conducts his campaign and the rewards he obtains once elected? Between his campaign and his continuation to higher office? Between his campaign and his interpretation of his own role as a politician? And so on.

Methods of Data Collection. Three key aspects of the politician's campaign can be examined: the amount of support he received from the party organization in his district; the proportion of time he spent discussing valid issues; his "fairness" toward his opponent. Although such items are difficult to measure, a careful study of an election campaign should provide certain objective standards that can be used to classify politicians in each of these areas. By dividing each category into a high and low rating, we can create an eight-fold typology for studying election campaigns. Each category represents a type of campaigner, and each can be labeled accordingly for purposes of analysis. Information for making the classification can be obtained from many sources—the candidates, local newspapers, magazines, autobiographies, campaign literature, and so forth.

The specific politicians we propose to study are the 143 senators elected to the United States Senate for the first time between 1946–64. There are many advantages to studying senators. Much has been written about them, and biographical information and data about their constituencies (states) are readily available. The *Biographical Directory of the American Congress, Statistical Abstract of the United States,* and similar sources contain the information.

The proposed research will be organized into three sections, one for each series of hypotheses described above. One section will analyze which type of politician tends to be which type of campaigner. Another will relate the campaigners to the types of states they come from. Finally, a third section will consider how each type of campaigner functions as a senator. Does he become an "insider" close to power and noncontroversial, or does he develop outside constituencies and little power within the body?

Implications and Explanations. Two theories will be used to interpret the data. Insofar as the campaign affects the senator's behavior, it can be seen as one of a number of stimuli acting upon him. In this sense, learning theory can help us relate the campaign to other determinants of legislative behavior. In addition, the legislator is treated in certain ways by his colleagues. Organization theory can be used to see how the Senate as a formal body reacts to new members and how it uses the completed campaign to evaluate the member who is entering its ranks.

The implications of the research proposed here concern a better understanding of the operation of democracy. The systematic information on different types of campaigners will contribute to a more enlightened view of the business of campaigning. It will suggest the conditions that promote more "rational" forms of campaigning, which should increase the accountability function of the campaign and guard against its irresponsible use.

THE EVALUATION OF SCIENCE

This illustrative research design has been presented in detail to clarify the various aspects of the scientific procedure. The final product of the research project is a research report, similar to the design except that it includes the data, analysis, and conclusions. In the final write-up, the types of campaigners are labeled and illustrated; the hypotheses are put in more specific terms (the wealthier the state, the more likely it is to produce candidate type A and C, but not B and D); and the 143 senators are studied in detail according to each variable. Charts and tables are included to show which hypotheses were verified and which were not. The theoretical discussion at the end tries to suggest why some hypotheses were confirmed and others were not.

Now that we have outlined the procedure for studying politics scientifically, it is easier to evaluate some of the claims made on its behalf. Certainly the idea advanced by some social scientists, that science means the end of ideological thinking and the end of political theory, is contrary to our view, even though, as the example suggests, one of the authors once was a practitioner of the scientific method. After tracing the antecedents of scientific political science to Max Weber, it is easy to see that the contemporary development of political science is also part of the anti-Marxist reaction. This suggests that the distinction some behavioral scientists make between science and ideology is a tenuous one at best. In fact, the behavioral revolution is embedded in political ideology.

The use of scientific methods is part of an attempt to understand political events in the world. In themselves, scientific methods do not suggest how those events should be interpreted (and the reason why they do not are subtle, but nonetheless ideological). Science is now in vogue, just as metaphysics and theology were once in vogue, because it is, ostensibly, an objective pursuit in an age that looks down on ideological biases. But, in fact, the scientific approach is actually embedded in an ideology without having the appearance of one. Hence, "scientists," who often do not even recognize the ideological bias in their own work, claim they are not "ideologues."

The contemporary approach to science in the study of politics resembles ideology in many ways. It suggests a certain amount of unwarranted certainty. Instead of describing the world in all its complexity, the behavioral scientist reduces everything to hypotheses and data, making things tangible that may very well be intangible. Problems of validity—whether the numbers actually represent the real situation—are generally passed over in the hopes that future scientists will solve them. Second, science possesses a world view and a history with which the current practitioner can identify. Younger ones trace their heritage through Key, Almond, and Dahl to Lasswell and Merriam. Older ones may even go back to Newton or Einstein, or other key figures who have contributed to the scientific world view. Thus, the contemporary scientist can turn to a number of classical texts for inspiration, although he chides the ideologists or theologians for doing the same thing. Third, science involves formula and routine. A given event can be studied in the context of a preexisting research design and interpreted in light of preexisting theories. In this sense, the scientific study of politics does not require a particularly high level of imagination or subtlety. As C. Wright Mills observed:

> Much of such work, I am now convinced, has become the mere following of a ritual—which happens to have gained commercial and foundation value—rather than, in the words of its spokesmen, a "commitment to the hard demands of science." [3]

The similarities between science and ideology are only part of the problem. Scientific political science, despite its claims of objectivity and nonpartisanship, is associated with certain political attitudes. This is not surprising, for if the scientific mood developed in reaction to Marxism, then we would expect its practitioners to be anti-Marxists (either of a liberal or conservative bent), and the few Marxists around to be antibehavioralists. Such, with almost no exceptions, is the case. Marxists tend to focus on total systems, examining major questions like the origin of the state or the relation between the political superstructure and its economic base. Behavioral science, by its very nature, is less totalistic. To collect data, it asks much narrower questions, questions that Marxists would never think to ask. For this reason, there is a correlation between one's approach to the study of politics and one's conclusions. Although the scientific method may be neutral in the struggle between liberals and conservatives, it cannot possibly be neutral between Marxists and anti-Marxists.

Of all the events studied by scientific political scientists, none has been more thoroughly examined than the act of voting. Since the 1944 presidential elections, a team of social scientists has been on the scene every four years, armed with surveys, samples, questionnaires, and an interest in why people make the decisions they do. With each election their methodology has grown more sophisticated, especially under the leadership of the Survey Research Center at the University of Michigan, which has trained most of these researchers. Out of these studies has grown a set of hypotheses about

[3] C. Wright Mills, *The Sociological Imagination* (New York: Oxford University Press, 1959), p. 72.

voting, extraordinary amounts of data designed to confirm or deny these hypotheses, attempts to generate broader theories to explain the results, and suggestions about the implications of the analysis for democratic theory.

Most people regard the voting studies as models of objectivity. After all, although studying something as controversial as presidential elections, the researchers scrupulously avoid taking sides among the candidates. This impression is reinforced by their books and research reports, models of clinical detachment and surgical precision. The candidate's programs are not evaluated. In fact, every effort is made (usually successfully) to let the respondents speak for themselves. The report is supposed to reflect their opinions on policy matters, rather than those of the researchers. Yet, certain biases inevitably creep in. Studying the electoral process, as we pointed out earlier, is in itself an ideological act. It emphasizes the importance of voting, automatically assigning it a crucial role in democracy.

Some critics argue that the real leadership of the United States exists outside the electoral process. Although one does not vote for the leaders of large corporations, they may be more powerful than the political officeholders. Therefore, these critics contend, voting studies implicitly support existing political reality and, for that reason, are not completely objective. Clearly, they are not as objective as their authors would like to think they are.

When they attempt to relate their findings to democratic theory, the authors of the voting studies usually reveal their own political values. For example, the second voting study, done in 1948, contained an explicit statement summarizing what the researchers believed their report implied in terms of values.[4] Many people had been under the impression that for a democracy to work well the citizenry had to be well read, rational, interested, and informed. The survey showed, however, that most voters were uninformed about the choices they made, generally expressing a wide variety of irrational explanations for their votes. Up to this point, the analysis was empirical. But what is one to make of the uninformed, irrational political behavior of American citizens? A Marxist would conclude that it was an empirical demonstration of false consciousness.

[4] Bernard R. Berelson, Paul F. Lazarsfeld, and William McPhee, *Voting* (Chicago: Phoenix Books, 1966).

The masses, he would say, were manipulated by their leaders into this docile state, characterized by misinformation and prejudice. The fact that most workers voted for the conservative candidate would be regarded by the Marxist as proof of his false consciousness interpretation. But the authors of the voting study were not Marxists; and their surprising conclusion was that irrationality, apathy, and misinformation were beneficial in a democracy. Contrary to all the usual precepts of democratic theory, they contended that an aroused electorate would destroy the passivity that is basic to the smooth operation of a democratic society. Democracy needs a cushion of nonvoters and ignorant voters to add stability. Any attempt to arouse the "masses" would destroy that stability and democracy as well. In this interpretation, the authors' value bias is clearly a conservative one, stressing order and stability. It is also elitist, viewing the voters and nonvoters as ignorant and uninformed in comparison with their leaders. A book such as *Voting* can profitably be read today as an excellent example of how a conservative ideology is masked behind an impressive array of charts and data.

More recent voting studies are less crude in proclaiming their values, but no less subjective. The 1964 election between Barry Goldwater and Lyndon Johnson, for example, is treated in an interesting fashion.[5] The authors show conclusively that Goldwater's assumption about "hidden" Republicans who would come out of the woodwork on election day to carry him into office was based on myth or wishful thinking rather than political reality. Not only were there no hidden Republicans, but nearly every strategic element in the Goldwater campaign was based on inaccurate appraisals of the American electorate. This was an interesting study that ran counter to the usual approach of voting study researchers by commenting on the specific issues of the day. Perhaps the authors felt that this election was so vital that comment was necessary. In any case, their bias is quite clear. It indicates how over the years the primary politics of the voting study researchers has moved from conservative to liberal, especially in the face of conservatives like Barry Goldwater.

This brings us to an important point. Since the ideology that is

[5] Philip E. Converse, Aage R. Clausen, and Warren E. Miller, "Electoral Myth and Reality: the 1964 Election," *American Political Science Review*, 59 (June 1965): 321–36.

most compatible with behavioral science is liberalism, critiques of behavioral science as an ideology are going to come from the groups most critical of liberalism itself—conservatives on the right and radicals on the left. We are speaking here of criticisms of science as an ideology, not of its vulnerability as an impossible goal. The science of human behavior has made impressive advances in its hypotheses, data collection, and predictions. We do not feel that it is somehow "wrong" to study human beings scientifically because they are so unique, individualistic, or complicated. And we do not agree with those who maintain that behavioral science has not been scientific enough and should become *more* rigorous and *more* scientific. But behavioral science is by no means objective; rather, it is part of the development of political thought, with its own ideology and preconceived ways of viewing the world. We should ask: Science for what and in the service of whom?

The fact that behavioralism as an ideology is criticized by both the right and the left is bound to be somewhat confusing. One school of thought, centering around Leo Strauss, sees the rise of behavioralism as a left-wing reaction against its own traditionalism, but a reaction that has become so established it can hardly be considered left wing any more. On the opposite end of the political spectrum, young radicals see it as the essence of a reactionary and right-wing approach to human affairs. To them, behavioral political science indicates the academic mentality of political scientists, who are too busy constructing abstractions to concern themselves with power and who holds it. Surprisingly, the conservative and radical points of view are actually quite compatible here. When Straussians charge that behavioral science is left wing, they are referring to the domination of behavioral science by liberals. When radicals charge that the dominant ideology of behavioralism is conservative, they mean that it supports the status quo, and liberalism is the basic ideology supporting the status quo in America today. The fact that the extremes of the political continuum join in this criticism shows, at least, that both ends place liberalism in the middle.

THEORY

One important consequence of the scientific study of politics is the demand for theory. This does not refer to the kinds of political theory discussed in Part II of this book or in the other chapters in

Part III. Scientific theories are of another order; they are attempts to relate the findings of specific scientific studies so that they form a coherent whole which explains other social phenomena. For science to do more than describe the world, scientific theories are necessary. A number of political scientists are currently working in this area. Two contemporary theoreticians, David Easton and Gabriel Almond, offer good examples of the process.

In 1953, David Easton published *The Political System,* the first of three books in which he develops his conceptual approach.[6] This first volume is partly a polemic against the traditional modes of approach. He castigates the profession for being too legalistic and restricting itself to the study of formal political institutions. He began to develop his own model of a political system, which has been elaborated in two subsequent volumes.

Easton defines a political system as a set of interactions among the actors in a society. But what distinguishes political interaction from all other kinds of social interaction is the unifying concept—"the authoritative allocation of values for society." By authoritative Easton means that the decisions are accepted as binding by those subject to the system; the subjects perceive the rules as legitimate. Since authoritative allocation of values also occurs in such institutions as the family and the corporation, some further limitations of the term political are required. For if such parapolitical subsystems as the family were included, the term political would become all encompassing, which would destroy the traditional understanding of political and also make the definition of political system useless as a guide for scholarly research. Therefore, Easton specifies that a political system deals with the authoritative allocation of values for the society *as a whole.* It would appear that such metaphysical categories as the "state" and "sovereignty," whose use was criticized earlier, have reappeared. In short, the definition of politics and the political is not much better than the following one: The authoritative allocation of values that the trained political scientists choose to study.

Putting aside this "boundary question," that is, setting limits to the domain of politics, Easton's political system may be described by the following diagram:

[6] David Easton, *The Political System* (New York: Knopf, 1953); *A Framework for Political Analysis* (Englewood Cliffs, N.J.: Prentice-Hall, 1965); *A Systems Analysis of Political Life* (New York: John Wiley, 1965).

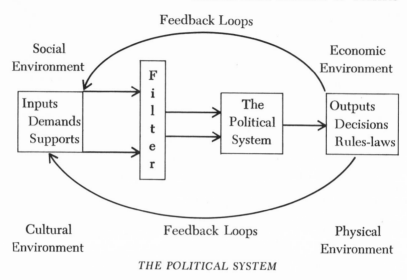

THE POLITICAL SYSTEM

A hypothetical illustration may be useful here. Let us suppose that the life span of individuals has been increased because of technological changes in the field of medicine. This change in the "environment" could lead to a political demand for inclusion of medical care for the aged within the social security system. This "input demand" is filtered by such mechanisms as political parties, congressional committees and the like, so that the flow of demands proceeds at a rate the political system can handle. (However, if the filtering systems are not operating properly, the demands may become excessive and therefore dysfunctional to the maintenance of the system.)

The ability of the system to process the demands is of course related to the "support inputs" going into the system (for example, have past performances led to diffuse support for the system or to distrust or hostility toward the system?). The system can rely on such supports as habit and tradition, but it must be remembered that drawing on supports is like drawing money from a bank account. Just as new funds must be added to keep the account balanced, new support must be added if the system is to maintain its equilibrium.

An output in this case might be the Medicare program, which will generate certain feedbacks. One would assume that a successful Medicare program would lead to demands for extending government-financed health care to other segments of the population.

Furthermore, successful Medicare might increase the level of support the elderly give to the political system.

One unique feature of political systems compared to biological systems is that they may alter their basic structures rather than disappear when faced with an extremely dysfunctional demand-support ratio. For example the Weimar Republic in Germany changed into the Third Reich of Hitler. Political systems in the Eastonian world neither die nor fade away; they only metamorphosize.

Ambitious as it is, Easton's model has certain severe theoretical and empirical limitations. Few people seem to know what actually happens in the political system itself—that is, what happens to demands when they enter the system as inputs and when they emerge as outputs in the forms of laws, decisions, and so on. Furthermore, Easton's model seems to possess an inherent, albeit implicit, conservatism, in which system maintenance becomes the goal and questions about the justice of the system are not considered. Since only some questions are asked, one might conclude that the questions *not* asked constitute the political bias or the model. Easton's model may help us understand reality, but it is not geared to changing it.

A similar conclusion emerges from the writings of Gabriel Almond. The theoretical model developed by Almond represents a functional approach to the study of comparative politics.[7] While somewhat less comprehensive than Easton's system analysis, Almond's model does provide a tool for comparative analysis which is not culture-bound and which facilitates a truly comparative approach. Almond wants to make meaningful comparisons between developing nations and "mature" industrial states feasible. He maintains that traditional approaches have failed to do this because, first, they are usually restricted to a country by country approach and, second, they have focused on formal institutions such as the executive or legislative branches of government, but failed to realize that the functions these institutions perform are often quite dissimilar. For example, one might assume, incorrectly, that elections perform the same role in the USSR and the United States.

[7] Gabriel A. Almond, "A Functional Approach to Comparative Politics," in *The Politics of the Developing Areas,* eds. Gabriel A. Almond and James S. Coleman (Princeton, N.J.: Princeton University Press, 1960); and Gabriel A. Almond and G. Bingham Powell, Jr., *Comparative Politics: A Developmental Approach* (Boston: Little, Brown, 1966).

In his initial writings on a functional approach, Almond suggested that certain functions must be performed in any active political system. Therefore, a study should begin by examining functions, rather than governmental structures. Almond identified seven functions that all political systems perform, no matter how primitive or how complex they are. The study of these functions is the study of politics. There were four "input" functions—political socialization and recruitment, interest articulation, interest aggregation, and political communication—and three "output" functions—rule making, rule application, and rule adjudication.

Political socialization is the process by which persons learn the political roles and values society assigns to them. Of the many institutions that perform this function, the family and the schools are regarded as the most significant. It is asserted that in primitive societies socialization ends early, while in developed societies, it continues throughout life; however, even there, it is the early years which are the most influential. Recruitment starts where socialization tapers off; that is, once an individual has learned the rules, he is allowed to play in the game.

Interest articulation is described as the process by which the people communicate their desires to the governing elites. Interests may be articulated through four types of groups: associated groups (labor unions, manufacturers or trade associations); nonassociated groups (those which one is more or less born into, like racial and religious categories); overt political groups organized for a special goal or purpose (a conservation lobby); and anomic groups (spontaneous groups or actions). In general, before articulated interests can be successful, a number of interests must be amalgamated. While in theory, various structures can aggregate diverse interests, it is the political party which is assigned this task in most of the "functional" literature.

The fourth input function, communication, is in many ways the most general and diffuse function. (In fact, political scientist Karl Deutsch would reorganize all of political science in terms of communication.) Almond appears to restrict it to its role as an integrating function within his broad structural-functional approach. Communication is the lubrication which keeps the other parts moving harmoniously.

The output functions of rule making, rule application, and rule adjudication follow so closely the traditional concepts of legislative, executive, and judicial functions that little attention is paid to them.

As influential as Almond's approach has been, it has four serious drawbacks. First, the whole grand scheme is not as culturally free as it would appear, in fact, quite the contrary. The model is clearly an abstraction drawn from Western democratic experience. The seven functional categories are based on an analysis of the highly developed, integrated, and formal political systems of the industrial Western nations, particularly the United States. And they are imposed on the unstructured, diffuse, and culturally distinct underdeveloped nations of the world. These nations are not considered aggregations of people, in Rousseau's terms, but articulated associations which, if not fully developed, are nevertheless in the process of developing a formal political system with its accompanying inputs, outputs, and feedback mechanisms. This is often accomplished by underemphasizing the ritualistic and personalistic character of the underdeveloped society. In the effort to develop universal categories, the all-important cultural distinctions are ignored.

Second, this parochialism becomes chauvinistic when applied to a comparison between developing and developed nations. It assumes that the good of all political development is for nations to become industrialized and "democratic" like the United States. In fact, this requirement accommodates the model. Third, in spite of its interest in development, the model is static rather than dynamic. It does not deal with change.

Finally, perhaps the most serious difficulty is that talking knowledgeably about functional analysis is much easier than actually producing a functional explanation. Where there has been a serious attempt to apply a structural-functional model to an underdeveloped nation, either the facts have had little relation to the model, or the data appear to have been forced to fit the model and are often distorted or ignored. Although Almond's scheme was supposed to facilitate comparison, most countries are compared only to the abstract model, not to each other.

CONCLUSION

To many who practice the scientific study of politics, the procedures and methods now being worked out have an intrinsic validity. In this age of science, scientific considerations dominate much of what we do. Science is seen by many as the product of our history;

this is where we have come, and problems that plagued nonscientists
—such as values and objectivity—no longer apply.

We reject this view. The demand for science and the contribution
of theories are attempts to understand political phenomena that
occur in the real world. And whether they are recognized or not,
questions of value and political choice appear in this world. This is
what we meant when we called science an ideology. The scientific
study of politics must show what it can contribute toward understanding the world and making it a better place to live. Because so
many scientists say that their approach has no contribution to make
in this area, we are suspicious of a purely scientific approach to
politics. We are not opposed to building theories; our complaint is
that the theories of Easton and Almond are inadequate because they
have tried to remove the political content from them.

The scientific study of politics developed at a time when ideas and
controversy were suspect in the United States. That is one reason
why political science seems to have so little to say about questions
of racism, exploitation, sexism, imperialism, war, oppression, repression, and other political phenomena. The only way we can hope to
understand politics, we submit, is by treating it politically. Instead
of emptying it of content, it has to be understood in political terms.
In the next chapter, we will examine the recent outburst of politics
in America and chart some of its implications for the study of
politics.

15 Politics and Permanence

WE HAVE TALKED a great deal about the end of ideology and the decline of political institutions in this book. If that were really the case, there would be nothing "political" left to discuss and everything we have written would be meaningless. Obviously, therefore, we do not believe that politics is about to disappear. But many other people seem to think so. One reason for writing this book was to underscore the need for understanding the foundations of politics, a form of human activity that will always be with us, at least in the type of world we have today.

In Chapter 2, we presented two definitions of politics: one emphasized conflict over power and one stressed conflict over the search for the good life. Under the first definition (which was rejected as the basis for this book), one of two things would have to happen to cause a decline in politics: either power would have to become unimportant or conflict over who has the power would have to decrease. Clearly, the first situation has not occurred. If anything, the amount of political power elites can mobilize is greater now than ever before. There are a number of reasons for this. More and more activity is defined as governmental, including things which were considered part of the private domain a few years ago. Furthermore, increased technology has enabled large organizations to do more things, simply because the means are now available for doing them. Man always wanted to go to the moon, but only recently could a government undertake that activity. So, political power is as important, if not more important, than ever.

A better case can be made about the decline of conflict over power. In the United States, questions involving the allocation of power within the elite are supposed to be decided by the political party system. When the Democrats win an election, they take power; when the Republicans win, the power is theirs. Sharp conflict between the parties is almost nonexistent, especially in matters of policy. Both agree on all the essential questions facing the political system. That was shown in Chapter 3. But, has conflict between the parties over their organization of governmental power declined as well? Do the parties disagree about which one should rule? There is a good deal of rhetoric which suggests that they do. The Republican minority leader of the Senate may debate the Democratic national chairman about which party is more capable of running the country. But this debate really has a flat and uninteresting sound to it. Recent experience has shown that both parties can run the country equally well, or unwell, depending on one's point of view, because neither party really "runs" the country at all. Insofar as we are governed, it is through private centers of power and by a trained bureaucracy that is unaffected by traditional party conflict. Anyone who focuses exclusively on the political parties as agents for the governance of a system might be tempted to conclude that, in the United States at least, politics is indeed disappearing.

There are other reasons, besides the similarity of political parties, for thinking that politics may not be with us much longer. Even the term "politics" has become a dirty word. Anyone who enters politics quickly learns to develop an apologetic style when people ask him what he does for a living. Resentment against politics and government is expressed in many ways. Consider the following figures from a national survey made in 1964:[1]

---

[1] Lloyd A. Free and Hadley Cantril, *The Political Beliefs of Americans: A Study of Public Opinion* (New York: Simon and Schuster, 1968), pp. 24–25.

	AGREE	DISAGREE	DON'T KNOW
Social problems here in this country could be solved more effectively if the government would only keep its hands off and let the people in local communities handle their own problems in their own ways	49%	38%	13%
The government has gone too far in regulating business and interfering with the free enterprise system	42	39	19
There is a definite trend toward socialism in this country	46	22	32

Similar polls have revealed a decline in trust, not only toward government, but toward the men who occupy governmental positions. Studying how the prestige of some seventy occupations changed between 1947 and 1963, two sociologists found that the office of governor dropped from second to fifth place, that of congressman from fourth to eighth, mayor from sixth to seventeenth, and county judge from thirteenth to fourteenth. The only government position that did not decline in status was the relatively nonpolitical one of Supreme Court justice; that remained first.[2] These polls clearly reflect the attitude of the mother, who would like to see her son become president, but recoils at the thought of him as a politician.

And other evidence is presented to show that traditional politics is declining in importance. The classic figure in American political history, the urban boss, is disappearing. He is being replaced by a variety of new political types, none as colorfully political. In some American cities reform groups have gained control of the city administration; much of their effort has been directed toward replacing partisan conflict in city government with a more equitable adminis-

[2] Robert W. Hodge, Paul M. Siegel, and Peter H. Rossi, "Occupational Prestige in the United States, 1925–63," *American Journal of Sociology*, 70 (November 1964): 286–302.

tration apparatus. Other functions of the city boss, particularly his ability to provide such benefits as food and money for his constituents, have been depoliticized and taken over, increasingly, by national administrations. Finally, those activities of the city boss that were related to winning elections are being performed by professional campaign managers and public relations experts, whose ability is based on academic expertise, not on the intuition and intense involvement of the city boss. All the evidence points to a significant decline in the role of the most political personality in American history.

At the national level, too, anything avowedly partisan is in disrepute. We tend to emphasize cooperation more than conflict. Since World War II, conflict between the parties in the area of foreign policy has almost completely disappeared. When President Truman assured the nation that he was going to be wary of anything done by our wartime ally the Soviet Union, almost unanimous cries of approval were heard from both parties. From then on, either foreign policy goals have been universally accepted, or when conflict did arise over them, it was not along partisan lines. This state of unanimity existed toward nearly all American foreign policy from World War II until Vietnam. Controversy over the country's role in Korea, and in such places as Guatemala, Iran, Greece, or Lebanon, was not aired. Furthermore, the public controversy over the war in Vietnam falls into the second pattern. Although the war was substantially Americanized during Democratic administrations, divisions over its propriety have not occurred on the basis of party. Many Democrats broke with Lyndon Johnson over this issue, while many Republicans supported him. But there were also Democrats who agreed and Republican dissenters. There was simply no correlation between support for Vietnam and party membership. The same pattern has taken place under President Nixon.

The pattern associated with domestic goals is similar, though not as pronounced. The Democratic party still considers itself the party of the little man and thinks that the Republicans are oriented toward big business. There is only a superficial truth to these characterizations. Most large corporations support both parties because it is in their interest to do so. Oil, the industry many observers consider the most powerful, habitually supports Democrats through its outlets in Texas (see Chapter 6). And Robert McNamara, the president of an automobile company, became secretary of defense in the Kennedy administration. On the other hand, the only secretary of labor who had been a union official, served under a Republican president. This pattern of similar support for the two parties is a reflection of their similar programs. Both parties generally agree that the welfare state must be continued; that corporations should be free to do what they like as long as their activities do not violate the law or the public interest; that the federal government should sponsor a moderate program for assisting citizens currently in poverty, provided that it does not interfere with the vested interests of any major segment of power in America; and that those who denounce these goals should be treated as irresponsible outcasts and pariahs. Partisanship is not expected to interfere with any of these goals. There may be slight disagreement between the parties on how to reach them: more Republicans may favor strong action against dissidents and weak action against poverty; more Democrats may take the opposite approach. But, just as in the case of foreign policy, there is little partisan conflict over the desirability of such goals.

All the evidence presented here to support the proposition that politics is disappearing has been based upon a definition of politics that we have rejected. From that perspective, the argument is persuasive. With the rise of bureaucratization and the emerging consensus between the parties over society's major goals, politics—defined as the study of who has power—is on the decline in all advanced, industrial systems. Most people in the United States, Britain, France, and West Germany do not care which party has power because it makes little difference to their personal lives. Their apathy is quite understandable. In the long run, the "great game of politics" is of interest only to those who are playing the game. Being a permanent spectator can be quite boring. People who have been excluded from the game naturally find it difficult to work up enthusiasm for the way it is played. So long as no major crises arise, everyone seems satisfied.

But we feel that the second definition of politics (discussed in Chapter 2) is much more helpful in understanding the contemporary world. When we speak of the permanence of politics, we are referring to politics in this second sense—conflict over the attainment of the good life. Before concluding that politics has suffered a sharp decline, we must examine the status of this second conception of politics. Perhaps, politics as the search for the good life has even increased in recent years.

Some people tell us that this second form of politics is also on the decline. We have already discussed (in Chapters 3 and 4) those who proclaim an end of ideology and found them to be premature. If ideology were really at an end, then politics as we have defined it would also, by definition, be finished, and this concluding chapter would be irrelevant. The "end of ideology" school believed that, because fundamental political problems had essentially been solved, political controversy would no longer involve *total*, competitive programs, but would focus instead on the narrower question of ways of reaching generally agreed upon goals. Daniel Bell has described this state:

> Few serious minds believe any longer that one can set down "blueprints" and through "social engineering" bring about a new utopia of social harmony. At the same time, the older "counter-beliefs" have lost their intellectual force as well. Few "classic" liberals insist that the State should play no role in the economy, and few serious conservatives, at least in England and on the Continent, believe that the Welfare State is "the road to serfdom." In the Western world, therefore, there is today a rough consensus among intellectuals on political issues: the acceptance of a Welfare State; the desirability of decentralized power; a system of mixed economy and of political pluralism.[3]

This sounds very much like our discussion of the decline of partisan controversy over domestic goals. Yet the focus is different. The earlier discussion was just about parties. The "end of ideology," on the other hand, suggests that the entire population fundamentally agrees upon goals. In other words, we should all be getting along better because we are in substantial agreement.

What evidence is there of a decline in ideology? Earlier we cited some figures showing that the American public was sharply divided over the role of government. These figures should now be contrasted with others from the same poll:[4]

[3] Daniel Bell, *The End of Ideology: On the Exhaustion of Political Ideas in the Fifties* (New York: Free Press, 1960), p. 402.

[4] Free and Cantril, *The Political Beliefs of Americans*, pp. 14–15.

	AGREE	DISAGREE	DON'T KNOW
The federal government has a responsibility to try to reduce unemployment	75%	18%	7%
The federal government has a responsibility to try to do away with poverty in this country	72	20	8

In addition, 63 percent approved of Medicare, 62 percent of federal aid to education, 75 percent of federally sponsored job retraining, and 67 percent of the Head Start Program.

These figures would appear to be contradictory—showing a lack of support for the idea of government but a good deal of support for the government's programs. They point to a remarkable consensus on the goals of what is called the welfare state, despite a good deal of publicly expressed disagreement. Combined with a consensus in foreign policy on the need for combating communism, an even greater consensus than the one on domestic policy, it is little wonder that some have concluded that ideology is on the wane. Yet this conclusion is inaccurate; there has in fact been an increase in politics in the last few years.

Since it did not take traditional forms, this recent outburst of politics went unrecognized, at first. For one thing, it occurred outside the political party system and had very little to do with the electoral process. Thus, the decline in partisanship mentioned above is directly linked to this new form of politics. Those who declared politics had ended were focusing on the traditional site of conflict, the political parties. When they found no conflict there, they concluded politics had declined. But, like a pillow, when you press politics down in one place, it will pop out in another. Since the parties were so similar, divergent views had to be expressed in other places—such as the civil rights movement, which transcended the parties and came directly to Washington; the peace movement, which tried to stop most of the fighting in Vietnam by working outside the parties or by using the parties but losing; urban riots, which, although they do not look political, are highly expressive actions of people pressing for a good life; student politics, a phenomenon which has now occurred in nearly every country of the world, regardless of ideology and stage of development. An examination of each of these movements will show how they signify a resurgence of politics.

The nature of racial conflict in the United States has changed within a few years from nonviolent and integrationist to self-defensive, coalitionist, yet separatist. It is interesting that both methods rejected traditional partisan conflict to work out new approaches toward the good life. The first method attempted to attain its goals was through moral witness and mass pressure. Moral witness was designed to shame the government into action. Accepting firehoses without protest, publicly declaring your tolerance for the man who is attacking you, hunger strikes—activities of this sort were designed to appeal to the consciences of those in power. The best example of mass pressure was the August 1963 march on Washington, involving over 200,000 people. Although there was no specific attempt to "lobby" in the traditional sense of the word, the marchers hoped to impress Congress and the president with the potential support for their cause. The speakers at the rally, including labor leaders, religious leaders, civil rights leaders, and politicians, tried repeatedly to make this point. In both cases, the political parties were virtually ignored.

When the emphasis shifted from nonviolence to self-defense and from integration to coalition, the lack of involvement with political parties remained. The new attitude took many forms: public declarations by what were called "black power advocates" suggesting that "whitey" was "gonna get it"; attempts to solve the economic problems by building up institutions in the ghetto; attempts to form alliances with white radical groups to work for change in local areas; unorganized, spontaneous violence against landlords, store owners, and police in major cities; and attempts to work through generally non-Christian religions to provide spiritual uplift for the American black man. All these approaches took place outside the political parties. In some cases there were attempts to win elections in local areas. Thus, the Newark Community Union Project tried to elect one or two state legislators from Newark's Central Ward. The rebuffs they met eventually led them to reject such a procedure in favor of what was called "direct action." Once again, traditional political activity was abandoned.

The peace movement resembled the first phase of the civil rights movement, except that there was more electoral activity. In addition to mass demonstrations and nonviolent resistance, there were also "peace candidates" who campaigned against both major parties in congressional elections. None of these candidates won. It is hard to say what their purpose was in running, except perhaps to demonstrate the futility of trying to change things through the electoral process. But much of this changed in 1968, with the McCarthy presidential campaign. Here, a candidate with a clear-cut program to end the war forced the incumbent president to bow out, won most of the primaries, but did not win his party's nomination. Once again, it seems that the movement was not as interested in electing its candidate to office as in demonstrating its potential strength to those who were already there. In other words, the electoral process was accepted, but its traditional purposes were rejected.

Student political activism grew out of the peace and civil rights movements, but it has recently become a force in its own right. In general, the rebellions have had two types of goals: some, like Berkeley in 1964, were designed to change the nature of one specific university; and some, like Columbia in 1968, focused on American society through an examination of the university. In neither case was the electoral process of any use because most students were excluded from the process by their age, and because the electoral process is not concerned with the power of large, public groups like universities that are outside public control. However, there is good reason to believe that even if both of these objections were removed, the movement still would have rejected the traditional electoral process. For those forms of political activity had much in common with those already mentioned concerning the civil rights and peace movements. There was a sense of urgency, a distrust of the parties, a feeling that using the electoral process condemned one to timeless impotence, and an implicit critique of all of American society. One of the ironies of this situation is that the student protest had a lot to do with giving the vote to the 18–21 age group. But, now, many of them feel it is meaningless and will not bother to exercise their prerogative. This is how political movements develop outside the major parties.

One other political movement is interesting because it works through the party system and the electoral process, yet presents a systematic critique of the American system of government. This is the activity at the right end of the political spectrum. The right views the Republican party as historically its own. Therefore, it feels an obligation to work within it to capture it. In both 1964 and 1968, this tactic proved successful; the right showed that, contrary to the expectations of political scientists, an ideological political movement could capture the presidential nomination of a major party and even win the presidency by forming alliances with other groups. Yet at the same time, some segments of the right reject this approach. Supporters of George Wallace, for example, accept the electoral process but reject the two-party system. At this writing, it seems that their approach is rapidly gaining converts, as evidenced by the election of James L. Buckley as senator from New York on the Conservative party ticket. Other segments of the right reject the electoral process and all political parties either by supporting violent means to gain control of the government or by attempting to influence policy makers through mass letter-writing campaigns and similar forms of mass activity. So it would seem, then, that conflict outside the party system occurs in every part of the political spectrum but the center.

It is important to realize how political all these movements are. Not everyone realizes it. In a book called *Anti-Politics in America*, political scientist John Bunzel attacks these dissident groups.

> Preoccupied with their own social diagnoses and cures, they are distrustful of politics. They cannot abide its mediocrity and are unconcerned with accommodation and conciliation. They have little interest in searching for acceptable solutions to difficult problems, in many cases preferring instead to impose their own preconceived solutions on problems. . . . They reject politics as a way of getting things done because it does not represent unequivocal evidence of moral excellence.[5]

Obviously, Bunzel has a different conception of politics than we do. If all groups just discussed were really antipolitical, then politics would be neither an inclusive nor a significant activity. If it is going to have any meaning at all, politics must include groups that reject traditional approaches but are based on the search for a better life.

And this leads us to the major conclusion of the book: politics as the search for the good life will persist so long as the good life has not been attained. This conclusion suggests that people are rational —when they are treated unfairly, they will seek ways to end that unfair treatment. Their search may be uneven; they may be quiet for

[5] John H. Bunzel, *Anti-Politics in America* (New York: Knopf, 1967).

some time, even generations. But they will not remain quiet forever. Although the world has never been perfect, someone has always been trying to make it perfect. That is what we mean by politics. As long as the world remains imperfect, this form of activity will continue.

We regard any suggestion that politics should cease as unrealistic. No doubt someone has told you, at one time or another, that the time for politics is over, that you and he should get together and cooperate. What he was probably saying was that you should stop trying to dominate him and let him dominate you. Those who call for an end to politics generally want to keep things the way they are. They are not seeking an end to politics but an end to challenges to their control. E. H. Carr has demonstrated that this "doctrine of the harmony of interests" reflects the self-serving outlook of the privileged.

> The doctrine of the harmony of interests . . . is the natural assumption of a prosperous and privileged class, whose members have a dominant voice in the community and are therefore naturally prone to identify its interest with their own. In virtue of this identification, any assailant of the interests of the dominant group is made to incur the odium of assailing the alleged common interest of the whole community. . . . The doctrine of a harmony of interests thus serves as an ingenious moral device invoked, in perfect sincerity, by privileged groups in order to justify and maintain their dominant position.[6]

Those who wish to end politics without the creation of a good life for all, then, are cheating those who do not share in the good life. They are also calling for an end to one specific type of politics. They are saying that anyone who challenges the status quo is being political, whereas anyone who upholds it is doing his job or being a good citizen. But politics cannot be defined in a way that excludes people who are doing political things. One consequence of the ubiquity of politics, then, is that it includes everyone in one form or another. And there are other consequences of our conclusion.

The law of political ubiquity holds for all political systems, not just this country's. This is even true of "totalitarian" systems, al-

[6] Edward H. Carr, *The Twenty Year's Crisis, 1919–1939: An Introduction to the Study of International Relations* (New York: Harper Torchbooks, 1964), p. 80.

though they are often alleged to have no politics at all. In Chapter 7, we discussed convergence theories stressing the similarity between those regimes called totalitarian and those called democratic. We will return to those theories here with the emphasis on the similarity in political processes, rather than the similarity in bureaucratic structure.

Both politics as the struggle for power and politics as the search for a good life exist in the Soviet Union. But the former is usually overdiscussed, while the latter is often neglected. It is now recognized that a one-party political system does not eliminate the struggle for power, but merely channels it into different directions. Thus, the deposing of Nikita Khrushchev and the retirement of Lyndon Johnson can be viewed as similar processes that took dissimilar forms. We do not know what caused Khrushchev's demise, but we can assume that he no longer possessed the confidence of a constituency within the Communist party, which is crucial to governing the country. Similarly, Johnson lost the support of his constituency within his Democratic party. Furthermore, both men lost power because of poor policies. Agriculture proved as troublesome to Khrushchev as the National Liberation Front did to Johnson. Finally, in each case the successors followed a policy of mollification, taking personality out of politics and trying to calm the populace in order to make a fresh start on the problems.

In many cases, Western writers treat power struggles within the Soviet Union as sinister and evil, while viewing similar struggles in the United States as the essence of democracy. Such a distinction is untenable. Wherever it occurs, politics as the struggle for power takes similar forms. Alliances are made and broken between the most unlikely of potential allies. Deals are made; deals are broken. Some people are adept at playing the game, while others find they cannot stand the competition and retire to the sidelines. Friendship and loyalty become secondary values, less important than the pursuit of power. Some attach themselves to the careers of others and follow them wherever they go. Some approach the struggle expecting to convert the participants to idealism and come away dazed and uncommunicative. Because the rewards of power are great, all other things become subservient to its pursuit. Few other subjects are discussed. Gossip runs rampant. Political capitals that have no independent cultural history are the dullest or the most exciting places in the world, dull to people with many interests, exciting to those obsessed with power. Such a capital is just as likely to be Washington, D.C., as Ankara, São Paulo, or a provincial capital somewhere in the Soviet Union.

All this is readily apparent to the observer who is looking for similarities among political systems. What is not so obvious is the similarity surrounding politics as the struggle for the good life. An American report on Soviet politics often depicts a situation of critical sterility; there seems to be little significant political discussion. Everyone adheres to the Communist goals and obeys the wishes of the regime in power. Freedom of speech, although recognized in the Soviet constitution, is nowhere a reality. Writers are sent to jail for expressing their opinions in print. Competing alternatives of the good life, the basis of what we have called politics, are not in evidence. Yet such a picture is incomplete. An examination of the situation in this country can provide realistic expectations for evaluating Soviet politics.

Most Soviet citizens agree that Communist goals are the only goals. Most Americans—probably about the same percentage—believe in capitalist goals. To argue that adherence to goals is voluntary in the United States and forced in the Soviet Union is to misunderstand the dynamic process by which regimes win support for their policies. Second, freedom of speech is also guaranteed in the American constitution, but that does not prevent the government from sending people to jail because of what they have written. Finally, competing alternatives for the good life in America were almost nonexistent in the 1950s. Ideologies were suspect. People with good, controversial ideas kept them to themselves. Few would publicly admit that the good life was worth searching for. We must not forget that politics is going through a resurgence after a period of decided quiescence. Very much the same thing is happening in the Soviet Union. The Stalinist period, like the McCarthy era here, was one of political repression. But a thaw has unquestionably taken place. From all available reports, ideas that would have been treasonable a few years ago are now publicly discussed in the streets and universities of Moscow. Students are attracted to new ideas and are expressing them. In spite of pockets of disapproval in bureaucratic publishing offices and university offices, intellectuals, especially younger ones, are asking questions that were stifled for a long time.

The resemblance to the United States is both appalling and exhilarating.

This is not to deny that there are differences between the two countries. Differences exist among all countries, which is one of the things that makes the study of politics so fascinating. Freedom of speech and freedom of the press have had a longer history in the United States than in the Soviet Union and are, therefore, more a reality here. Many government officials in this country are forced to tolerate dissent because it is supposed to be tolerated here. So there are very real differences. The search for the good life may be somewhat easier in one country than in the other, but this does not mean that it does not exist in both—simply that it takes different forms. The presence of the search in both countries is much more striking than the differences in procedure.

One final consequence of the ubiquity of politics is that it will not disappear in the near future. This may sound rather obvious, but there have been predictions to that effect. Consider the following statements by prominent American political scientists:

> Thus, in the political sphere, the increased flow of information and more efficient techniques of co-ordination need not necessarily prompt greater concentration of power within some ominous control agency located at the governmental apex. Paradoxically, these developments also make possible great devolution of authority and responsibility to the lower levels of government and society. . . . This development would also have the desirable effect of undermining the appeal of any new integrating ideologies that may arise, for ideologies thrive only as long as there is an acute need for abstract responses to large and remote problems.[7]

> If one thinks of a domain of "pure politics" where decisions are determined by calculations of influence, power, or electoral advantage, and a domain of "pure knowledge" where decisions are determined by calculations of how to implement agreed-upon values with rationality and efficiency, it appears to me that the political domain is shrinking and the knowledge domain is growing. . . . If leaders and other legislators are less bound by the domain of pure politics than we had thought,

[7] Zbigniew Brzezinski, "America in the Technotronic Age," *Encounter*, 30 (January 1968): 16–26.

then they are freer to be guided by the promptings of scientists and findings from the domain of knowledge.[8]

Predictions of this sort fall into the "harmony of interest" category discussed earlier: they are more the wishes of their authors than scientific predictions of future events. We feel that it is much safer, as well as more scientifically accurate, to repeat our conclusion, that as long as there are some who do not share in the good life, politics —the search for the good life—will continue.

We have discussed many things about politics in this book. We outlined the Western tradition of political thought, which raised intriguing questions and provided some diverse answers. We have described the scientific study of politics and seen that it has no final answers. We have looked at some of these questions in terms of contemporary political institutions and found few answers there, either. But we have discovered something: that the search for these answers brought us into the world of politics. In writing our book, we took a political step by calling these things to your attention. The next political step is up to you.

[8] Robert E. Lane, "The Decline of Politics and Ideology in a Knowledgeable Society," *American Sociological Review*, 31 (October 1966).

Annotated Bibliography

WE HAVE FOUND from experience that long lists of books, while impressive to either the reader or the student, are often not very helpful. There is so much given to read that the best solution is often not to read any of it. Therefore we have decided to keep our erudition to ourselves and to make our bibliographies short and highly selective. Instead of trying to cover the subject matter of each chapter thoroughly, we will instead present, for each section, a few books that particularly appealed to us and that we thought students might want to know about. Reading a few good books carefully is better than knowing about many books of mixed quality.

PART I

Part I deals with the meaning of politics. For those interested in pursuing that subject, the following might be found helpful.

Birnbaum, Norman. *The Crisis of Industrial Society*. New York: Oxford University Press, 1969.

> *Although difficult to read, this book does contain one of the better attempts to define politics in a way that is relevant to an understanding of it in a complex society.*

Crick, Bernard. *In Defence of Politics*. Baltimore: Penguin Books, 1964.

The kind of politics defended in this book is the kind that is concerned with adjustment, compromise, and conciliation. The author has little faith in those who demand too much from politics, and this bias harms his whole treatment of the subject.

Gramsci, Antonio. *The Modern Prince and Other Writings*. New York: International Publishers, 1959.

Gramsci was, after Lenin, one of the most important twentieth-century Marxists. This book contains his only writings in English, and they are informed by a conception of politics that is much broader than Weber's or Crick's. Although written in Fascist Italy, there is much here that is helpful in understanding politics in the United States.

Megill, Kenneth A. *The New Democratic Theory*. New York: Free Press, 1970.

An important attempt to learn about politics from the radical movements of the recent past. This book shows that a politics that makes serious demands for a better life can be a liberating politics aimed at making democracy a meaningful term once again.

Weber, Max. "Politics as a Vocation." In *From Max Weber: Essays in Sociology*, eds. Hans Gerth and C. Wright Mills. New York: Oxford University Press, 1958.

This is still one of the best treatments of the meaning of politics. It deserves its status as one of the classics on the subject.

PART II

This section of the book deals with political institutions and how they function, particularly in the United States. The following books explore different questions raised in that section.

Baran, Paul A., and Paul M. Sweezy. *Monopoly Capital: An Essay on the American Economic and Social Order*. New York: Monthly Review Press, 1966.

Though the authors tend to get overly technical, and although the book is not well integrated, it contains one of the few important attempts to come to an understanding of contemporary capitalism and how it functions as a political system.

Cleaver, Eldridge. *Soul on Ice.* New York: Dell, 1968.

This is more than an eloquent plea by a black man on the plight of one powerless group. It is a serious attempt theoretically to understand racism and how it becomes institutionalized into a powerful oppressive force.

Domhoff, G. William. *Who Rules America?* Englewood Cliffs, N.J.: Prentice-Hall, 1967.

Despite a careless job of research and a failure adequately to define what a ruling class is, this little volume is filled with information on one segment of the powerful and how they live. Its popularity, in the face of its flaws, indicates how important the subject is.

Dubofsky, Melvyn. *We Shall Be All: A History of the Industrial Workers of the World.* Chicago: Quadrangle, 1969.

Many books on the powerless could be recommended, but this study of workers who decided to do something about their powerlessness by forming the Industrial Workers of the World is exciting, exhaustive, and moving. It also reveals again how those in power respond to such a movement.

Edelman, Murray. *The Symbolic Uses of Politics.* Urbana, Ill.: University of Illinois Press, 1967.

This book contains an interesting description of how demands for reform in America are rarely met fully, since those in power are more often concerned with giving the appearance that reform has taken place without actually changing anything.

Engler, Robert. *The Politics of Oil: The Study of Private Power and Democratic Directions.* Chicago: University of Chicago Press, 1967.

An exhaustive coverage of how one industry has turned the political process into a service for its own ends. This book demonstrates, by case study, how political decisions in the United States benefit a few continually at the expense of the many.

McConnell, Grant. *Private Power and American Democracy.* New York: Knopf, 1966.

The best available book on interest groups and how they function in America. The author convincingly demonstrates that many private groups have assumed governmental powers with very few checks upon how they use them.

Miliband, Ralph. *The State in Capitalist Society*. New York: Basic Books, 1969.

Here we have a series of replies to those who argue that there are few political problems left in capitalist society. Although the book does not offer a theory of its own, it is the best statement of a Marxist on the state in English, and it is also notable for its emphasis on means of compliance which are not violent.

Mills, C. Wright. *The Power Elite*. New York: Oxford University Press, 1956.

Mills's book started recent discussions of power. It is flawed by an inadequate theoretical conception and by an all-too-broad notion of power, but it is still one of the liveliest, most informative books on the subject, still well worth reading.

Morgan, Robin, ed. *Sisterhood Is Powerful: An Anthology of Writings from the Women's Liberation Movement*. New York: Vintage, 1970.

A series of essays of varying quality from the women's movement. The feeling after reading this book is that relations between the sexes may contain the most important political problem of all.

Preston, William, Jr. *Aliens and Dissenters: Federal Suppression of Radicals, 1903–1933*. New York: Harper Torchbooks, 1966.

This book shows what happened when the American government decided forcibly to repress challenges to its power. It is hard to read this book and still believe that freedom of speech is a right that any American has.

Weinstein, James. *The Corporate Ideal in the Liberal State: 1910–1918*. Boston: Beacon Press, 1969.

By concentrating on the years of the Wilson administration, the author shows how the modern corporate state came into being. It is a valuable study of political change.

PART III

Barker, Ernest. *Political Thought in England, 1848–1914*. 2d ed. London: Oxford University Press, 1928.

At the time Barker was preparing this volume many new social and natural sciences were clamoring their compartmentalized views of human nature, causing a complete dissection of ac-

ademic opinion, and creating general intellectual chaos and confusion. We find here an attempt to reconcile many of the new economic, social, psychological, and political ideas of the day in a manner complementary to all schools of thought.

————. *The Political Thought of Plato and Aristotle.* New York: Dover, 1959.

This book is more than an admirable exposition of Platonic and Aristotelian philosophy. It is concerned with the intellectual environment which inspired and influenced the classical writings and with the practical impact they had on the modern world. Especially note the fascinating account of the histories of the Republic and Politics.

Cabban, Alfred. *Edmund Burke and the Revolt against the Eighteenth Century.* New York: Macmillan, 1929.

Cabban writes on the array of edicts to which Burke exposed, in the eighteenth century, the influences of Locke upon his politics and thinking, the general intellectual foundation of Burke's political philosophy, and the association of Burke with the thought of Coleridge, Wordsworth, and others.

Canavan, Francis. *The Political Reason of Edmund Burke.* Durham, N.C.: Duke University Press, 1960.

This work is a startling example of new interpretations of political philosophers and the resurgence such interpretations may have on political philosophy in general. Canavan here challenges the accepted version and understanding of Burke's philosophy and conclusively demonstrates how an opposite view can give sound perspective to the entirety of Burke's ideas.

Cassirer, Ernst. *The Question of Jean Jacques Rousseau.* Translated by Peter Gay. Bloomington, Ind.: Indiana University Press, 1963.

Cassirer confronts courageously the conflicts and dilemmas in the writings of Rousseau which create difficulty in discovering a coherent and definitive meaning. His success may be due to the seriousness with which he takes the reflections which Rousseau made on his own work.

Cole, G. D. H. *A History of Socialist Thought.* London: Macmillan, 1953–60.

This five-volume work, which deals with the entire spectrum of Communist and Socialist movements from the earliest nine-

teenth-century precursors to modern socialism, reflects the gen-
ius of a rare and versatile scholar, one who possesses the unique
and eclectic talents so required to undertake this monumental
historical task.

Crossman, R. H. S. *Plato To-Day*. London: Allen and Unwin, 1937.
In this uncompromised work Plato is brought "home" to us in
a more realistic manner than in those years when Crossman was
philosophical commentator for BBC. Crossman maintains a fluid
style as he allows us to understand precisely what Plato might
have said about the twentieth century if he were alive today.

Gay, Peter. *The Enlightenment, an Interpretation*. New York: Knopf,
1966.
An interdisciplinary study and broad interpretation of the En-
lightenment. His argument is tactfully waged against scholars
who have sought to reify our understanding of the Enlighten-
ment through a polemical and conservative critique.

Halevy, Elie. *The Growth of Philosophic Radicalism*. Translated by
May Morris. Boston: Beacon Press, 1955.
This is an exciting book which gets strength from its emphasis
on Bentham's work. The influence of Smith on Bentham, of
Bentham on Ricardo, and of Bentham on the radical school
which grew as a direct result of his discoveries is an illuminat-
ing display of a proper sense of historical perspective and
analysis.

Hook, Sidney. *From Hegel to Marx: Studies in the Intellectual De-*
velopment of Karl Marx. Ann Arbor, Mich.: University of Michigan
Press, 1962.
A classic study dealing with many of the most important ideas
in Socialist, idealist, and materialist thought. Hook supplements
the argument for a radical and dynamic interpretation of Hegel-
ian philosophy by his reference to the dialectical process as
"teleological metaphysics."

Lowith, Karl. *From Hegel to Nietzsche*. New York: Holt, Rinehart
and Winston, 1964.
This work stands apart as a landmark in studies of nineteenth-
century social philosophy. In two parts, Lowith first tackles the
idealism of Hegel and Goethe through the rejection of this
rational school by the right and left Hegelians. The second part
explores an existential conflict having roots in classical philos-

ophy as the contradiction between the sphere of the public and private lives. Lowith confronts a more critical dilemma between the "Bourgeois and Christian" world.

MacPherson, Crawford B. *The Political Theory of Possessive Individualism: Hobbes to Locke.* New York: Oxford University Press, 1962.

His theory of possessive individualism is designed as an aid to help us better understand the seventeenth-century political theorists. MacPherson succeeds through this assumption by clearing up many of the problems that have plagued us when reading Locke and Hobbes.

Marcuse, Herbert. *Reason and Revolution: Hegel and the Rise of Social Theory.* Boston: Beacon Press, 1960.

This extraordinary work is much more than an exposition of Hegelian philosophy and a documentary on the social theory which grew out of it. It is, as Marcuse states in the opening paragraph, a "hope that it would make a small contribution to the revival . . . of a mental faculty in danger of being obliterated: the power of negative thinking." Marcuse has given rebirth to the greatest of all methodologies, the dialectic.

Plamenatz, John. *Man and Society.* Vol. II. New York: McGraw-Hill, 1963.

Although Plamenatz's treatment of such theorists as Marx and Hegel, Hobbes and Locke, is exceptional, his analysis and examination of Machiavelli is especially so. His critical commentary is difficult reading for the uninitiated, but with time and effort spent, the book promises to be a rewarding venture.

Wolin, Sheldon S. *Politics and Vision: Continuity and Innovation in Western Political Thought.* Boston: Little, Brown, 1960.

For those who are aware of the argument between the behavioralist and political theorists, as well as between theorists themselves, this is a well-written and widely read volume on the changes in political philosophy and what and why a certain dimension of traditional thinking has been discarded.

PART IV

This section contains chapters on the reaction against Marx, alienation, science and scientific method, and the ubiquity of politics. The following list follows this general order.

Arendt, Hannah. *Between Past and Future: Six Exercises in Political Thought.* 2d ed. New York: Viking Press, 1968.

> *In many respects this series of essays is a continuation of thoughts presented in her* Origins of Totalitarianism *and* The Human Condition. *This is most clearly seen in the essay, "What Is Authority," and we find here as before brilliant insight into and grasp of the overwhelming problems facing contemporary civilization.*

————. *The Human Condition.* Chicago: University of Chicago Press, 1970.

> *The distinction among socially necessary labor, work, and action appears as a modification of ideas presented by three great economic philosophers many years past. However, if this distinction is seen as an expository device to pursue her thesis, it takes on the aura of genius and originality, especially the implication of contemporary work ethics.*

Aveneri, Shlomo. *The Political and Social Thought of Karl Marx.* Cambridge: Cambridge University Press, n.d.

> *This is a fascinating attempt at a unification of Marx's thought, showing how some basic themes, including alienation, dominated all his writings. Although difficult, it is one of the better one-volume treatments of the subject.*

Bay, Christian. *The Structure of Freedom.* Stanford, Calif.: Stanford University Press, 1970.

> *Bay goes far beyond the highly confining borders of contemporary social science and determines a new approach to political analysis through his application of sociology, psychology, and political science. He has produced what appears to be an entirely new concept of freedom and new criteria for evaluating the degree of freedom in a democratic society. His section on basic security and psychological freedom maximizes the actual and potential freedom we all possess and unnecessarily sacrifice.*

Blauner, Robert. *Alienation and Freedom: The Factory Worker and His Industry.* Chicago: University of Chicago Press, 1964.

> *Although marred by a definition of alienation that is too subjective, this is one of the few books that tries to talk about alienation in the work place.*

Gerassi, John. *The Coming of the New International.* Cleveland: World Publishing Company, 1970.

This book is a testimony to the outbreak of politics all over the world in the late 1960s. It contains essays on revolutionary movements in America, South and North, the Third World, and the Socialist countries. One comes away feeling politics is very much a permanent activity.

Gouldner, Alvin W. *The Coming Crisis in Western Sociology.* New York: Basic Books, 1970.

Another very good critique of scientism in social science. It contains a humanistic vision of what sociology should be like and why it is worth aspiring to.

Hughes, H. Stuart. *Consciousness and Society.* New York: Knopf, 1958.

Contains a good discussion of the writers who followed Marx and tried to answer him in different ways.

Kaplan, Abraham. *The Conduct of Inquiry: Methodology for Behavioral Science.* San Francisco: Chandler, 1964.

There are many books on how to make a science of society. This is one of the better ones, and it is interesting to read it in terms of the criticisms made by Mills, Gouldner, and Marcuse.

Lipset, Seymour Martin, Martin Trow, and James Coleman. *Union Democracy.* Garden City, N.Y.: Doubleday Anchor, 1962.

An empirical study of one labor union that demonstrates that Michel's Iron Law of Oligarchy has its exceptions.

Marcuse, Herbert. *One Dimensional Man.* Boston: Beacon Press, 1964.

This is a famous book which supposedly exercised a major influence on the New Left. Its best parts are criticisms of the kinds of mentality that are dominant in contemporary social science. It should be read in spite of its difficult style, for it is full of insights about how certain kinds of thinking can be oppressive.

Marx, Karl. *Economic and Philosophical Manuscripts of 1844.* Edited by Dirk Struik. New York: International Publishers, 1964.

The various debates about the meaning of alienation tend to revolve around this early work of Marx, which brilliantly traces the problem to capitalist society and what it does to the people who work in it. It is must reading.

Mészáros, Ivan. *Marx's Theory of Alienation.* London: Merlin, 1970.

An extremely difficult book to read, but it traces the concept of alienation historically and shows how Marx's treatment of the concept was original for its time and extremely relevant to the present.

Mills, C. Wright. *The Sociological Imagination.* New York: Grove Press, 1961.

In many ways, this is Mills's best book. Although somewhat old by now, it is the best criticism of scientism around. It also contains insightful and humorous treatments of pseudo attempts at theory building.

Wolff, Robert Paul, Barrington Moore, Jr., and Herbert Marcuse. *A Critique of Pure Tolerance.* Boston: Beacon Press, 1969.

All three essays provide valuable critiques of tolerance, and also provide indirectly, such as Marcuse's short essay, "Repressive Tolerance," or directly, such as Wolff's, "Beyond Tolerance," well-founded objections to pluralist democracy. Wolff offers thoughtfully constructed theories on pluralism. Unfortunately, "Repressive Tolerance" has served almost singularly as Marcuse's Achilles heel, because it has made this great political philosopher vulnerable to unjustifiably harsh and polemical liberal criticism.

Zeitlin, Irving. *Ideology and the Development of Social Theory.* Englewood Cliffs, N.J.: Prentice-Hall, 1968.

This book covers much the same material as Hughes's, but it focuses more directly on the political controversies between Marx and the anti-Marxists.

Index

293